FEELINGS IN HISTORY

FEELINGS IN HISTORY, ANCIENT AND MODERN

BY

RAMSAY MACMULLEN

2003

CONTENTS

PREFACE

WHAT is the mental experience, what is the under-standing, that we enjoy when we read the past as if it were a novel? This is the question at the heart of my essay; and at the heart of the question are feelings — those that we discover in the historical record and their match that we summon up in ourselves as we read.

I invite reflection on my question and the subordinate topics it may introduce; but I do so not as some oracle or authority. Where I take up the science of the mind, in my second chapter, it is not to tell specialists anything they don't already know; nor do I take up classical philology in the first, or what are called "emotion studies" or the French school of the *Annales* or the antislavery movement, in the third chapter, as bits of history (intellectual) to be discussed as such. No, these various subjects are broached not with the idea of offering readers useful information, but only as illustrations in an argument — a means of showing *how the role of emotions has been treated over the centuries, historiographically, or has been neglected or distorted; or properly ought to be treated.*

There is a reward to be hoped for in the discussion: more truth, as I will argue — a deeper level of historical understanding. My core question concerns motivation, after all; and motivation is surely an all-important matter. Indeed, it must be the chief object of historical inquiry. No account which fails in this regard can hope to satisfy. So much being said, however, most history that we read somehow strikes us as unsatisfactory. The cause lies in the very thing that confronts us in our daily lives: the difficulty, not to call it impossibility, of knowing what goes on in the recesses of another person's mind, or even of our own.

i

To the extent that conduct is directed by merely *rational* calculation of profit and loss — good or bad consequences, in whatever way we can predict them — then a description of the circumstances surrounding a choice may be good enough to suggest the motive at work. It is a given, let us suppose, that John Doe once had bills to pay, too little money, and no custom for his business in hardware. Let him stand for a group or community. He re-settled to another town where there was much building going on. Why would he and his like choose to move? The historian supposes, "To sell more and pay his bills." Readers assent. They are right, so long as John considered money alone. "To pay his bills:" historians fill most of their page with just such simple assumptions based on what they take to be the logic of the situation. Regarding John Doe, Napoleon at Waterloo, the Westward movement, they are all the same.

They shed no light, however, on major turning points which were entirely irrational and emotional in the lives of Paul Gauguin, Albert Schweitzer, or Ernest Henry Shackleton, to instance three people who made a difference, in different ways. Their like who are less known and therefore less conveniently offered as illustrations can be teased out of the record, to show the same behavior. Calculation in any ordinary sense of that term did not direct their decisions.

The fact is no new discovery. I may instance a throw-away line from Sir Lewis Namier: "Although we know that men's actions are *mostly* conditioned by factors other than reason, in practice we have to assume their rational character."[*] I supply the italics to bring out the point: that in the view of so keen an observer, more than half of motive is irrational.

We know this is so from looking within ourselves. We know, too, that something better than the ordinary historical account is possible because we have read historical fiction, or fiction without any pretense of touching on matters of historical significance — still, narratives that may read like his-

---

[*] Namier (1953) p. 1078. He was advocating consideration of "passion", "unconscious promptings" and "modern psychology."

tory: *August 1914, The Duke's Children, Henry Esmond, Waverley.* Or like social history: *Eugénie Grandet, Buddenbrooks, The Forsyte Saga.*

These offer an account that *can* satisfy, with the whole truth. For fiction is free to supply the colors that characterize and more properly explain people's acts, meaning, those feelings for which historians can generally find no place. Historians at least in recent times omit what may not be recorded openly or at any length in the pages of the past; they omit what cannot be handled in a fashion approximating to logical discourse. In this way they fall short of verisimilitude, they fall short of that truth on which ordinary readers will bet their bottom dollar: history is feeling. It is feelings that make us do what we do; and feelings can in fact be read. But the reading of them requires writers and readers to join their minds in ways that have long been out of fashion among students of history.

To examine these various ideas and assertions comprehensively would be beyond anyone's powers. Imagine it: the whole of the past record of all peoples, and every manner of incorporation of emotional life into written accounts — an impossibly huge matter to consider. I can sense the impossibility even if I look no further than the books that happen to be on my shelves because they were written by my friends.

These open a view on an almost limitless horizon. At the same time, however, they suggest an organizational principle: discussion of my core question cannot be approached in just the same way in ill-documented times as in the better documented. The Sui or T'ang dynasty, early Islam or Byzantium — despite whatever A. F. Wright or F. M. Donner or E. Patlagean discover — will not allow the same questions that can be directed at nineteenth and twentieth century Zionism (with D. Vital) or at the Franklin-Roosevelt years (with F. B. Freidel).

If then I am to address my chosen subject at all, I must do so in a way that takes account of this broad difference in surviving evidence between periods richly recorded, and the relatively impoverished.

I must first write off, from ignorance, all but Western civilization. Within its boundaries, among periods that can count as "better documented," I can claim acquaintance only with U. S. history in the earlier decades of the nineteenth century, through books I have written recently. Here, however, there is material readily available to illustrate what role emotions play in the flow of events and how they may be incorporated into the narrative. So, most of my third chapter. As to "ill-documented" eras, another recent book of mine gives me an acquaintance with Rome from Cicero into the opening years of the Christian era. For my first chapter, here again, I can find an illustration of how emotions are handled, both in the stream of historiography that feeds that period and in the modern use of what it affords. The two chapters, presented in their proper chronological order, are divided by an intervening one which comments on the first and leads into the third. Finally, a very short Conclusion sums up the whole.

And the point of it all? With what assumptions about human behavior should we visit the past, and with what powers of our minds at the ready? I return to the heart of my essay, where my preface began, hopeful of drawing in to my inquiry anyone who likes both truth and fiction.

CHAPTER 1:
HISTORY IN THE
ROMAN REPUBLIC

ABOUT the nature of our urges to act, about people and
their emotions as they make events, about the best ways
to turn these all into a narrative, is there nothing at all to be
learned from Antiquity? Nothing Classical? The challenge
answers itself.

But to give the answer some focus, I direct it at historiography leading up to the decade around Caesar's death. There
are reasons to commence with Thucydides, so far back. Aside
from his intrinsic interest and preeminence, he served as a
model to Sallust, the best-known historian of Caesar's lifetime; so, too, to Caesar himself on occasion, for example,
when Caesar describes the feelings that attended a particular
moment of drama in the 40s BC at Marseilles. With
Thucydides, too, began the flow of accounts of events with
which historians in their own lives were familiar and thus
enjoyed the right to speak about the actors' emotions: as,
next, Polybius could do, himself another grand figure in
Classical historiography. He directs the flow into the history
of the Roman Republic; and following him, by a natural
continuation, are various intermediate figures in the debate
that went on among them all on the very question of my

essay: what is or what should be the relation between fact and fiction? Where do feelings fit in? The debate can be illustrated out of these writers' historical works as well as in critical discussions of the times.

At the end, in the decade around 40 BC, a convenient illustration for my analysis can be found in the role and motivation of Caesar's heir and in the manner these are presented — first, by contemporaries; then, in an instructive contrast, by the preeminent modern authority, Ronald Syme. The contrast will, I hope, justify the attention given to the practices of Antiquity in this first chapter, where, instead, some more theoretical discussion might have been expected. I like an argument that stays in touch with specific illustrations and documents.

1. THUCYDIDES

Thucydides, possessed of a mind so wonderfully endowed, by Zeus! for the practice of his art, found in the powers of reason all that is needed for the understanding of the past. Or he seems to do so, on first reading: in history there is no place for emotion.

Is this what he really believed? On the whole question, his primacy among the Ancients entitles him to be heard; but he must be heard also because some of the later writers in whom I am interested looked back to him more or less explicitly as a model.

"On first reading" he seems to credit reason with all that an historian could require. Why else would he burden his pages throughout with exact figures? — how high are certain walls, how great their circuit, how many persons or ships involved, how many hours or days, at what cost of talents, how many killed, captured, or enslaved. To learn such things, so much to be relied on, so well above all argument, he must regularly have interrogated contemporary witnesses, so that he could then shape his interpretations on a basis of indisputable data. His reader in the same fashion should benefit, too. Indeed, there is usually more benefit in his pages than one can at first take in. "It may be, for instance," said Burckhardt, in all seriousness, "that there is in Thucydides a fact of capital importance which somebody will note in a hundred years' time."[1]

And this overwhelming abundance of hard evidence is offered without apparent distortion, inviting equally objective analysis and doubly necessary to historians: for they must be able to grasp the past situation that dictated a given response, just as actors in the past grasped and must have responded to it. To know their situation is to know their mind. Hard evidence thus suits the purpose. It would suit a political scientist, equally, or a scientist of any other sort — Thucydides himself being so "scientific," so "rational", as modern readers describe his work. Sir Ronald Syme concludes, "Thucydides insists all the time on reason." It may be seen in his favorite characters. Pericles stands out among them. "Intelligence is the supreme virtue."[2]

So, Syme. Yet even in acknowledging the power of a mind ever at work in Thucydides' account, readers may discover much more besides, as they allow their own minds to sink more deeply into the historian's. Some will use the very word "depth" to describe their experience.[3] A familiar point of entrance is offered by the so-called Melian dialogue. Here Thucydides, quite at home among the Sophists of his lifetime, portrays his countrymen in formal debate with representatives of the little island community of Melos. Should it join Athens' side or count on security from Sparta? The Athenians are all brains and logic; the Melians, muddle-headed sentimentalists. They are held up to ridicule, asserting as they do against all possible belief, "We feel encouraged, after all, not without good reason."[4] Before many pages have been turned, they have been rebuked for their folly by their extermination.

Which is the point of it all — for Thucydides' readers are chilled to the bone by both tone and outcome of the story, as he intended. Inexorable rationality, the Athenian way of mind, is held up to them for detestation. In just the same way, they are chilled by the savage impatience with which, earlier (3.37.2; 3.40.2), the Athenian Cleon brushes aside compassion or anything except the calculation of material interest, as he argues it out before the assembly; and his opposite, the politician Diodotus, accepts the terms of the debate and, himself as well, denies appeal to any pity or indulgence. In question were the people of Mytilene, to be exterminated or not. A modern consensus has it that Thucydides *meant* readers to react as they do. The consensus must be right. Pure reason in the service of force *was* inhuman, and he evidently felt it to be so, himself.

Or again, consensus points to the tragic idiocy of the Athenians planning their great Sicilian expedition, every part of it so prudently predicted and made secure against mischance, yet destined as every reader knew to end awfully: a work of characteristic irrational audacity of which an Athenian commander had actually boasted to his troops on quite a different occasion.[5] Off it went, that great fleet, freighted with youth and hopes, a grand brilliant terrifying spectacle assembled out of the strength of an imperious state — a time, a moment, of a whole people a-tremble with the drama of it, and readers too, because they know, and the dramatist counted on their knowing, its fate (6.30.1ff.). Reason betrayed them all.

At moments, Athenians understood, and made fun of Sophists, the local Wise Guys, for their funny ways: Antiphon, Socrates, Anaxagoras, Hippodamus, Protagoras.... But this was of course more likely to be the verdict of the masses, not of Thucydides' sort.

To revert to the Sicilian expedition (6.24.3f.), and his manner of presenting it: "A passion to sail out seized on everyone, ἔρως... ἐκπλεῦσαι, the older men in the belief they would subdue those whom they sailed against (or at least so great an armament would not meet with disaster), while those who were in their best years were possessed by the desire for foreign sights and scenes and had good hopes of suffering no hurt;" and the common soldiers looked to get rich, one way or another. At work thus were strong feelings, in a mix differing as people were differently situated: an optimistic expectation of whatever conquest might bring, glory or wealth, and the sheer spirit of adventure. Such were the causes of the sailing, as the sailing in turn was the cause of the decisive weakening of Athens. They dominated the course of action as the historian understood and traced it.

But an explanatory choice like this is not compatible with the view of Thucydides as a scientist of any sort, one who merely laid things out and added them up; for the feelings that invested the Sicilian expedition — feelings, the reality of which he presents as fact and the consequences of which are to be understood as historic — cannot be turned into figures. They are beyond quantification. To be estimated they must rather be *felt*; and the historian must be ready to help the reader to do this, by his art.

The art at work, far from being accidental or exceptional, was recognized if its purpose was not well understood by Plutarch (*Moral.* 346f.). He saw how "the best historian is the one who, by a vivid representation of emotions and characters, makes his narrative like a painting. Thucydides, for example, in his writing is constantly striving for this vividness" — Plutarch uses the word ἐνάργεια, *enargeia*, "realism" such that one can almost see the thing — "wanting to turn his readers into spectators, as it were, and to reproduce in their minds the feelings of shock and disorientation which were experienced by those who actually viewed the events." This verdict in agreement with such writers as the Augustan Dionysius of Halicarnassus has been noted by A. J. Woodman, who makes a strong case for the natural placing of Thucydides in the flow of Athenian drama quite as much as under the influence of the Sophists.[6] But it is not the historian's strategy for explaining past events but his style of presentation that Dionysius admired. The choice of words, their power to thrill and evoke, counted most, or only; and in the sequel to Thucydides it was rather rhetoricians who saw themselves as his inheritors. I return to the point a little later.

It has been perhaps no very contrarian insight, to view Thucydides as more than a collector and supplier of facts upon facts — himself, all rational, cool, and objective, all admiring of reason. Given the colors he lavishes on certain favorite scenes such as those debates instanced above, or the Sicilian disaster, readers can hardly help responding emotionally; and it is natural to suppose, not only that they were meant to do so, obviously, but that the author himself was deeply engaged with his subject matter in the same way.[7] W. R. Connor spoke out for this interpretation, saying at one point, "the emotional power of the work is not to be denied, repressed, branded as modern sentimentality or condemned as a form of 'brain-washing'. The ancient critics recognized Thucydides' ability to recreate the *pathos* of events, that is, to lead his readers to participate vicariously in the sufferings of the war. That experience is at the center of any reading of Thucydides and is the product of the shaping of the text to involve and implicate the reader, both mentally and emotionally."

A great divide separates this perception from Sir Ronald Syme's. Connor's is one which must be defended in a realm beyond reason; for consider how reserved Thucydides always is, how rarely he reveals that self about which the modern reader claims knowledge. How can anyone be sure what his personal feelings were? In answer: only through the assumption of our common humanity. It cannot be easily supposed, because it cannot be felt by any of us, that an author could write as this one did, except in the grip of just such emotions as his readers experience, vicariously. Our assumption is readily supported by common sense — to say nothing of the material presented in the next chapter.

And there is a very occasional glimpse afforded of Thucydides' feelings, explicitly. There are the closing days of the commander Nicias' life at Syracuse, first, in the few moments before the final fight, and then after his capture and death, where we are told (7.69.2; 7.86.5):

> Nicias, driven almost out of his mind by the situation,
> and seeing the real dangers and their imminence and
> how short a time before the setting out, suffered the

torments usual in major engagements. Everything to
be done by his forces was, he thought, still not ready;
everything to be said had still not been said enough.
Once again he called on each trireme captain singly,
addressing them by their fathers' name, their given
name and tribe, that they should live up to whatever
good fame each had won, and not bring to naught
ancestral virtues so marked in their forebears. He
reminded them of their fatherland, the freest ever, and
of the unconstrained choices it afforded in one's daily
life; he added all those things that men in such situations as those present will say, oblivious of what might
be trite and usual, in similar terms, for every cause:
appeals to wives, children, and ancestral gods, which
men will shout out, in the consternation they feel,
thinking them of some use... [And thereafter, the
Athenians being defeated and Nicias taken] Thus he
died... Of an ending so unhappy, he was the least
deserving of all Greeks of my time; the whole course
of his life had been governed by the rules of virtue.[8]

The estimate of Nicias' *areté* in terms of the author's own
lifetime amounts to a personal endorsement both of Nicias
and his code. The code is a real thing. Moral neutrality apparent so often elsewhere in the work is not what it seems; it is
rather a faithful representation of the various actors in the
events believing themselves to be men of virtue, as we all do,
all, honorable even among thieves. It is these latter delusions
that Thucydides understands, enters into, and faithfully
records, like a novelist, only appearing to be amoral — save
once, where he plainly sides with Nicias.[9]

He knows his subject's moral values, he knows, too, the
thoughts that lie behind Nicias' frantic exhortations to his
ship-captains. But how is it possible for such thoughts to be
known? The answer is wrapped into the account itself: they
are simply to be found among "all those things that men in
such situations as those present will say." Thucydides knew
them from his life's experience. He sensed them in Nicias
with a probability amounting to certainty because of the

common humanity he shared with the commander as with all those men he had observed in war before. It was this experience he applied to his description of the pre-battle moments.

His description is wonderfully vivid, wonderful mimesis. But "if vividness or the sense of actually being there is the main source of Thucydides' ability to persuade," a critic may object, "I don't see how one can easily distinguish his performance from that of a novelist, who also deludes us into believing."[10] A very fair question — indeed, almost exactly the case, with a cavil only at the word "delude". The historian in real life feels what he believes others are feeling, he compassionates (if that is within his powers), he remembers his own experiences and the affect of them, he attributes what he remembers to others as he observes or describes them in similar situations, later, and he is quite easy in doing so because his results, in his view, achieve verisimilitude. They are exactly like the truth. A novelist would make just the same claim; for if he cannot persuade, he fails to draw us into the story; and psychoanalysts make the claim, too. Otherwise they would be out of business. I revert to the point in the next chapter (at the end of the first section).

What was not noticed by Plutarch, however, nor since Plutarch, is what Thucydides *does* with the feelings he observes, or supposes.

He makes his account dramatic, yes, he engages our feelings, and this was perceived by his later admirers to be the chief gift he left to his art; but it was a literary gift. In addition, he uses feelings to explain events; he suggests the equation, emotion=motivation. The "why" of what happened needs to be sought, as he saw, not in calculations of material advantage but in people's feelings, though the latter may be expressed in acts served by such calculations. In his deeper insight, Thucydides is not a literary artist but an historian.

For example: when he reaches back to his country's past, he must explain the downfall of the Pisistratid tyranny. It was a work of assassination. Harmodius and Aristogeiton were the heroes, both "in a fury, the one, an erotic one, the other, an indignant one aroused by insult" (δι'ὀργῆς, ...ὑβριζόμενος, 6.57.3) which the tyrant had offered to his sister.

Or take the origin of the whole Peloponnesian war, from the top down. It is Thucydides' view that it started with Corinth and Corcyra. Corinth acted "out of hatred of the Corcyreans, because of their contumacious behavior, though they were her colonists" (1.25.3; again, 1.38.2); and the latter then ask Athens for help, offering assurances of properly grateful feelings in the future (1.32.1, χάρις; emphasized again, 1.33.1, 1.33.2); which the Corinthian envoys would counter by saying the Corcyreans had violated all decent expectations, were dissident and hostile, and "we do not send out our colonies to suffer outrage at their hands" (1.38.2, ὑβρίζεσθαι).... We have these rights to assert against you [Athenians], quite adequate in terms of Hellenic laws" (1.41.1), which is to say, serving as a basis for indignation if Athens should offer to intervene on the Corcyrean side. When Athens nevertheless does intervene, that is the first cause of the war (1.55.2) — for thereupon "the Corinthians set about their revenge," ὅπως τιμωρήσονται. Later, though the contestants interrupt the war with a truce, it all comes apart in a series of incidents, and fighting resumes, because of the Athenians' "believing themselves to be wronged" (the phrase at 5.42.2 and again at 5.46.5) and acting on these occasions "angrily," "outraged." It is all one flow of feelings, mostly anger.

Near the end, the intervention of a *tertius gaudens*, a happy Third Party in the war, is determined, "it seems to me," by fear. So hazards Thucydides (8.56.3), trying to read the mind of the Persian governor who has in charge the regions on the edge of the Aegean.

The role played by all these feelings may be called primary. They make people break out of their routines, they destroy the status quo. Yet they are not irrational, not engines of madness. Rather, for Thucydides, they are the constituents of ordinary and surely reasonable behavior — reasonable in the sense that he and his readers or anyone at all could easily understand them. There follow then those feelings of a secondary role, governing choice of means rather than ends. In war, for example, once arms are engaged, the two parties are moved by military considerations, which may be scientific in some sense, rationally calculated. Then Syme's view comes closer to the truth. But the underlying emotions of course persist, unspoken and perhaps aggravated, providing the energy necessary for the demands of war.

As in its grand lines, so in detail, Thucydides' history unfolds in the same way. In the Greek world, divided among hundreds of sovereign entities, two parties might most easily become three, or many. In explaining how this happened to amplify the fighting, he has many stories to tell. They start with feelings. These are the passions at work in states like Locris (4.24.2), Camarina (6.88.1), Argos (7.57.9).... Anger over disregarded rights moves Aigina, citing a treaty (1.67.2); Megara's rights by treaty have also been violated by Athens (1.67.4), so the two are ready for a fight. The Spartans declare in favor of their own intervention, since their allies have been wronged and they "should seek retribution immediately (1.86.3, τιμωρητέα ἐν τάχει); for let no one offer to teach us that we should think things over, when we are an injured party, ἀδικούμενοι." The Athenians on the same occasion say in agreement (1.77.4), "People who have suffered injustice, ἀδικούμενοι, are more infuriated than when they suffer violence; for the one seems like being cheated by an equal, the other, like being compelled by some greater force."With the exchange of such sentiments the two major powers become directly involved against each other.

The Spartans are beset by their anxiety over Athens' strength (1.88.1, φοβούμενοι), the rest of Greece is in a state of suspense fed by, or feeding, rumors and oracles (2.8.1), and a minor raid on the island off Athens' harbor causes a panic in the city (2.94.1, ἔκπληξις). Cruising warships on the Aegean west coast generate "a great fear" (3.23.2, μέγα τὸ δέος). Throughout the surrounding years, that is, the Third Book, fear is woven into the narrative.[11] In its terms general conduct is shaped.

In this Third Book, Athens begins its recovery from a most devastating plague, and confronts a land invasion as well; and this time is one well chosen for revolt by a major member of its empire, Mytilene on the island of Lesbos. The Athenians succeed in taking the city. They must then consider what to do with its citizens. Answering Mytilene's treachery in the moment of their own distress, no punishment at first seems adequate but the harshest. Revulsion, however, soon sets in and the decree is recognized for what it is, "savage and monstrous" (ὠμὸς καὶ μέγα, 3.36.4). Comparable is the Spartan treatment of the Plataeans at about the same time, upon their surrender: they are asked "only the one single question" (τοσοῦτον μόνον, 3.52.4), had they individually done anything to *help* their captors — though, as they say in protest at what amounts to a death sentence, they had expected treatment that would be "better in accord with law... Hellenic law forbids our slaughter."[12]

In such ways did the pressures of war produce a change in behavior, resulting not from calculations of military advantage but from passions aroused by conflict; and these Thucydides examines immediately afterwards in his treatment of the Corcyrean revolution. He sees that, in terms almost of the *longue durée*, such changes were quite as important, in event-historical terms, as any single battle or decree, and he charges his analysis with words like "savage", ὠμὸς, retributory revenge, ἀντιτιμωρήσασθαι, and a whole vocabulary of moral and social description (3.82), to explain how the world he had known became quite different, and horrible. The root causes were (3.82.8) the passions for wealth and supremacy, and their derivative, passion for political strife.[13] To such new imperatives men could bring themselves to yield by calling their bad acts good; and so they could spare themselves some of the pangs of shame and rejection. Treacherous cunning was, for example, really intelligence; and so forth.

These Corcyrean pages are too well known, however, to need more than a mention (often imitated, by the Roman Sallust, for one); but subsequently, as Thucydides makes plain, the new world, war-made, is to be taken for granted in his work, along with the operation of more ad-hoc reactions to war's dictates, to defend oneself or hurt the enemy.

The explanatory role that Thucydides discovers in men's feelings bears out the view of Hegel to be quoted again in the chapter that follows: "The first glance at History convinces us that the actions of men proceed from their needs, their passions, their characters and talents; and impresses us with the belief that such needs, passions and interests are the sole springs of action." This, anyway, was how Thucydides saw it. Such is his settled view and means of explanation.

In his treatment of feelings, so as to explain decisions, he does not ignore the distinctions among the different kinds, or their separate origins. Sometimes hope governs action, sometimes shame, sometimes loyalty as an expression of good feelings, friendship, gratitude, or pity;[14] anger is most often provoked by some hostile act not deserved, *indignus* as it would be in Latin, hence, "indignation" (but Greek lacks the specific term);[15] and settled hostility is "hatred" which explains policy choices; or it may be, revenge for past wrongs.[16] Moods are important factors: fear, or optimism or despair.[17] Instances have been given, above. There may be a mix of feelings in a population that leads to joint action, as in Athens' sailing upon Syracuse, or among the Acarnanians going to war (7.57.10); these, Thucydides takes the time to disentangle; and a single individual may of course act from mixed motives, too, as does Tisaphernes (8.87.3) or Alcibiades (6.15.2), the latter, partly indignant at a rival for an insult offered him (like Harmodius, above), partly driven by desire for wealth and fame. He was closely involved in the later turns and twists of the war, so that his personal character had historic significance. This, Thucydides goes on to sketch and then to follow out its tendencies in a public career.

The tendencies of the Athenians as a people were not very different from Alcibiades'. Thucydides gives many pages to that composite personality, very much as a sociologist would; pages likewise to the personality of Sparta at least as seen by an ally, Corinth (1.67.4ff.); and a passage on a people of what is nowadays central Bulgaria, the Odrysii, among whom prevailed "something common to the other Thracians: to take rather than give; and it was more disgraceful not to give when asked, than to ask and be refused. But they observed this generally as each individual was able. Thus nothing could be done [among them] without offering presents" (2.97.4). Anthropologists know of peoples in modern times sensitive to similar norms or terms of approval; Poseidonius who will appear later was likewise a collector of peoples for description and analysis of their ways.

In all spheres of past action, then — the general, the particular; the long-term, the short-term — Thucydides makes plain his assumption that emotions determined, or participated very significantly in determining, decisions of historic interest. They *were* motivation. His insight certainly does not exclude prudential or materialistic calculations. These generally govern the flow of conflict, once begun, on which ancient historiography loves to dwell. But such calculations — the desire for what wealth or victory or safety affords — give only an external, active form to deeper-lying urges.

2. POLYBIUS AND POSEIDONIUS

The flow of conflict was nowhere traced with more fame than in the *Iliad*. The ancients counted Homer a historian, and why not? Only Herodotus was credited with founding the tradition in prose. Next, Thucydides, in the canonical series. He was the first to write of a living war, not an old one.[18] He had immediate followers to pick up where, by his death, his own narrative had been broken off: Xenophon, Theopompus, the so-called Oxyrhynchus historian; prominent among the successors to these were Ephorus and Duris, whom Diodorus of Sicily refers to (15.60.5f.). He knows also a number of others of his craft. Looking back from his own day, Augustus' time, the known series can be seen as in fact a very broad stream. Our record supplies above 600 names with thousands of titles to their credit. From surviving whole works, from substantial parts of others (however capriciously saved), and from references later to this or that numbered Book among the not-surviving, a rough estimate of the total output can be made: some 400,000 pages, were it all in our hands, down to Augustan times.[19]

The sequence Thucydides-Ephorus-Polybius-Poseidonius-Diodorus links the principal names in a chronological series. Poseidonius with his *Histories* in fifty-two books ranks as the grandest of these, indeed grander than any others at all that we know of.[20] But Polybius wrote on a vast scale, too. He took into his view not only the Greek but the entire known world of his times. He could pick up at least one stream of national narrative from a point where a predecessor had left it;[21] but other starting points he had to invent from their internal logic, because they hadn't been explored before. Several streams were dominated by monarchies, requiring a more biographical approach than Thucydides had any need of,[22] inviting not so much biography, indeed, as tragedy.

The picture of the second-century Philip of Macedon is treated by Polybius in this fashion, as high drama.[23] A man increasingly governed by the passionate element in his own nature, jerked about by unreasoned impulses and quite untrammeled, whatever he felt, he had the power to impose on others. Others could only react: so, for illustration, he is "highly elated" by his capture and cruel treatment of Cios (15.22.1), but his indifference to how this might be seen by his victim's friends makes them his enemies, including Rhodes, "roused to savage hatred" (15.22.2ff.). The Rhodians "henceforth considered him to be their enemy and made their preparations accordingly" (15.23.6). Therefore they appealed to Rome, and drew in that greater power.

The train of events is driven by emotions, but perhaps not well understood; for Polybius like ordinary observers of the time has much more trouble penetrating the mind of a monarch than of some more accessible figure in politics. Puzzled by the dynamics of Philip's reign, he resorts to abstraction: "perhaps it may be said of all kings that at the beginning of their reigns they talk of freedom as a gift they offer to all and style all those who are thus loyal adherents, as friends and allies; but as soon as they have established their authority they at once begin to treat those who placed trust in them not as allies but as servants" (15.24.4). And again (7.13.7; 7.14.6), to explain the degeneration "from king to tyrant," he can only conclude, "of such decisive importance for young kings, as leading either to misfortune or to the firm establishment of their kingdom, is the judicious choice of friends who attend them."

Philip draws Rome into hostile action against the Aetolians. They "had unjustly deprived him" of two prizes of war, and he appeals to his Roman friends "to participate in his indignation;" and they think "his indignation was not without good cause." Besides, the Aetolians had shown themselves ungrateful to the Romans (21.31.3ff., 7). And another king, Eumenes, rejects peace terms because the conditions are ill suited to the dignity of himself and his allies (οὐτ' εὐσχήμονα, 21.10.5) — that is, shame would attend their acceptance. Polybius judged Eumenes to be particularly conscious of his image, particularly ambitious for glory (φιλοδοξότατος, 32.8.5). Personal feelings turn into history when they are regal.

So great a thing as the Hannibalic war, according to a favorite explanation, could arise from a single person's "passion for gain and power." That was what Fabius Pictor offered his readers; but Polybius saw rather baffled fury at defeat, the "passionate feelings" of one great leader added to those naturally felt by his nation, "longing for revenge" and angered at deceitful treatment.[24] To the next generation, the same feelings were passed on, and acted out in moments of savage fury. The relatively minor war of Rome with the Illyrians arose from their ruler's infuriation at the insulting treatment offered by a Roman envoy (2.8.12); where, later, events were governed by the personality of another local dynast, "a man possessed of a spirit of adventure, but quite irrational and without judgement; and this dogged him all through his life"

(3.19.9).[25] By a similar misfortune, the neighboring Aetolians fell under the leadership of young Dorimachus, "of a violent and aggressive spirit," who affronted another people, himself in a fury, while they, in their response to outrage upon outrage at his hands, deride him; and "on this account alone," that "he bore so ill and angrily what they had said," Dorimachus roused his people to war.[26] Polybius' own state, the Achaean League, though it elected its leaders, responded to one, Aratus, who acted from personal pique or something stronger ("incensed and exasperated") against the Aetolians, and so commenced hostilities (4.7.8); which in turn initiated the so-called Social War (4.13.6). All these are instances of what, above, in Thucydides, were called "primary" feelings: at work in the initial rupture of a previously peaceful relationship, or of some other established routine or course of action.

Relations of monarchies with democracies were seen by Polybius as more likely to be controlled by the former, who sought friendly relations through open-handedness on a grand scale; and to this, which was much more than the purchase of goodwill, all alike gave the name "greatness of spirit."[27] The city-plans of scores of Hellenistic *poleis* reflect the feeling and its expression through royal gifts of colonnades and the like. Democracies for their part responded with votes of honors and other high compliments; which might be rescinded out of injured feelings (e.g. 28.7.5f.), just as a king might expect a compliment and not get it, or at least not one that he felt was adequate, and so *he* reacted against the offenders out of his indignation (ὀργῇ: 4.47.7; 4.49.1f.). Such were the vicissitudes of international relations.

As rulers in monarchies had personalities, so whole peoples, likewise. In Thucydidean fashion, Polybius characterizes the Carthaginians and Romans, both demonstrating greatness of spirit (but the Carthaginians', verging toward mere love of domination), while the Aetolians were savage-tempered, impulsive, aggressive, not to be trusted for a minute; or the Cretans, given over to selfish rivalries.[28] Emotional tendencies similarly were at work within smaller groups: armies are characterized as of this or that mood or morale; the Achaeans are

thrown into a wild panic, a general Terror; the senate of
Rome or Carthage, or the assembly of the Acarnanians or
Achaeans, which Polybius knew so well, will be filled with
hope, or despair, or rage; or they may be filled with an ambition to act, and be seen to act, on the highest moral level.[29] It
is in such ways that the historian explains the turns and twists
of his story.

"Most men endure hardship and danger," says Polybius,
"for profit's sake;" but the passage is exceptional and the
exception proves the rule; for he is speaking only of those
who are enrolled as mercenaries in the armies of Carthage
and the eastern monarchies he was familiar with, and then, as
they behaved at the prospect of pillage.[30] As a general motive
he is more likely to offer the aspiration for what is noble.[31]
Even in regard to booty, Roman military discipline was fully
capable of insuring a civilized sharing-out; and, as is
explained in his best known pages, the Roman constitution
likewise insured or encouraged many virtues: for example
(6.55.4), to be seen in Horatius Cocles' heroic behavior and
"the eager emulation in achieving noble deeds engendered in
the Roman youth by their institutions."[32]

Moral considerations enter into conversation between
states, and reflect feelings; for no feeling is more fundamental in a social animal than the urge to seek and to win others' approval, and nothing is more likely to achieve this than
deference to shared norms. Polybius can be readily believed
in his report of a moral element in international dealings:
for instance, when the Rhodians (21.23.5) assure the
Roman senate that it "had really wanted... obviously, praise
and glory among men.... You went to war with Philip and
made every sacrifice for the liberty of Greece; for such was
your purpose; and this alone — absolutely nothing else —
was the prize you won by that war" (at which, we can imagine the senators' surprise and gratification, while not
unconscious of their real concern all along: *maiestas*). Such
noble conduct! of a godlike quality.[33] It had its secular
rewards, too, establishing their good faith among their
allies.[34] Similarly the Achaean assembly was reminded that

its decisions could always aim at what was honorable, so long at least as it was not reduced by circumstances to the consideration only of selfish interest (24.12.2).

"Good faith among allies," where the Greek word, πίστις, must translate Latin *fides*, at one point gave rise to a seriocomic imbroglio: certain Greeks (the execrable Aetolians, in fact), being defeated, approached the Roman commander for terms of surrender, and heard his invitation to do so "on terms." This, they thought meant one thing, the commander, another, extremely different. When it was too late, they understood their mistake. "But this, they said, this isn't right! And it isn't Greek" (20.10.6) — a misunderstanding like that of the Rhodians, just above.

And, for another illustration of the urge to seek approval, and of cross-cultural confusion: Polybius won the friendship of Scipio the Younger when the lad was in his late teens.[35] Scipio opened his heart to the older man, revealing his unhappiness about what people said of him, and more specifically, in asserting the interests of his family in political court battles, that he was seen as less of a man than his forbears. In his "ambition for repute," φιλοδόξεῖν, driven by the "urge and eagerness for everything noble," he sought and welcomed Polybius' help in improving his fame.[36] Polybius offered advice under three headings: self-restraint, manly courage, and greatness of spirit. As to the first, Scipio must abjure the imported indulgences that were all the fashion among young noblemen; as to the second, he must go boar-hunting like any Hellenistic prince (or like his mentor, who happened to be an enthusiast for the sport); and as to the third, in financial affairs that involved very large sums and ambiguous obligations, he must offer to his society quite the grandest gestures, on an extravagantly un-Roman scale. So he was remade, against the *mores* of the time. Polybius' readers may be reminded of the characterization of Philip or Eumenes, mentioned above; for Scipio in Roman history enjoyed a career of truly regal significance, and that significance the historian must explore to its depth; but with the difference, that here he really knew his subject and could describe his emotional and moral development in convincing detail.

The moral qualities that Scipio demonstrated in his youth evince a reasoned control, the reverse of which — acting from plain passion — Polybius often accuses. Illustrative passages are many.[37] They may be assembled to form a picture of Polybius the scientific, the cool intellectual, as has been done for Thucydides by some of his readers — a Symean picture.[38] But a generous amount of unadorned fact in Polybius' text and the intelligence pervading it weigh very lightly against the vocabulary of explanation in the overview attempted above: he uses a string of terms like "indignation", "resentment", "eagerness", "gratitude", "pity", and so forth. He sees or indeed feels their significance. To moral qualities themselves, and the overarching idea of the honorable or morally beautiful, he is himself committed in an emotional way; he loves what is noble, *to kalon*; and he discovers it in the common actions of humanity, to "respond to kindness and tact, often with a long-term loyalty...," and "naturally admire generosity, thinking it noble (καλόν)..., [and to] have a natural compassion toward people who are in great difficulties or who are suffering from oppression," and so forth, across a range of affective evidence.[39] A. M. Eckstein is the critic quoted.

Still further: Polybius offers a profusion of passages not only describing people in the grip of feelings, but so presented as to engage readers sympathetically — passages "intended," as Eckstein puts it, "to move his audience..., to awaken feelings of pity" or some other emotion.[40] In the wake of the naval engagement off Chios (16.9.8f.) the number of bodies floating about could only induce "horror" and "a spirit of no ordinary despondency," as the historian well knew; so he offers the sight out of his set purpose; or again, he goes into the treachery that leads up to a massacre, and asks, "can any indignation be too strong?" (2.58.8). He loads the Aetolians with abuse for every possible cruel, uncivilized, immoral trait of character, so as to bring the reader into the mind of the admired Aratus, the Achaean leader. Aratus is "incensed and exasperated" at them just as readers are meant to be (4.6.11f., 4.7.8). And another rhetorical question to rouse excitement at the onset of a great battle: "Is there anyone who can remain unmoved in reading the narrative of such an encounter?" (15.9.3).

At the same time, emphatic attention is given to previous historians like Phylarchus who exemplify how history should *not* be written: *not* merely to titillate, chill, horrify, for the sake of the emotions in themselves, as a playwright is free to do — but never an historian. Truth, first; then, such evocation as flows from human nature responding in the reader; and there is in truth more than enough to engage an audience — enough, of which Polybius makes full use within his chosen bounds.[41] They do not exclude invention, for instance, in a commander's speech to his troops before going into battle, so long as it seems to suit the occasion; and the historian had heard many such, and sought out reports of still more.[42] *Enargeia* may and should engage the feelings.

After an interval of rhetorizing practitioners dominant over many generations of history-writing, Polybius thus appears the first "worthy extant successor to Thucydides."[43] Historians thereafter took his seriousness seriously, beginning with Poseidonius, and of course drew on him for fact; or they acknowledged his canonical status, as Dionysius of Halicarnassus did in ending his own work at the point in time where Polybius had begun.[44] But casual readers were best pleased by the emotionally engaging moments, and these were the most remembered and imitated.[45]

I come now to the next in the series of Greek writers who constitute the back-bone, as it were, of the historiographical tradition. Poseidonius, nicknamed "The Athlete" for physical prowess that was to carry him through much hard traveling and no doubt dangers, too, began life in Syria and ended it at a ripe old age in Rhodes. There for many years he had taught in the Stoic school. In his lecture-room Pompey had sat, and later Cicero, among many others. Students do not always hear what is said. Granted, it was philosophy. Their teacher's historiographic interests, picked up in the 80s, he pursued in silence until at last the *magnum opus* was published toward the end of his life in the 50s BC; and it was then rapidly passed over by the reading public. Its sympathies were too large, too theoretical. It had grown out of and reflected journeys in his homeland, and in Dalmatia, Italy, north Africa, Gaul, Spain, Egypt, and Sicily, to say nothing of a familiarity, extensive if perhaps second-hand, with the further lands of the Near East. In Sicily, he had investigated the recent outbreaks of rebellion among a huge servile population. It afforded a view of slavery which he had thought about carefully, without illusions, as he knew it also in other countries.[46]

In Gaul, he found much to remark on among the peoples to the north, remarks here also that were distinctively detached, detailed, and often analytical. Caesar for his Gallic Wars — the reality, or the *Commentaries* (6.11ff.) — knew them, but just what use he made of them is not clear. They recall Thucydides' reflections on human nature at large, in passages well known (e.g. Thuc. 2.97.4, above, on the Odrysii; 3.45.3 in the mouth of Diodotus the Athenian speaker; 3.82f., in Corcyra); but Poseidonius had more exotic manners to describe, far up among the lands along the Danube and Rhine, in communities where duels to the death broke out over one's share of the meat-course at public banquets, and enemies' heads were mounted proudly over one's doorway — a sight by which he "was at first nauseated, but afterwards took it lightly."[47]

He was observant of childhood, and his work was later drawn upon in describing "the natural affinity to pleasure and victory" among the young, "just as at some later time they show when they grow up that they have a natural affinity towards moral values. Part proof of this is that they are ashamed of their mistakes as they grow older, are glad in noble actions, lay claim to justice and the other virtues and often act in accordance with their notions of these virtues" (notice the wry, restrained "often").[48] The prominence, here, of terms for affects fits the thought of an author who wrote a major study *On Emotions*, applying to the subject a great deal of common experience as well as, and sometimes opposed to, the philosophical traditions in which he had been trained. Among feelings, he distinguishes desire and anger, "universals" as this idea is discussed in Chapter 2, below. He has theories about the physiology of emotions, too, and their relation with reason, denying them the quality of judgements.[49] In this study he follows on a line of research and conjecture in which Aristotle's name is perhaps the best known, for pages in his *Rhetoric*; and later there were works by Theophrastus also *On the Emotions*, and competing discussions by Epicureans and Stoics.[50] The latter at the beginning were inclined to deny reality to feelings, and to try entirely to suppress them, because they were all wrong; but a later Stoic like Poseidonius wanted to understand as much as to control. In that sense, he was to a degree Aristotelian. Hence, his attention in his travels to ethnopsychology as he could pursue it among very different peoples, and his speculation that they lived according to their different value-systems, in response to the necessities of their physical or political or social surroundings.[51] He appears unique in the attention he gives to such connections.

Within his prodigious intellectual production, it is his *Histories* in which Poseidonius considers these matters quite as much as in his Stoic studies. But how much, and in what ways? The *Histories* survives only in fragments, of which one alone is long (too long to quote) while the others lack a context and were chosen by the excerptor for reasons not always relevant to history at all. As a specimen of them, an anecdote about a workforce of men and women for digging: "... and one of the women whose birth pains had started went off from her work nearby, gave birth and returned straightaway, not to lose her pay," and so on, to the end of this little tale; or the description of the army sent to war by Apamea, its men "clutching belt dirklets and javelettes covered in rust and filth, with wee stetsons clapped on their heads and sunshields," and so on, to their very "flutelets and solo recorders, instruments of revelry rather than of war."[52] Of portraits of individuals, those of Marius in his final days, and of Marcellus a hero against Hannibal, can be more or less understood and savored still, though not quoted for us quite verbatim.[53] They are characteristic in their respect for small details in which meaning can be found, and in their wit and high colors. Any

Poseidonian views on individual motivation, however, are lost beyond recovery. His excerptors cared not for these. They preferred and preserved oddities, anecdotes, items very strikingly expressed.

3. ROMAN WRITERS

About the time that Poseidonius set about the writing of his *Histories*, Sempronius Asellio was beginning his *Histories*, too.[54] The moment may serve me for a transition to the stream of Roman historiography within which Caesar, Sallust, and Livy stand out; for they survive in a quantity more than ample to justify discussion, below.

Asellio also serves to introduce the subject of rhetoric in Latin historiography; for, in an excerpt found among the quite insignificant remains of his work, he ridicules as infantile the bare-bones style of the old-fashioned Roman annalistic and promises instead to provide his readers with both the narrative of events and the plan and method behind them, *quo consilio quaque ratione*.[55] The terminology, making him sound very much like Polybius, belongs to the standard rules of oratory, in which of course educated Romans like Greeks were thoroughly grounded. Now, "the plan and method" giving rise to an event, if they are to be revealed, must require some searching into the actors' minds, some characterizing and attention to the nature of the impulses at work; in short, some psychology. This teaching was intended to equip one (as young Scipio had realized he was not equipped) to handle oneself well in court, to talk round a reluctant jury, dramatize the doings, good or evil, of the defendant or accused; all this equally before a political audience; and for success in the attempt, one must have some mastery over narration, plus color. These were basic rhetorical skills useful also in history.

The reformer Gaius Gracchus a generation earlier, in the 120s BC, owed his success in public life as much to oratory as to anything else; and some little snippets of this survive in quotations. They suggest just what narration plus color might be like. One is an anecdote told of a plowboy on a road in southern Italy curious about a company of men carrying along a litter, and he asks, perhaps with a foolish grin on his face, *per iocum*, just what is it they have inside? — whereupon the young lordling lounging in the litter gives orders to his men to have the boy beaten to death. The story horrifies, the horrification was intended to arouse Gracchus' listeners against the class and conduct that the nobleman represented. Or again, quoted by Cicero: after Gaius' brother had been beaten to death — he too, but in a riot action — Gaius asks, "Where shall I betake myself, unhappy man that I am, *quo me miser conferam*? Where shall I turn? To the Capitol? But it is wet with a brother's blood. Or to my home? — that I might behold my mother a widow weeping and abject?" To which Cicero need hardly add "the fact, that this was all done by him in such a way, using his eyes, voice, his gesture, that his very enemies could not hold back their tears."[56]

Another famous speaker, this later one contemporary with Asellio, was Marcus Antonius, grandfather of *the* Mark Antony. Cicero imagines him in a *conversazione* placed just toward the time when Poseidonius and Asellio were writing. Antonius there serves as spokesman for Cicero's own ideas on oratory. He is glad to be drawn out on the proper employment of feelings by speakers, not excluding what they themselves feel; for "do not suppose," he recalls about a well-known moment in his career,

> do not suppose, then, that I myself... did without profound emotion, *magno dolore*, the things I did when choosing that famous case, in which my task was to maintain Manius Aquilius in his civic rights. For here was a man whom I remembered as having been consul, commander-in-chief, honored by the Senate, and mounting in procession to the Capitol; on seeing him cast down, crippled, sorrowing and brought to the risk of all he held dear, I was myself overcome by compassion before I tried to excite it in others. Assuredly I felt

that the Court was deeply affected when I called forth
my unhappy old client, in his garb of woe..., tearing
open his tunic and exposing his scars. While Gaius
Marius, from his seat in court, was strongly reinforcing,
by his weeping, the pathos of my appeal..., all this
lamentation... was accompanied by tears and vast
indignation on my own part, *dolore magno*.[57]

The impression conveyed by such passages as these few is
indeed affecting. In that fact it fairly illustrates the flow of
feeling into oratory as that art reached Rome from Greece.
But it had in Greek hands long flowed into history as well.
In Cicero's dialogue, Antonius indeed assumes that history is
a branch of oratory, an art in which is included the power to
arouse the entire range of responses in the audience; and the
same power, as is plain although not specified, must be exercised likewise in historical narration; for the audience must
be given the plan infusing an action (or at least those great
actions which deserve to be recalled) and the manner in
which they are carried through, along with the characterization of the actor. Antonius' vocabulary here exactly recalls the
terms of art that Asellio uses, quoted above.[58]

And beyond the work of evocation that proper history
should perform, it should make real and vivid whatever is
described, through the telling use of detail — so Antonius
recommends: *enargeia*. By this means it will serve his particular purpose; for he himself reads, he says, "for the pleasure of
it, when there's time."[59] He certainly does not mean, by *delec-
tatio*, anything very intellectual; more like the enjoyment of
reading fiction. The emotions are stirred. His confession is
very much in the tradition of Duris, even though it is pre-
ceded by praise of Thucydides for that writer's ideas, sharp
clarity, and generous provision of sheer fact.[60] *There*, there
would be intellectual enjoyment; but *enargeia*, it will be
recalled, is the lifelike quality that makes an audience see a
scene in all its smallest points and, perhaps, its poignancy, so
as to experience it wholly.[61]

Affect must not be laid on with a trowel, as, for example,
Duris had done. His was a name that might be used to focus

scorn for bathos and melodrama — thus, by Polybius and others.[62] But Polybius and his like were themselves a largely disregarded minority, from Duris' day on into the Augustan times that interest me — witness Antonius. There should be room for historiography that appealed to a "mass audience," "middle-brow culture," as it may be described, in contrast to the cerebral reader that Thucydides was thought to require.[63] So long as history avoided distortion in the sense of outright falsehood or slanted treatment of the past, let it attempt the overwhelmingly evocative reconstruction of the past. Faithfulness to the basic facts must be the foundation, true, but the superstructure might be as elaborate as the writer wished.[64] It failed if it did not persuade; it would not persuade if it contradicted common experience; but it need not be, as a "scientific" definition of "the truth" would require, every bit attested by known records.

From the earliest years of his oratorical career, Cicero demonstrated his powers of dramatic narrative. One has only to think of the more highly colored parts of his eloquence against an evil governor, cruel beyond measure, "so that the cry and supplication, 'I am a Roman citizen,' which has so often to so many in the furthest corners of the earth brought aid and safety among very barbarians — this cry only the more quickly brought them a harsher death and agony...," etc., etc.[65] Better than any Roman alive, Cicero could have fulfilled Antonius' prescriptions, and he knew it, and he intended to do so; they were after all his own prescriptions.[66] But after the 50s BC when he drew them from Antonius in the *De oratore*, his life was too interrupted for this effort. Incomplete *Commentarii* on his consulate were never published. Other Romans — his own brother was one, and his dear friend Atticus, and Cornelius Nepos — wrote *Annales* or similar accounts, long lost;[67] and Caesar wrote *Commentarii*.

These last, indeed, survive: the famous Rhine bridge and all. They are of course not a history book in quite the measured, responsibly researched and ripely pondered form of the works in Greek so far considered. They serve, however, to show

in some detail how the author approached the task of historical reconstruction, motive included; and that is my concern.

Caesar's first encounter with the peoples to the north was
through reports. The Helvetians' migration was moved by
their desire for land, sharpened by indignation; for what they
possessed was not proportionate to what they deserved
according to norms or expectations ruling their world; and
besides, "they were a people in love with war."[68] So the Gallic
wars all began. Afterwards, he began to know these men and
others face to face and as individuals. They were proud war-
riors, given always to aggressive assertion of their desires and
their sense of power, and this could only seem arrogance,
especially provoking because they claimed more than they
had any right to.[69] To the contrary, it was the Roman state
that might rightly claim respect proportionate to its strength.
Nor was it to be borne by such as Rome and Caesar that the
Rhine should be crossed by mere slap-together boats; it must
be a bridge that carried them over.[70] What was Rome's due
even in defeat was intolerably denied in the humiliation
inflicted on her legions, years earlier, or more recently, by
"most shameful hurt" done to her allies.[71] Where the senate
and people had actually offered a hand of friendship to one
of the tribes, or done one a favor, why, then to bear arms
against Rome was intolerable;[72] and it was a disregard of
legitimate expectations if emissaries to a parlay were
threatened, or a truce violated, and the whole Roman army
saw it as such, and reacted with fury.[73] The army had its pride
not to be denied; it would not yield where shame would
attend retreat.[74]

In these various contexts, Caesar explains how events are
set in train by very much the same feelings that other writers refer to: that is, anger, especially exacerbated by the sense
of not getting what one is entitled to; the desire to have
(whether land or booty); and the desire for approval, protection of one's image, sense of shame — all these, social feelings. Explanatory passages are, however, not many. Perhaps
that is because the *Commentarii* is so nearly a war narrative
and nothing else, the raw material for a history; and, once

hostilities commence, there is little further to be said about motive; for each side is understandably reacting to what the other does and aims only at the one end, victory.

The same may be said of his account of the *Civil Wars*; or it is simply his style. In any case, he makes little attempt to explain what happened. At the start, he must say why his enemies forced his hand (as he saw it), under the influence of several different motives: grudges long-nourished by some of the troops that followed Pompey, while others were drawn in by fears or desire of reward in money or higher rank; individual leaders also drawn in by grudges and, in addition, by resentment at political defeat, or by hope of a rich province to milk during a term as governor, so as to pay off debts; or dread of suits, for the same cause; and Pompey himself "because he wanted no one to be on a level with his own *dignitas*."[75] What then could Caesar do except defend himself against the insults and injuries offered to him, as he explained to his men? And against the fact that Pompey was "wholly corrupted by jealousy"?[76]

Hostilities once under way, an early focus was the city of Marseilles. While it professed an equal obligation to both sides, nevertheless it joined Pompey's, by a piece of treacherous deceit that Caesar can only consider a wrong done him, and so begins a siege. There ensues after a time a naval battle in the harbor which he cannot resist describing as Thucydides did that of Syracuse', visible to watchers on land, and "all the men of more advanced age with their children and wives... were stretching out their hands to heaven or visiting the temples," and so forth, in a piece of not very successful pathos.[77] By these displays the Caesarian forces were little affected, feeling rather "angry bitterness at the revolt, at the contempt shown to themselves, and at their drawn-out labors of war." Later again, they responded with equal intensity of feeling to the sense of wrong and shame.[78]

Finally, there is a stirring moment as a final battle is about to begin, where a devoted centurion promises victory to Caesar, so thus "he will regain his *dignitas* and we, our freedom" (3.91). Whatever may be intended by this last word, or how ever defeat might bring with it slavery ("slavery" is more often what men speak of in Polybius' scenes of war-fears), *dignitas* at least is a well known Roman term. It was the generally acknowledged perception of a person's "clout" or place in the world, a possession of supreme value, as dear as life; it was the equivalent of that respect for which a member of a New York street gang will kill, if he is "dissed"; or for which Jewish students at German universities, long ago, learned to duel, so that they could assert their honor in the face — very precisely in the face — of their Christian fellows.[79]

Caesar, not only by this moment in his account but repeatedly in public settings before civil war broke out, defined his choices in terms of *dignitas*. He must defend its possession, so far as he could claim it. His men understood this, his friends and even his enemies understood without necessarily approving. While *dignitas* might indeed serve its possessor to protect, to render help, to stand up in any company, to deter attack or avenge insult, in sum, to assure all sorts of political and material rewards, what explained its role in motivation was its roots in one's sense of self, one's sense of approval and of rights. To *dignitas*, then, under attack by humiliation and insult, Caesar could appeal without apology before any audience, as also when he acted as historian to record what was said of the origins of strife by his supporters. His appeals are generally taken at face value by his modern readers.[80] Rightly. That is, private passions did really split the state, at least as writers of the time saw it.

Sallust, Caesar's younger coadjutor, when he retired from politics and took up history-writing in the later 40s BC gave prominence to *dignitas* in his pages. It was the possession of everyone who was anyone. Lentulus had had it, Cato the younger, Lepidus, Memmius, even the degenerate revolutionary Catiline had once had it and lamented its loss.[81] It was perhaps too close to be recognized as a social construct, energized by its affective core elements; but still, its importance to the individual was evident, and Sallust saw, too, its importance to society as a whole. An aristocracy that lost its *dignitas* to pleasures was done for — like Rome's, in his judgement, looking back.[82] The same thoughts, floating up on clouds of cigar smoke from the depths of leather armchairs in the best of clubs, are familiar to this day: once we were a great people, all disciplined honest patriotic folk, but now.... Sallust had ease and leisure for such profound reflections, strolling about in his quite gigantic gardens, a private Versailles. They lay just on the north side of the capitol, bought up with whatever wealth had come to him, no questions asked, in the course of his governorship of north Africa. As a moral and social philosopher he comes forward generally in the prologues to his books, rehearsing in his inimitable style a mishmash of philosophical commonplaces à la Grecque. "He was certainly no deep thinker."[83]

But the question, how do norms and institutions actually work, so as to produce characteristic tendencies toward one kind of behavior over another? — this more trenchant question did occupy him in several passages. Among them, drawing on Polybius' Sixth Book, he recalls how "the outstanding men in our nation like Quintus Maximus, Publius Scipio, and the rest used to say that, looking at the death-masks of their ancestors, their spirits were inspired with a burning desire to earn honor... — memory of their deeds caused the flame."[84] Similarly, he sees how the necessities of war, which are institutions of a sort, teach their own special reflexes — just as Thucydides had seen.[85] He draws on the Greek historian most noticeably for features of his style of composition, but for comment on *mores* as well.

And Sallust also takes up a trope of Roman moral history going back to the Hannibalic war: that a nation is well served by the existence of external threat, which induces a certain mentality, keeps the people virile, religious, united, ready for anything. "The Carthage fear" once served this purpose; but supremacy everywhere in time induced degeneration.[86] In his *Bellum Jugurthinum* and *Catilinae*, the two accounts for which he is best remembered — and remembered not only because they alone survive in their entirety — Sallust had chosen topics that invited such moral assessment: the corrupt mishandling of a foreign prince; later, an insurrection, by the rotten part of the nobility. Where it was a group that served him as protagonist, explanation could only be through a general indictment of what Thucydides or Polybius would have called *pleonexia*, excessive *desire to have*, without specification of just what might be desired. Our English "greed" does not have quite the same broad force as this, nor *avaritia*.[87] It was the latter passion, "without limit or restraint," which beset Rome's chosen from the days of Jugurtha to Catiline and beyond, and explained prevailing conduct, as Sallust describes and indicts it.

Where it is not a group but an individual that he focuses on, he uses both settled character traits and the passions of the moment to show where events took their rise. One actor is by nature "fierce", another "quarrelsome". The vocabulary is little varied since conflict is what most often makes for drama, and drama is what Sallust supposed makes for history. If it is missing from an occasion, speeches will whip it up; and the side to support is never left in doubt, between the good and the evil.[88] By any historian of Catiline's insurrection, a great deal of good and evil and richly artistic name-calling could be found, of course, ready to hand in Cicero's actual speeches, on which in fact Sallust draws heavily; but he succeeds in presenting an equally clear choice in his account of the Jugurthine war.[89] More than other authors, he intends not only to record or portray emotions, as an essential part of the story, but to stimulate them in his readers.

Particular provocation of strong feeling in the past is occasionally explained, for example, by a public insult rubbed in with some additional remarks, this being the cause of the whole Jugurthine war, or a memorable anecdote confronting the burning ambition of Marius with the obstacle of Metellus. Metellus, serene a-top a tower of ancestral and fraternal consulates, himself at the moment commander in the field, denies to Marius a leave of absence, to run for consul. Time enough for that some other year, he says, when my son (then a mere lad) will be ready for the canvass, too. It was a taunt "which set Marius fiercely aflame both for the office he sought, and against Metellus; and as a consequence he allowed himself to be swayed by desire and fury, the worst of counsellors" — with historic consequences.[90]

At one point an African king, fearing for his safety at the hands of another, his neighbor and kinsman, is imagined inviting protection: "It belonged to the *maiestas* of the Roman people to prevent such a wrong, and not to allow the kingdom of anyone to grow great through a crime."[91] The appeal is well conceived, given a natural sympathy to be felt for the petitioner's rights and the rule of law; hence, shared indignation; but in addition, an aim at the characteristically Roman love of acknowledged supremacy, "greaterness".[92] As boys once wrestled and struggled until one said "uncle", "I give up," so Rome would not lay down her arms until a challenger acknowledged her supremacy, for good and all. Then she might be gracious; the Greeks learnt she might even leave them their freedom, within the terms of their subordination. This seemed to them a miracle.

Turning to Livy, last among the three Latin historians to be considered here: "greaterness" is given a prominent place in his pages. It figured formally in terms of surrender, for example, those he records of the Aetolians: "to preserve inviolate the rule and greaterness of the Roman people." Among the claims of individuals, it is naturally limited to those who were of the highest rank and office; and he indicates there was some agreeable thrill to the acknowledgment of it, when the Roman populace saw it accorded to their consuls.[93]

Desire for glory he sees often as moving the Romans to action, especially in the earlier centuries of their history; indignation worked, too, especially (as very often) when roused in the cause of right; and rightful wrath, proper shame, various other emotions are held up for admiration and as determinants of whatever behavior Livy is recording.[94]

Opposite qualities he notes generally with their ill consequences: rashness, lust....[95] Roman noblemen in their competition for office trod on each others' aspirations, or toes, and were furious, too, and wanted to get even from then on: they became known enemies, and *inimicitiae* often split the state, resulting in a dramatic tension between the natural urges of the individual and the requirements of good citizenship. On these, Livy lingers.[96] Loss of face, public *contumelia* of some sort, stimulated the desire for revenge, an emotion nowhere more openly acknowledged than by the *grande dame* of a great house, writing to her son, "You will say, vengeance on one's enemies is a lovely thing. To no one more than to myself does it seem a great, a lovely thing, so long as it may be pursued without harm to the state."[97] Here, the tension is explicit. *Inimicitiae* — quite as characteristic an element of Roman politics as the much more often studied *amicitia*, that is, "friendship" in its technical sense of an alliance or claim on support — *inimicitiae* were its equally Roman opposite,[98] and offered to the historian an opening for excitement in the narrative, for strong personalities, passionate impulses, all, roused by what was of peculiar interest to an aristocratic audience, just as duels were for newspaper readers of, let us say, the decades around the turn of the nineteenth century.

Feelings such as these derived from a person's sensitivity to the community all around and its judgement of behavior. They were social, expressive of a need for approval. Social also were the feelings, and consequent expressions, of gratitude for favors granted, ties of friendship resulting, expectations of dutiful behavior or of anger at someone who fell short, desire for respect that depended on influence over others' choices of action, and irritability on this front, where one's influence might be disregarded — so, from all these various emotions, a Roman vocabulary: *amicitia, gratia, beneficia, fides, clientelae, pietas, dignitas, contumeliae, maiestas.* It is only because historical interest focuses so much on politics that these terms of a meaning particular to Roman society figure so much in both the ancient and modern historical accounts. They serve as a reminder of the affect surrounding and giving energy to the narrative. Both the reality and the terms in which contemporaries presented it in written form acknowledged the sources of action.

Social in another sense are the feelings that sweep through a crowd, a mob, an army, a whole people, as Livy describes the moment: fury, terror, pity, hope, joy, nervous tension.[99] So

moved, the actors decide to fight to the end, to bury a Vestal
alive, to enter the war on the speaker's side. That is how events
take form. In conveying their feelings, Livy may heap words
on words, for example, of execration — the enemy to be
attacked are traitors and brigands, breakers of sacred truces,
sprinkled with the gore of their own fellows, faithless allies
and cowardly foes, and so forth (4.32.12). Fear and shock
greet the sensational news of a conspiracy of noblewomen to
manufacture poison, for what purpose is not clear; and some
of the accused commit suicide (8.18.6ff.); while abhorrence
greets equally sensational report of homosexuality, aimed at
the innocent or active at the center of a new cult, to every
good citizen's consternation.[100]

In a Livy-study still seen as very well judged and thoughtful, P. G. Walsh acknowledges the effect of such highly colored choices of topic and language. "The 'thrills and chills' are
continually emphasised" — but not mechanically produced;
rather, felt by Livy himself.[101] The reader may picture Livy
acting out as he composes, certainly trying the sound of his
sentences aloud (because they would be dictated to an
amanuensis) and perhaps, like Dickens exclaiming or crying
as he spoke. He projected himself into the scene he was
describing just as Antonius had done and recommended to
other practitioners, and wanted his audience to do so, too: to
feel. Such were the teachings of rhetoric. Of this art, Livy was
the first historian to be a complete practitioner rather than a
politician who was also a speaker — and a speaker, everyone
in his Rome must really be for any success. The rhetorical
character of Roman historiography may be judged from the
examples touched on, omitting Caesar's distinctly different
genre of composition and different objectives: but including
Sallust, Livy, and Cicero as he appears potentially. The latter's
notion of how history should be written is quite clear in his
various literary treatises. Minor figures could be added, too,
without our noticing much more than their similarity to
these earlier ones.[102]

It is easy to agree that surviving historiography in Latin
admits much more emotionality than Greek; but within the

Latin as in the Greek, the different kinds of emotionality need to be recalled: what the writer ascribed to actors in the past, what he felt in himself, and what he aroused in his readers. The three kinds were noted in my discussion of Thucydides, and one or the other in Polybius or Sallust. It is easy to agree, on the other hand, that a stretch of narrative by Sallust, Livy, or Cicero, as compared to Thucydides, Polybius, or Poseidonius, is far more likely to contain far more of the third kind of emotionality: reader–affect. The Latin writers offer a more or less constant play of affective stimuli, directed at the moral sense as often as at simple compassion.

To the modern mind, this characteristic of all surviving ancient historiography but of Latin in particular is disturbing; for it is natural to ask if the truth has not been lost in drama and sensation. The substance of what happened — has it not yielded to mere art? Has not vividness, *enargeia*, mimesis, *exaedificatio*, come from within the mind alone of an artist, not from the field–notes of the scientific observer? And perhaps Syme was right in what he chose for praise in Rome's best known historian, at the end of a monumental work on that author, Tacitus? —"Men and dynasties pass but style abides."[103]

To which, however, there is a reply: even in the most rhetorizing of historiography, the artist could claim to know (though in Livy's handling of remote centuries, we cannot agree that he did know) the world he was describing. It was in some real sense his own. His handling of his drama must offer no point of contradiction to common experience, as his audience would define it — who were also of that same world. And in this bargain, this contract, between audience and writer may be found some considerable comfort even by the most cautious skeptic today.

For consider the contrary: that a person engaging in the various actions chosen for description and accepted as fact really felt nothing at all. Insurrectionaries had no deep grievance! — nor negotiators who flung out of a meeting, nor assemblies that shouted their decrees of war or death. Such a possibility, to readers of Thucydides or Sallust alike, evidently seemed impossible. It could not be imagined. Therefore the supply of feelings by the historian was needed to represent the whole real truth. And it must be conveyed *with its emotions in their proper force*, too. The sense of force is essential. Exactly this, the arts of dramatic presentation could supply. The objective, however, which the better Greek historians realized — our full understanding of what happened — was not what the worser, and the Roman, aimed at — mere delectation.

4. AUGUSTAN HISTORY

From the generation after Caesar there survives a pair of Greek historians of which no very long analysis is needed. The first, Diodorus of Sicily, in his *History Library* begins his account with some hundreds of pages on the Greece of mythology. Thereafter, true to its title, from an assortment of sources the work gathers an unmethodical account of classical and Hellenistic times to the edge of the Gallic wars — mostly a flow of events with little of the psychological elaboration that would serve my inquiry; and in the latter books, known today only from fragments, he draws chiefly on Polybius and Poseidonius, whom it has seemed best to address directly (above).[104]

Nevertheless, there are many relevant passages here and there. They touch on most of those sorts of feelings already discovered in Diodorus' predecessors. A revolt, for example, takes its start in someone's feeling of being wronged by the unfair division of a political inheritance, just as wrongful, despotic conduct will rouse resentment from the injured, and eventually they will rise against the ruler. Such reactions are explained in terms of "hatred", "anger", "outrage", and the like; or (very much less often) someone in power will show mild or generous behavior from friendship or gratitude or the sake of good repute.[105] There is an admixture of social feelings in Diodorus' treatment of causation, and a clear tracing of events to their roots in an emotional impulse of some sort.

Long-nourished anger is seen in search of vengeance; or to explain someone's conduct, that person's violent nature is described or an unreasoning desire for good fame; and of course mere greed for gold is a motive on occasion, too.[106]

Whole groups or assemblies yield to their moods and feelings: to pity, hope, excitement, panic fear;[107] an entire people may be shaped by anxiety, or the lifting of it (by the reasoning seen above in Sallust and others, that it was good for the Roman moral backbone to have to worry about Carthage).[108] Occasionally Diodorus philosophizes about emotions: for instance, pointing out that resentment of treatment from other people depends on one's sense of one's place in society, high or low.[109] He wants his readers to think. It is, he supposes, a purpose of history to make one do so: to reflect on human behavior in all its varieties and settings, so as to learn from others' experience and thus become a better human being.[110]

Yes, but history has a second purpose also, to provide agreeable sensations, "thrills and chills" as one critic put it (quoted above). Otherwise we hardly need details of hideous tortures and mutilation, so drawn out as they are given us at 33.14.1ff., or again, in Agathocles' reign, replete with savage acts, revenge, flight, despair, when "reverence due to the gods was overthrown by men," with villains in positions of power "respecting neither common humanity nor solemn compacts nor gods." The situation must be brought out to us in all its lurid colors. We enjoy our horror. Diodorus continues, "it was reasonable to suppose that the husbands and fathers would suffer something worse than death when they thought of the violence done to their wives and the shame inflicted upon their unmarried daughters." This much could be assumed. Yet a sober writer, he warns, "must keep our account of these events free from the artificially tragic tone that is habitual with historians, chiefly because of our pity for the victims, but also because no one of our readers has a desire to hear all the details when his own understanding can readily supply them."[111]

What is easily recognizable here is an attempt to rise a little above the melodrama of writers like Duris, whom
Diodorus nevertheless uses,[112] along with a dozen others of
his predecessors; for he was determined to separate himself
from the over-wrought, emotive excesses of the rhetorical
style. In the attempt he does in fact succeed. Given his choice
of emphasis, so often war, which must inevitably include violent actions and emotions, success on his own terms could
not totally exclude thrills and chills. He could, however,
aim for and does achieve a balance — a balance between the
inclusion of affective elements so as to explain, and so as to
stir his audience.

His successor on the other hand preferred what Diodorus
rejected. The writer was Dionysius of Halicarnassus in his
Roman Antiquities. His work runs through the earliest centuries of Rome down to 265 BC, the point at which Polybius
picked up. Dionysius had no more to work with for these
times than the most exiguous state records, with an admixture of legend. This, however, he judged adequate to support
a superstructure, an *exaedificatio* with its affective elements
made up from whole cloth — foundations and superstructure together constituting history as the teachings of rhetoric
defined that genre.[113] Imagined speeches stretch to a great
length; posturing and bathos, well represented. Imitating what
was common in his models, Dionysius emphasizes outrage
and moral norms, international or individual, to explain
indignation and induce sympathy;[114] emphasizes also resentment and hatred, as his models do; and sees all his dramatiz-
ing of actors' emotions as psychological analysis —which of
course it is not, where it must be simply invented.[115]

In discussing Thucydides, Dionysius like his contemporaries in Rome (notably Sallust) most admired not that
author's challenge to the reader's intelligence, but points of
style, techniques of expression, and rhetorical brilliance.[116]
For Dionysius, these may be enough to move a story forward
by moving readers with it. Affective color provides narrative
energy. Illustration may be found in the Coriolanus-chapters
(small wonder that Beethoven looked here for a classical

inspiration): they are sometimes awash in tears. But notice, Coriolanus sets off a great war, through a passion for revenge.[117] He and his passions do make history.

At this point, now, to bring my list to an end, I look last at the *Life of Augustus*[118] by Nikolaos of Damascus, asking: is there affective material here convenient to a summary? — something that pulls together what has been noted in the whole of the list, which may be of use to historians?

The reasons for pausing on this particular short, generally colorless work lie not so much in itself as in its subject. The period is so well documented that the account can be cross-checked and augmented; and the protagonist is of course uniquely significant. Born in the year of Cicero's consulship (63 BC) as "Gaius Octavius," later "Gaius Iulius Caesar Octavian(us)" upon his adoption by his great-uncle Caesar (and conventionally "Caesar" himself thereafter), he eventually received the title "Augustus". As that last, it is convenient to speak of him throughout.

His family belonged to the lower ranks of the oligarchy, and was on the rise through his father's career; but this was cut short. Augustus was left fatherless at the age of four or five. His was a peer-community which set great store on successful engagement in public life and the achievement of high office; and the boy grew up knowing his father had been deprived of a consulate only by the mischance of a premature death. In his circle of kin, however, everything possible was in fact achieved by Caesar, Augustus' great-uncle, the most electrifying presence (or absence, in the 50s BC) that anyone could possibly imagine; and by this godlike person Augustus was taken up in his later teens to a position of public and remarkable favor, with all possibilities widening before him. He was moreover surrounded by men who in one degree of fervor or another admired the leader in their midst and thus fortified whatever awe, gratitude, and affection a boy in such a position of privilege must feel toward such a cynosure.

Being settled for some months in northern Greece in an encampment of the legions he was to accompany on a great campaign, when Caesar should join it, at Caesar's death Augustus had to rethink his life.

All this familiar tale I recall only to make obvious the emotions that one would expect to find in an eighteen-year old at such a juncture: a mix, surely, of passionate grief and rage; and taken for granted must be a particular direction for rage, to inflict punishment on Caesar's killers. The expectation of vengeance in a Roman's moral world has been noted above. The mix that we might expect, then, with no teaching needed from any ancient sources, would be enough to indicate what particular actions in turn should follow from Augustus. In fact, however, as history unfolds in Nikolaos, what one would expect is precisely what one finds.

The general expectation of vengeance to be exacted from the assassins appears immediately in the aftermath of the Ides of March, when the news reached Augustus and his friends advised him on how best to respond to it (Nik. 16). At the same time, avengers were expected to come forward in Rome from among the persons who had benefited from the dictator's favor. For the moment he deferred action, despite further expressions of loyalty from the army and promises of support in avenging Caesar (§17); but he did decide on a return to Italy, and sailed to a port near Brundisium. There, he heard more of Rome: "that the populace from the warmth of their feelings to the dictator were angry about the assassination" (§17), and "when the young [Augustus] heard this he was moved to tears and sobs by the memory and love for the man, which stirred his grief anew" (§18). Letters from home advised caution, but his mind was filled with high deeds and resolution. By the act of testamentary adoption he had been lawfully confirmed in the honors of his new father and "it was most right and proper to accede to him and to avenge him, who had suffered such horrible things."[119] Learning of his resolve, his mother "dared not dissuade the lad from attempting high deeds and embarking on a just revenge."[120] So far, reactions highly charged but predictable.

Their predictability derives in part from what readers today will think of as universals in human behavior; but in part, too, from the particular ethical habits of the Roman time and place, where obligations to one's house and ancestry were deeply felt, as by both the elder and the younger Scipio, and where it was seen as utterly disgraceful not to feel and act out one's gratitude for favors received.[121] No one had received more than Augustus.[122] *Pietas* dictated his response. "One must sacrifice to one's parents not lambs and kids but the tears and [court-] convictions of their enemies."[123]

From Brundisium he journeyed slowly north to Rome. There, in reaction to the Ides of March, the members of Caesar's interest, "Caesarians" in the language of the time,[124] had agreed "that they must have satisfaction for him [their leader], and not do anything else, and not ignore his unavenged death;"[125] but the moment and its passions devolved into compromise — at least among the leaders. On his return to the capital, Augustus saw he "was the one person remaining to avenge his father" (§28). Instead of joining him, Antony, the chief Caesarean, did everything he could to ignore, humiliate, and isolate Augustus, even accusing him of a plot against himself; at which Augustus "was filled with righteous anger" (§31).[126] He had no reason, either, to feel very friendly toward Cicero at the time, for offering a quip, a merry pun at his expense, which was both treacherous and humiliating, and circulated widely.[127] Still, he controlled himself. He was to do that often, for example, when his enemies ignored and insulted him even after his victories on the field; but "while [Augustus] Caesar bore the outrage, *iniuria*, by ignoring it, *dissimulando*," his soldiers could speak for him. The moment recalls one much later when he thanked an ethics-professor for a piece of advice on the control of one's rage: "I still need you around."[128] He felt; but he didn't show it.

Nikolaos makes clear that there were strong passions at work among the civilian masses both in the city and in Campania, where Augustus next repaired to recruit some military force.[129] It was his cause they mostly favored. Readers are prepared for this strength of feeling by what are, in a rather spare account, heavy words scattered about: "impious", "sacrilegious", "outrageous", and so forth, to suggest how the tyrannicides were viewed, what perceptions kept the situation at a boil, and why the year 44 BC should have ended in a renewal of civil war. For by December Augustus had an army, Antony had an army, Decimus Brutus had one which he was supposed to yield up to its lawful commander, all these in Italy, while, overseas, there were other forces in real truth beyond any constitutional control, and likely to be hostile to some of those at home.

Of constitutional control, Cicero had come forward as champion, delivering the series of his anti-Antony speeches called *Philippics*. He well knew how much easier it was to make a man look bad than an abstraction look good; nor was abstraction in the style of Roman politics. Influence over other people's choices operated in Roman fashion through networks of obligation, seen from beneath, or of favor and patronage, seen from above; in any case, personal. What was thus created by the tireless intelligence and energy of Caesar, as an instance, never resembled what we would call a faction, with implications of its being outside the received boundaries of political power, nor, certainly, was it what we would call a party; no, it was simply "the Caesarians," just as there had been *Pompeiani*.[130] They stood for no policy. Accordingly, Cicero's oratory must naturally be *ad hominem* in a familiar but far more than ordinarily outrageous, venomous, slanderous style. The reply when made was in proportion.

That is, when Antony, still rabid and furious, was in a position to assert his *dignitas ad lib.*, he had Cicero pursued, rambling among his villas to the south, where the old man was stopped, and killed, and his head and hands cut off, those hands, it was said, with which the *Philippics* had been indited. To the orator's head, on Antony's orders brought to him in Rome, Antony "directed many bitter insults," while his wife Fulvia "after abusing it spitefully and spitting upon it, set it on her knees, opened the mouth, and pulled out the tongue, which she pierced with pins."[131] The reported scene gives force to the general impression conveyed by Nikolaos, that events were borne along chiefly on passion.

And it recalls another moment, another death, some months earlier in 44 BC: this, of Trebonius, a man who owed

to Caesar all his progress up the rungs of power, even to a
consulship. Serving subsequently as governor in the east, one
morning, still a-bed in his palace, he was caught by a centurion of Caesarian forces. He demanded to be taken to the
centurion's commander, Dolabella. The centurion answered,
    'Off you go, then, but leave your head here, for we're
    under orders to bring that, not you.' So saying, the man
    cut off his head straightway, and early the same day
    Dolabella directed that it be set up on the praetorian
    throne where Trebonius had conducted his judicial
    business. The soldiers in their fury, along with the
    crowd of camp followers — since Trebonius had taken
    part in the assassination of Caesar by distracting Antony
    in a chat at the doorway of the senate chamber while
    Caesar was being killed — inflicted various kinds of
    outrage on the body and passed around the head from
    one to another along the city pavement like a football,
    for a laugh, and so crushed and broke it to nothing. In
    this way, the first of the murderers paid the price.[132]
Once again, here, a glimpse of the force of feelings stirred by
the Ides among the troops.
    Indeed, they dominated the whole decade of the 40s.
Time was when the senate's vote had declared a war along
with the conscription of military forces under some commander it chose for them, and all was well, and Rome was
great and glorious. The power networks partly inherited,
partly woven wider, by the heads of great families served
them at the polls, not in arms against each other. By the 40s,
in contrast, the more civilian senators can only have seen in
these instruments of greatness — the legions above all — a
thing alive and with a mind of its own; rather, a heart of its
own. Where were its affections lodged? Which side was it on?
To judge from Cicero's correspondence, he and his like were
gripped by the most anxious uncertainties, continually asking
each other, What news, what rumors of fealty, and to whom?
Their situation was hardly dignified, indeed, humiliating.[133]
And whose opinion could one trust? Not even the military
experts, not always. After the Ides, Pompey still believed he

could, with a stamp of his foot, raise an army of volunteers anywhere in Italy. His boast proved ridiculous.[134]

It was also humiliating to make appeals to a mass of otherwise no-account men under arms. Historians, Nikolaos among them, supply many speeches of this sort. Cicero, saving his pride, boasted derisively how he used the occasion of one to bamboozle certain legions.[135] In Rome, the legions were a worrisome presence or worse, especially if they could be turned against himself as being in some way responsible for the assassination.[136] Even Augustus and Lepidus had trouble with their men; other commanders had to reason and persuade instead of command.[137]

Principally what prevailed were the sympathies of Caesar's veterans as such. In Nikolaos (§18, Dec. 44), we find Augustus' friends of the opinion that "the soldiers would most gladly follow where Caesar's son was their leader, and do anything for him;" or later (§29, Sept. 43), after Antony clashed with Augustus, "his father's soldiers bore ill the scorn that Antony displayed" for them, "though at the beginning they reproached themselves for having quite forgotten Caesar while they ignored the insults heaped on his son." It was then that they reconsidered and protested and brought about a reconciliation between their two leaders; but in a subsequent scene outside Augustus' house, "one of them at the top of his lungs shouted to Augustus to take heart, knowing they all were a part of his inheritance, for they remembered Caesar as on a plane with the gods and they would do and endure anything for his successors." Or, for a third illustration: in advertising directed at Caesar's veterans (§31), "they should remember Caesar [as Augustus'] father and in no way utterly betray the man's son."

Loyalty to Caesar quite dominates the decade, from beginning to end. The strength of the feeling may astonish, but it is agreed on by contemporary observers like Cicero, by historical accounts thereafter, and in many modern interpretations, too.[138] It could be confused, when a choice had to be made between Antony and Augustus. This was repeatedly the case in the sequel to the Ides of March. Nikolaos gives it some place in his account (clearest at §31.136). Even so, however, the stubborness of the men's attachments may be perhaps judged from the great amount of money needed to win them over from one loyalty to the other.

In explanation, Appian describes how "officers who had served under Caesar... judged he [Antony] should rein in his outrageous behavior [toward Augustus] both for their sake and his own — he who had served with Caesar and so obtained everything good he now enjoyed."[139] What was asserted and would readily be understood by him as an important element in a soldier's beliefs were the claims of gratitude, no different after all from any Roman's, in or out of military service. A commander only deserved more than anyone else, by virtue of rank; and his claim had only to be asserted.[140] It would speak to the heart: of soldiers, high officers included, who recalled Caesar with affection, and in convincing terms, and reacted with the more passion against those who, being favored and advanced by him, nevertheless slew him.[141]

The bond to a commander such as Caesar was tied to the expectation of a reward, in cash or land, and this receives mention in the historians.[142] Most desired was a plot of land to live on. In Campania many demobilized men by 44 BC had been assigned a plot or were awaiting an assignment grouped, as Appian explains, in their old legions.[143] Caesar more than any writer, but also the continuators of his *Civil Wars*, quite richly, and Livy, with Appian later, all inform us about the vibrant and keenly felt sense of unit that animated legionaries. They acted out their sense through demonstrations of bravery before their fellows, as did their officers, too, or through the avoidance of disgraceful conduct in combat.[144] Ultimately, the determination to fight and not to run was understood then as now to depend on such social feelings, making men responsive to each other as to their commander as well. Hence the prominence of the word "shame" in the historians' explanations of brave acts. Horrible as war was, yet emotional as well as material rewards could inspire even "a wonderful loyalty... and longing to fight together once more under his [Caesar's] name." So Nikolaos explains.[145]

Nikolaos, it is nowadays agreed, wrote his *Life* while the subject was still alive. The fact might give it particular reliability; but then, he was drawing with the least possible change on the subject himself, Augustus' *Autobiography*.[146] Did it not distort what really happened in order to favor the writer? So far as concerns Augustus' motivating emotions, the Greek edition by Nikolaos gives prominence to Augustus' sense of obligation toward his adoptive father and his desire for revenge — prominence which, however, is no cause for distrust; for, after all, the same feelings animated people in very large numbers whose relationship with the dictator was comparatively remote. Augustus must be granted the anguish he recorded. It was properly Roman to express one's grief and pain; instances of this have been seen and noted, above. Anger it was not in Roman fashion to express except when it was possible through action. Before that moment, raging about with no target or effect revealed only one's lack of *dignitas*; so it should be kept in; and Augustus was of a type to do this, as has been seen. But he made no secret of his determination to avenge this adoptive father, and manifestly devoted himself to that end immediately and for years. Besides his anger, and his anguish compounded of grief, gratitude, and loss, finally, he made no secret of an ardent desire for the world's applause. Our own term for this, "ambition", is somewhat too darkly colored, too selfish in its means and ends; whereas *gloria* was an approved objective for Romans, attested among all ranks of aspirants from non-commissioned officers on up; and this, too, has been seen in Nikolaos. To sum up, then: the natural fit between the emotions and impulses that any observer would expect in a teenager of Augustus' particular experience and situation, and Nikolaos' account, can be seen and tested in the text quite satisfactorily. Thereby we can understand what happened.

His is not our only source, of course. Cicero has often appeared, above, and Velleius, a generation younger than Augustus, and Appian: Appian, writing toward the mid-second century AD but weaving Caesar-contemporary memoirs into his narrative.[147] What survives to explain Augustus in affective terms, and to explain Antony, too, and the tyrannicides and army officers down through the ranks to individual speakers, and to show us initially why they all did what they did, seems as worthy of trust as most of ancient history — or rather more so.

And the fit with the traditions of classical historiography or, more properly termed, common sense, seems satisfactorily firm. The story of Caesar's heir from its beginning to the point at which Nikolaos leaves it, in the midst of a now-declared war, is determined throughout by various feelings moving the various actors to whatever fateful decisions they take, just as actors in events before them have been seen to play their parts according to their passions, clear back to the earliest times of the Roman people. At any rate, this is how the ancient historians tell it.

But modern historians? Quite the opposite.

So many of these have looked back to Augustan times, of course it is quite impossible to characterize or speak about them all. Compared to the regurgitative resources of classical scholarship on such a grand topic as this — young Augustus — the four stomachs of a cow are as nothing. Choosing one single interpretation is, however, not too misleading, given the fact of its very peculiar authority. I refer to Syme's 1939 study, *The Roman Revolution*, on which was founded his extraordinary career among academics, and an extraordinary fashion, or acquiescence, within the field. His book, after its various hardback editions and printings, and a dozen paperback reprintings, still remains in the 1990s a "classic", its author "the Emperor of Roman history."[148]

What is the truth about Augustus' times as Syme sees them? His readers will first be struck by the exceptional and almost universal nastiness of the Romans involved in any way in the events that Nikolaos and others deal with. Syme's detestation for the actors in the narrative has of course been noticed.[149] It takes in whole classes: "the propertied of the *municipia*…, avid and unscrupulous in their secret deeds," freedmen who "as usual, battened upon the blood of citizens," and "the army… now recruited from the poorest classes," who "from personal loyalty might follow great leaders like Caesar or Antonius" and after the Ides constituted "a

solid block of vested interests" in their post-war pay-offs, but
beyond that, "became truculent and tumultuous. Not without excuse: their Imperator... had been treacherously slain by
those whom he trusted and promoted. The honour of the
army had been outraged. Though Rome and the army were
degenerate and Caesarian...." So even this more intelligible
Roman mass does not escape derogation.

Yet the quoted words are almost all that Syme assigns to
the military, anywhere. It hardly appears in a flow of events
which its attachments may more truly be seen to control —
attachments which Syme's favored characters themselves, senators and the like, watched and talked about with anxious
interest. *His* interest rather centers in senators and the like,
themselves, almost exclusively, as his readers have often pointed out and as he is ready to declare, all history being the history of oligarchies; so that, being asked why the great mass of
humanity finds no place in his work, he replied, "It bores
me." So might a driver, "in ignorance sedate," suppose a car
moves forward when he or someone in the driver's seat presses the pedal. Truly the car moves because a spark is ignited
and causes an explosion someplace the driver may not know
much about.[150] The driver may perhaps describe the result.

The oligarchies Syme describes at different times suffer
depletion, and new memberships accrue from the favor of
new leaders: "the bulk of Pompey's personal adherents...,
hungry sons of a poor and populous region;" Caesar's train
packed with people out for "rewards of greed and ambition;"
joining Augustus, "the avid, the brutal and unscrupulous,...
those who had nothing to lose," while his "Senate was packed
with ruffians;" no worse than "young *nobiles* [who] went in a
body to the camp of Brutus and Cassius, eagerly or with the
energy of despair."[151]

The tyrannicides upheld a constitution which was no
more than "a double coating of deceit" — this judgement in
a chapter devoted to exposing the entire hypocrisy and
emptiness of whatever this group held up in words and ideas
as their fighting cause, or their opponents, likewise, who tried
to trump them with the same cards. "Roman politicians,

whether they asserted the People's rights or the Senate's, were acting a pretence: they strove for power only."[152]

A view of the actors of the past like Syme's may supply striking, even brilliant, assessments; but no one would call it empathetic. He favors the word "cool" for his own and his recommended appraisal of past events, the cool observer being detached, disengaged, able to discount the sources in favor of a truer sense of what people and their proclivities were really like. In the five hundred pages and more of *The Roman Revolution* the reader will not easily find more than a dozen occurrences of affective words, "anger" or the like. Not that all insight is abjured: Syme can see Augustus' "inner scorn (but public respect) for names and forms."[153] How is Syme able to reach into the secrets of the man's mind? Generally, by assuming the worst, after the best has been discounted. This key he applies throughout the book, for example, in that chapter ("Political Catchwords") analyzing what Cicero and others like him were fighting for or advertised as their ideals (which of course we are not to take at face-value).

Among those who achieved real power, Syme has a good word to say of Marcus Brutus as "firm" and of Asinius Pollio as "honest;" and of Caesar he attempts a balanced treatment, while still characterizing the dictator and others as driven essentially by "ambition".[154] Alas, throughout the period dealt with, "politicians… were acting a pretence: they strove for power only." No trace of belief in anything but this can be discovered, under "cool scrutiny;" no true attachment to anything, despite all the slogans and the posturing.[155] This it was that "provoked civil war" — indeed, directed the path of every prominent individual's career. This and nothing else made history. Augustus himself comes in for vigorous and consistent denigration: in his later decades, regularly "despot"; in his earlier ones, "adventurer", "revolutionary", "demagogue", the favorite terms, with their adjectives; but also, "his ambition implacable."[156]

Where this frightening figure surpassed all others was in his reasoning: thus he grew and reached his acme as "a chill and mature terrorist," able in his ascent to apply "a rational

calculation of persons and interests," able to estimate appeals
to the honor of Caesar's veterans as "an investment," "crafty",
"cool and circumspect," with "more skills, fewer scruples"
than his enemies.[157] He knew as his historian knows that the
worst in men is the truth about them.

But in applying to *The Roman Revolution* the sort of analysis to which the ancient authors were subjected, a very puz-
zling contradiction appears: the essence of explanation (not
to mention ornament, "thrills and chills") is, in the one, feelings; in the other, totally absent. The affective element and its
illustrative role in Nikolaos is ignored by Syme; ignored in
the same way is the tradition of all those other writers who
went before him. Over the latter half of the last century, evidently Syme's choice of method suited the prevailing taste —
witness his fame and position, witness also any sampling of
writing in the field that one cares to make.

Why should the study of Roman history have taken this
odd direction, to the denial of the sources (which really do
have a lot to tell, or to suggest)? The answer, I think, lies in a
well-seen assumption among the moderns, or at least among
academics, that causation, meaning motivation, can only be a
rational thing. Only in rational terms, then, the past must be
explained. Any alternative is naïve, a surrender to ornament,
to *exaedificatio*, "thrills and chills." Whoever expects to find
explanation among these has failed to look beneath the sur-
face, trusts the sources like a child, just isn't up to any prob-
ing and sophisticated study of the realities. Not least, in the
study of Augustus: since motivation arises in the intellect, not
among the emotions, an "adventurer" who can entirely master them or never had them in the first place will naturally
come out on top, in the worst of all possible worlds: as
Augustus in fact did. Q. e. d.

But whether this modern equation, motivation=calcula-
tion, is closer to the truth than the alternative suggested
above, emotion=motivation, remains to be tested in the next
chapter. It will be clear at the moment, however, that I myself
prefer the truth taken for granted by the historians that the
school of Syme draws on, and then ignores.

CHAPTER 2:
"Scientific"

THAT Symean sort of historical analysis which came up for discussion at the end of the preceding chapter — analysis in which "cool" is the watchword and affective coloration is excluded — puts inquiry on a good sound rational footing. It was and is of our own times, our scientific times. Let the Ancients believe that decisions are attended, and not only attended but governed, by *feelings* not by *thoughts*. Such a belief may have served a Nikolaos; it might still do for the careless layman; but by serious historians today the Symean choice will be preferred. Wrongly.

Those serious historians will naturally focus on decisions that may be said to have made history, that is, the decisions and consequent actions of individuals able to direct whole groups in the course of change, or the decisions taken within such groups in and by themselves. Both are seen to move according to the calculation of their interests — interests narrowly or broadly materialist, political or economic. To this as the key to understanding motivation we are generally used.

In contrast, the Ancients. To defend their hoary teachings in our own day — impossible! Indeed, I cannot imagine any success, unless I can somehow show that the ancient is also the modern. But exactly this proposition is what I attempt in the present chapter.

And the turn of the millennium seems to favor my attempt. Views counted as enlightened and of the times, not only in Syme's day but still in the present, have come under attack. The signs of this are noted at the beginning of the first section, below. Over only the last decade or two in the last century, more and more often remarked on by people engaged in ethnopsychology, neurobiology, sociology, psychology, anthropology, and market behavior, all seriously scientific — among these various specialists a consciousness of change asserts itself, almost a sense of revolution. They see a new consensus emerging.

So far as it concerns my chosen subject, how to read and write history, this consensus seems to me most easily understood through the words at its very center: *thoughts* and *feelings*. Just what is their nature? Surely the "-ologists" should be heard on the matter.

Even without their help, we can address a few preliminaries. At the start: whenever we call up to the forefront of our consciousness the two terms in question, we sense at least one clear fact, that *thoughts* are relatively easier to explain. *Feelings*, on the other hand.... We may imagine or recall inflicting some nontrivial punishment on the bad behavior of a child, or deciding to take up our parent's line of work, or perhaps not flinching from some serious physical risk; or when we made a will. We read in memoirs how it was that the boy signed up for war. All such moments, invested as they are with emotion, seem too complicated, too mixed of different and converging or conflicting strands, too much involved in influences from our past and our values, to be given any one name — duty, patriotism, or whatever we might choose — in ordinary English.[1] But such is the kind of consequential moment with which historians are most often concerned. Their job cannot be easy.

In the second place, historians confront the problem of translation. Other cultures have each their own ways, to be acknowledged; differences are real and hard to bridge; and may be expressed in another, strange language, or in a choice of words that have changed meaning over time, much or subtly. Actors in the past might, for instance, say they acted at the urging of their *dolor* or a *grief*. Both words are English of a sort, hardly in use since the seventeenth century; but one was once also Latin, the other, also French. They serve as reminders that language is a living, slithery thing, and apparent equivalents from one to another are tricky. So, then: problems in translation.

Least real of the difficulties is the radically epistemological. We are reminded by arguments exquisitely clever that we ourselves stand in our own world, the past in quite another; and the various forms of communication between the two, mostly written, can never be unproblematic. A vast amount of distortion at their point of origin must be conceded; a vast amount of ourselves will intrude on our interpretations of them. Any true understanding is literally beyond our reach.

Such arguments are unanswerable. Also, academic. There is a countervailing calculation: that, on any given day except weekends, thousands upon thousands of narratives of past events will be formally presented and considered in our criminal law courts, and a decision will be agreed upon as to what really happened, *wie es eigentlich gewesen*, in a famous formulation. The truth will be established beyond a reasonable doubt. If we perhaps wonder exactly what might be *reasonable*? — well, it is whatever a reasonable person would believe and accept. American law politely refuses to say any more. At that point of demonstration, the matter is left, and a jury will, at that same point, agree to put a man in jail for life or even do him in, once and for all.[2]

Is this not then as good a standard as may be reasonably demanded of historiography, on which no life depends? It looks for a degree of truth — an approximation to reality — that is itself a reality familiar to everybody and generally accepted, as opposed to whatever is sought in theoretical ideals and models.

1. THOUGHTS AND FEELINGS

At a respectable distance from ourselves, in 1831, giving weight to the arguments of Marxism and therefore of historical philosophy *par excellence*, Georg Wilhelm Friedrich Hegel insisted to his readers, "The first glance at History convinces us that the actions of men proceed from their needs, their passions, their characters and talents; and impresses us with the belief that such needs, passions and interests are the sole springs of action." Still further, while it may be allowed that some few persons in the past have been "moved by a liberal or universal kindness — benevolence, it may be, or noble patriotism," these same springs are more generally the cause of disasters, chaos, destruction, cruelty. "We assert then that nothing has been accomplished without interest on the part of the actors; and — if interest be called passion, inasmuch as the whole individuality, to the neglect of all other actual or possible interests or claims, is devoted to an object with every fiber of volition, concentrating all its desires and powers upon it — we may affirm absolutely that *nothing great in the World* has been accomplished without *passion*."[3]

More recent opinions to the same effect were recalled in my Preface; to which, from among the social sciences, add Robert Zajonc at the turn of the millennium declaring, "It can readily be argued that of all major psychological processes, emotions are of prime importance.... Emotions, then, are primary."[4]

Zajonc goes on to call attention to the very presence of the subject of emotions at all, in a particular handbook of social psychology to which he contributes. The topic in previous editions had never been given a place. His own chapter is near neighbor to another more traditional one on decision-making. There, the author has 45,000 words at his disposal to describe and explain how people decide to act, in whatever direction; but he sees no cause to mention emotions. Instead, he takes as what he calls a *metaprinciple*, a supreme truth, "that there is some good reason for most things that people do... even when people seem to be behaving irrationally or unreasonably." They are guided by "expected utility" and "cost-benefit analysis."[5]

This serenely Symean idea he pursues in ways familiar to analysts of market behavior. Market behavior of course includes such events as the great depression of the last century, in addition to all sorts of other phenomena, past and current, great and small, of the sort equally studied by historians. Analysts, however, being surely more numerous, far better funded, and even keener in their investigations, must have something to teach the historiographical guild. The chief lesson they would impart is that very *metaprinciple* just referred to. "Virtually all current theories of choice under risk or uncertainty are cognitive and consequentialist. They assume that people assess the desirability and likelihood of possible outcomes of choice alternatives and integrate this information through some type of expectation-based calculus to arrive at a decision." "The presumption in academic finance has long been that statistical evidence overwhelmingly supports the efficient market hypothesis."[6] So consensus carries us back to Weber, back to Schumpeter, back to the "rationality postulate," back to the necessarily supposed cool calculating individual whose mind can be read at any remove, through attention to the economic quanta. Doubts that all individuals are always cool are addressed by aggregation: let them be whatever they want, enough of them lumped together will nevertheless come out the way theory requires (and one could say this as truly of wars and elections, as of big swings and panics on the market). It is a rare voice raised in protest: protesting that as many brokers in a given year will come to work buoyant and ready to buy, as those who are edgy and ready to sell out wholesale, and they must therefore be moved as much by the one feeling as by the other — feelings being always a part of behavior. The warning comes from a sociologist.[7]

And long ago, at a point between Weber and Schumpeter, a sociologist took the time to study the affective nature of business relationships, investments, and sales-decisions, shaped by shows of friendship, congeniality of values, and so forth — today, all worked out on the golf course, quite familiarly.[8]

Market analysts have naturally listened carefully to psychologists, to test their own insights — psychologists, who have in the past generally confirmed the *metaprinciple*. "Within the cognitive paradigm," that is, "of the person as computerlike," "emotion, motivation... represented no more than error variance.... No wonder emotion and motivation were effectively ousted from the content domain of cognitive psychology;" or again, "Until recently, emotions attracted little attention from decision researchers. Decision making was viewed as a cognitive process — a matter of estimating which of various alternative actions would yield the most positive consequences. Decision makers were assumed to evaluate the potential consequences of their decisions dispassionately."[9] What we would certainly like to believe of ourselves as rational beings, looking into ourselves, was thus pronounced to be right all along: *feelings* and *thoughts* are two different and quite generally opposed mental activities, and our major choices in life, those that deserve record and drive change beyond obedience to biological urges, obey our reason. We are back at the beginning of my first chapter, and a supposed Thucydides.

Were all this expert opinion to be taken as is, historians in the exercise of their craft could hardly expect to find much in emotions beyond occasional ornament for their more self-indulgent paragraphs. Properly professional ones would aim at a spare, Euclidean style.

However, from the 1970s among psychologists a growing suspicion could be sensed that the consensus had been wrong. Even some market analysts could be found, expressing doubts.[10] What was increasingly studied and seen to count was the blurring together of the two sensations familiar to us all: our *considering logically* something we've noticed or recalled, and our *being moved* by it — moved to what in a technical phrase is often called a state of mind, or, commonly, a feeling.

Of course, there is a complicated story of research and discussion behind all this. It begins with tentative studies early in the second half of the last century,[11] and was advanced thereafter by Zajonc (1980), in a much-cited article — if some one voice needs to be, or can be fairly, singled out for mention from the growing chorus of contributions and debates. But to make clear its course, perhaps the most useful starting point lies even further back in time, a century behind

Zajonc, and not with cognition but with emotion (or "feeling" or "affect" — notice, I use the three words interchangeably, as some psychologists prefer, but most do not).

In 1884, William James published an article which, more or less reprinted in a later book, and then brought out together with closely compatible work by a Danish scientist, was for a time very influential; and then too strongly attacked; and so it faded out of mind, until the latter twentieth century.[12] Then the Jamesian theory or approach, as it was identified, was revived, either to serve as a classical starting point and validation of new work, or as a great monument of doctrine to be challenged. In either case, it came to life again.

It declared "that <u>the bodily changes</u>" we are aware of and call emotions "<u>follow directly the</u> PERCEPTION <u>of the exciting fact, and that our feeling of the same changes as they occur</u> IS <u>the emotion.</u>"[13] Now, here began the teasing apart of the thing commonly called emotion. Counter-intuitively, what the layman would say was (for example) his "anger" proved really to be a set, perceived by him, of various goings-on in his body: visceral, pulmonary, vascular, muscular, glandular, and so forth. Without these, "anger" would be, said James, quite unimaginable. We simply could not bring it before our minds. And another fact, too: that the sensations defining anger were beyond our control, they were irrational, a response of autonomic systems. Thus, emotions themselves must be of the body, "hard-wired" in the term sometimes used in this connection.

The importance of this perception for historians, so far as it has stood up, bears on the question of universality. For the moment I defer this matter.

Jamesian description did not fit everything most naturally called emotion. It didn't fit the long-matured feelings characteristic of adulthood or of enduring situations — Hamlet, or depression.[14] No laboratory devices would reliably detect these. And what might be subjectively reported as two different feelings might show up in laboratory measurements as apparently identical sets of bodily changes.[15] A one-to-one correspondence of outwardly detectable somatic change and inwardly perceived affect could not be demonstrated. So the whole subject was seen to be interesting, that is, more complicated than had been realized until recent decades.

Nevertheless, testing did demonstrate a great deal of correspondence, even if not complete and perfect, and, still more clearly, a basis of emotions in chemical balances and nerve structure. Neuropeptides, for example, played a key role. Areas of the brain, notably in its lower parts, could be stimulated electrically to produce what the subject will say is an emotion; control for positive emotions is localized in the left brain, negative in the right; and, if areas are destroyed by trauma, the subject will say he feels different — reduced in his capacity for sadness, regret, anguish, embarrassment, pleasure at art or music.[16] In the brains of infants, electrical discharge is measurably different if they are approached by a stranger instead of their mother.[17] And of course the flow of adrenaline can be shown to increase measurably with some emotions like anger, as sadness measurably raises blood pressure.[18] Discovery of structures and processes basically similar in mammalian brains underlines the biological character of feelings; and, while animals can't be made to speak about their feelings, their actions can sometimes be best, or only, explained as moved by what humans call the spirit of play or joy, panic or separation, care or nurturance, rage or anger, fear or anxiety, lust or sexuality, and "seeking" or expectancy — meaning, "the urge of all mammals to explore their environments," as Panksepp puts it: the spirit of adventure and curiosity.[19]

Anyone who has ever owned a pet could tell, or has heard or read, stories illustrative of "the fact" that animals have feelings. By which are meant, with whatever exaggeration, feelings like humans'. So the layman's knowledge chimes with the scientific. Further: if it seems so natural to attribute to a raccoon or fox or elephant the same inquisitiveness that we ourselves may feel, surely it is far more "reasonable" to attribute it also, across the centuries, to Frederick II in Palermo, or any other exotic experimentalist of the past. Historians certainly do that.

It would be natural, next, to look for some usefulness in the biology just described, serving the purposes of survival. In this regard, Darwin in 1872 offered an important contribution: a book comparing facial expressions of animals with humans. To this, recent work has added arguments for the cross-cultural identity, among humans, of (for example) the bared teeth of anger.[20] Similarly, for happiness, surprise, sadness, fear, and disgust — these being sometimes claimed for the list of our most basic emotions. They are expressive of reactions not really under our control, "hard-wired" like other phenomena defining emotion. Even an infant born blind (and deaf) will show them. They must be innate.[21]

True, the arguments can be disputed; definitions — of "basic" and of "emotion", too, for that matter — can be disputed; cultural differences in the display of certain feelings can be shown; certain others can be instanced, like hope, which display themselves on the human face not at all, or at least not in any recognizable way. Nevertheless, something like anger really is intelligible to everyone in its display, whether a photo of an actress portraying it is shown to someone in Hokkaido or in Tierra del Fuego. The idea gets across. The phenomenon must surely be useful to our species. A face that threatens can prevent more combat than is really necessary. Accordingly, such a face can be shown to rivet attention beyond other expressions, in measurable ways. It evidently serves communication even with other species; but principally, expressions, like other gestures, "broadcast internal states among conspecifics."[22] As still further proofs that emotions have somatic meaning, the left side of our face is ordinarily more expressive than the right, because of the circuitry; and we cannot control such visible reactions, sometimes, in panic or rage, because their initiation is hard-wired.

We owe it to James that a very much deeper and more important service to survival has also been identified in the psychological-physiological linkages just reviewed; or perhaps it should better be said that the service has been recognized and explored as a consequence of revisiting James. Briefly: "bodily changes" to which he called attention — "somatic markers" in today's terminology— speed up our responses to things that happen around us. Speed saves lives.

How does this happen? To things we perceive, in our reaction, we attach the sensations that James points to, like so many tags or labels in our filing system, our memory. The tags are summary things, indicating the response, positive or negative, which we found most to our advantage, at the first appraisal. Thereafter, without our needing to think a second time at any length, they tell us promptly what to do. As Zajonc puts it, "the rabbit cannot stop to contemplate the length of the snake's fangs;" or, less dramatically in Oatley's words, "basic emotions... make the system capable of rapid and unified response... without parsing, interpretation, or other computations that could be lengthy."[23] Efficiency of response is feeling's first, principal contribution to survival.

As a sign of its primacy in our reactions, we notice how often we recall something wholly, or almost wholly, as an emotion, when all other detail has vanished from our memories; or, in what we can recall more fully, the details that were most emotional will stand out the most clearly.[24] It is feeling that then dominates or chiefly characterizes our field of consciousness, and we describe it, when we are asked to think about it, as particularly vivid.[25] Vividness, we may say, has emerged in the course of evolution as the key to remembering. We could never retain or recall every particular in our experience, nor do we need to. What we need are instantly retrievable judgments of "good" or "bad", of objects to be sought or to be avoided. As one or the other label is attached to a memory, evaluation can thereafter be instantaneous and our choice of action, similarly.[26] It is in the somatic marker that the necessary quality of vividness lies: in that cold clenching in our stomach, the lump in our throat, our difficulty in drawing a breath, blushing, or the other physical attendants of fear, sexual desire, hunger.

Very good. But what is undeniable about some certain feelings, we cannot accept regarding certain others. The variety of our responses will not all fit within this one Jamesian and post-Jamesian picture.

The snake that threatens a rabbit, and does so in a flash, or any similar danger that presents itself to us all of a sudden, may well produce bodily changes that are instantaneous and beyond our control, and it is at least understandable to say with James that these changes *are* the emotion which we subsequently remember. But there are also responses, perhaps resulting in equal "markers" or bodily changes that are by no means instantaneous. They arise from an appraisal: a "mental evaluative process" in Damasio's phrase, a perception attended by reflection. We consider just what would be the consequences of a situation and our best reaction to it; we deliberate, searching among past experiences, looking toward a given outcome, trying to sense its likelihood, trying to feel how one or another result would sit with us, the whole process lasting a half-second, it may be, or a week, and ending in an affective tag — a tag to be affixed, in the simplest situation, to something observed which will satisfy a pressing need or presents a pressing danger; or affixed, where it is a complicated matter, to a sense of how we may expect to feel, given a certain outcome. Will the sensation be a good one or a bad? Taking this into account, what is our feeling at the moment of decision itself? Negative or positive? In plainer words, then, should we *do* it? Let the evaluation be made possible in part by the markers, nevertheless, it is not autonomic or automatic. It is a form of cognition.[27]

Plainly, among inner sensations that are counted as feelings, a variety distinguishable each from the other has been identified, occurring in a flow; but there is no unanimity about the order of their flow. What began with James' contention that the physical ones came first, then awareness of them (which was emotion), and rational appraisal only thereafter, led into renewed research, more carefully targeted experiments, attempts at finding better names for the phenomena identified, and still, disagreements. Perhaps disagreements should be resolved by an elastic definition: feelings are a complex of several elements.[28] Which of them should we call "emotion"? The peaceable answer is, all of them, as parts of one process.[29]

From these findings, the kernel that historians may notice is the admission of feelings into the description of decision-

making, either through the dissolving of unreal distinctions
or a fuller accounting of realities. The upshot is a "blurring
together of the two sensations," logical consideration, and
emotion (referred to above at note 7).

But it should not be assumed that the scientific consensus
necessarily diminishes the role of thought, to the degree the
role is blurred. On the contrary: the same affective element
that adds speed, is seen to add depth and refinement as well.
It calls up to the evaluative moment a part or the whole of
what is lodged in memory — whatever is tagged similarly to
the affect aroused by the stimulus of that moment. What is
recalled represents experience. Among the most cogent findings were those of Damasio, working with subjects who had
lost the use of brain-areas associated with feeling; for, among
these subjects, what could be noted were "decision-making
failures."[30] The failures are explained by the lack of a social
element, to which I return in a moment.

Something must be conceded to the view of endless centuries: that emotion is the enemy of clear thought, whereas in
reason we have the best servant of our interests. Damasio
leaves room for pure logic in thinking about things like chess
strategy or bridge-building. Such mental activity makes use
of experience with little or no affect. If emotion were
attached, it would detract — as pride of profession, in the
novel, was attached to the building of a bridge over the River
Kwai. Madness! In experiments where subjects were offered
prizes for playing a game well, and their play was influenced
by affective input, they lost; they had become optimistic
beyond any justification in the proven odds; as, suffering from
some mild depression, they did better, since their calculations
were not distorted by our normal motivation to maintain
self-esteem; while, in other experiments, subjects primed for
a choice by relevant rousing or moving experiences — pho-
tographs or movies or moments of directed recall — made
decisions influenced by the feelings stimulated in them, and
did the worse for it.[31]

But Damasio was able to show that, much more often,
there was rather a price to be paid through the loss of affect-

capacity; and experimental results confirm the finding.[32] "We sometimes delude ourselves that we proceed in a rational manner and weigh all the pros and cons of the various alternatives. But this is probably seldom the case," Zajonc concludes; and it is well for us; for, as loss of affect-capacity can be shown to be bad for our decision-making, so input can be shown to be good.[33]

Psychologists rarely look so closely into these phenomena among large groups as among small ones, or among individuals in controlled settings; so they rarely connect their findings with events that are of interest to historians; but even on this level of magnitude, an occasional risk-taker will offer an opinion.[34] Political pollsters are free to go further, indeed they see no risk in the matter at all. Movements and voting and demonstrations naturally reflect likes and dislikes or stronger feelings still.

"Action-readiness is the central core of emotion;" "Emotions serve to establish our position vis-à-vis our environment, pulling us toward certain people, objects, actions and ideas, and pushing us away from others."[35] Commonly then follows a plan in which further stimulation of the initial feeling produces little change in the response, because the decision has been taken; but there will be an account taken of the difficulty of action, in physiological preparedness.[36] Working together with "an attractive female" by (evidently male) collaborators produced greater readiness for effort than with a "less attractive." The state of mind was affected, that is, the attitude, which is a sort of emotion.

Among emotions, very little self-study is needed to persuade us of their variety. Attitudes differ from moods, moods from passions, one passion from another. There seem to be endless shades and types, whether we consider the quality that distinguishes each, or its intensity, or its internally perceptible manifestations. From a huge number of studies, produced at a sharply increased rate from roughly 1980 on, perhaps it is enough to show only one picture to suggest the nature of the conceptual problem — this, from J. A. Russell:[37]

Fig. 1: Russell's circumplex

Russell, like many others before him and since, wanted to reduce the data descriptive of emotions (in an inclusive sense) to some order — some form, the simplest tolerable, that would allow their heterogeneity to be grasped. No exaggerated claims were made for the result. Subjects were asked to look into themselves and report what they found under the heading of twenty-some "emotion-related" words chosen to give a comprehensive view across the whole gigantic lexicon of English. The words were to be rated along two bipolar scales, the vertical measuring arousal, the horizontal measuring pleasure (or degrees of liking or dislike). The resulting circumplex was used also to show perceived closeness of one term to some other, not quite synonymous. Russell's data could be checked in various ways, for example, through quantifying adrenaline-release in subjects in a crowded as opposed to an uncrowded commuter train, with correlation to their self-report of stress on a scale of descriptive terms.

Similar scales, unipolar or bipolar and based on self-report-ing, are often used for so-called valence measurement. It may need to be said, too, that self-reporting is the ordinary way of getting at feelings, whether in subjects or in investigators themselves, and that bipolar scales which are essentially arbi-trary in various respects (like the Richter scale, too) are also routinely used without uneasiness.[38] Action-readiness, howev-er, could be measured by physiological changes, as in experi-ments of the sort mentioned just above (at n. 33); and, with its rates of heart-beat and blood-pressure, it recognizes what James called "bodily changes" — emotion itself, or rather an aspect of the more complicated process called emotion.

There will be, of course, in anyone's offhand catalogue of feelings, some that lie beneath the level of somatic marking. Russell's circumplex serves as a convenient reminder of the tailing off of arousal states from, let us say, anger to apathy. Historians might at first sight disregard the latter, because it could lead to nothing that should register in the historical record; but in fact (e.g., accidie, below, chap. 3) there are muted feelings that do register. Furthermore, much experi-ment has shown how lower states of arousal influence the higher, as increments at particular moments (above, n. 28), and thus as elements in decision-making. That they may not originate the way anger does, in our perceiving physiological changes, does not make them any the less emotions.[39] We quite naturally use the same vocabulary to describe their onset: "I *felt* entirely cool about the problem," or "at peace," or "rather optimistic." In just such words we might describe an electorate on the eve of a vote, a crowd gathered for a demonstration, and call it all history.

The fact that feelings play an important part in choice most decisively brings them under the historian's charge; but beyond that, there is a final consideration: the part they play in every-day life. They are essential to our interaction with our fellow-beings, in the forming of our opinions about each other as in the marking of our memories for ready recall, according to their affective quality. By introspection, we who are not Basque shepherds or Trappist monks discover in our minds a constant

agitation of thoughts about our fellows, because not a day —
for most of us, hardly an hour — passes without some form of
human contact. "What then did he really mean?" "What will
they think?" "Aren't all slick types the same!" "How could she
have done that?" "Was it as good a meeting as it seemed?" "Is
he actually my type?" "What a fool I must have seemed!" "I
can't stand the way she looks at one." "I think we just click." It
is not the denotation of our contacts with others but rather the
feel of them that counts: "22 times more variance is account-
ed for by the tone of one's voice than by the content of the
utterance when people are asked to interpret utterances."[40] In
this continually ongoing happy or frustrated or anxious review,
our "thoughts" *are* feelings.

The processes of review and evaluation here involved I
described in layman's language in my first chapter, apropos
Thucydides' insights into the drama of Nicias' closing days.
Description in technical language is not much different:
"...one [who is the observer of an emotional moment] is
interpreting a vicarious feeling aroused in oneself by the
other's expression of feeling. Through introspection one
comes to realize that this feeling is not an endogenous mood
or affect, arising from purely inner processes. Rather, it is
vicarious feeling, or representation of another's feeling that is
a function of being receptive to another's self-expression."

We look, then, or we listen or we read, and then we practice — empathy. Empathy is in all of us, a capacity inborn
and hardwired, whether or not well exercised; and it is
important to note, here at the end of this first section, that its
accuracy as a historian might use it can be tested and generally approved.[41]

2. PROBLEMS IN TRANSLATION

With various degrees of richness in different societies, the
interior life is reflected in their words. To describe all our

own emotions, English offers an estimated 500 to 2000 words; Tahitian, far fewer, reserving affect-terms for the sharp sensations that come at the first onset, while emotions that linger long are thought of as illnesses or witchcraft. Yet the Tahitians' and other peoples' limited vocabularies of feeling should not be taken as proof that theirs is an emotionally impoverished life, any more than a highly descriptive vocabulary necessarily shows its users to enjoy an exceptionally rich one.[42]

There are other non-Western people among whom the word best translated as *anger* also means *sadness*, and still others who group anger and envy under a single term, and anger also under emotional violence of any sort such as striving or passionate energy (the Ilongot on the Philippine island of Luzon). For the same Ilongot, *liget* in the sense of *passion* or *feelings* or, almost, our colloquial *juice*, serves for *anger* also, and for *irritation, violence....*[43] "Without *liget* to move our hearts," they say, "there would be no human life." It is the feeling of being moved, without further differentiation. In Micronesia, Ifaluk *ker* most nearly approaches *happiness* but with overtones of disapproval: it is a thing close to immoral; while Ifaluk *song* that may be translated *anger* means, really, *admonition* or *reproach*.[44] It is a particular subspecies, the anger which is justifiable, akin to *indignation* (and Latin *indignatio*). *Popokl* for the New Guinea Hageners denotes "outrage over the failure of others to recognize one's claims," another subspecies of indignation; *musu* for Samoans is a subspecies of anger, the reluctance and resentment which are felt at having to do what is expected of one.[45]

Australian aborigines discriminate within sadness: they reserve *wtzilpa* for that particular concern that we feel when we think of our homeland and relatives, *wurrkulinu* for that felt over kinfolk, excessively, *vilunuyiluru*, dejection from too much worry over absent or distant ones, for example, if they are in the hospital, and *rulatjarra*, sympathetic grief for sick or deceased relatives.[46] To the Japanese, it is amazing that neither English nor any other Indo-European tongue has any term at all to describe how we feel when we behave coquetishly or in a puppy-like way toward someone whose love we feel sure of. It is *amae*. Nor have those outside of Japan any way or word to express the uncomfortable sense of being beholden, *oime*.[47]

In Spain, the discomfort an audience may feel as witnesses of a terrible performance has its own terminology, for which Anglophones lack any equivalent. It is "an anthropological finding that psychological expressions of men's self are contained in language," French or German or English, each choosing different parts of the spectrum of feelings to designate by a word: pleasure, anxiety, and so forth.[48] The various emotional states, however, are entirely familiar the world around, and can be successfully translated with the help of scenarios: so-and-so is what you feel when such-and-such is the situation.

Inevitable, all this — inevitable, given the variety of human societies. The continuum of affective experience is infinite, beyond the capacity of any people to devise the language that will either encompass or properly sort it out. Certain tiny elements will be dignified with designation, and assigned an agreed-upon noise — a word. Other elements with an apparently equal claim to notice will be wholly disregarded; or — common feelings though they are — they may be treated as minor variants, lumped under some single affect-term. But, as Alexander Johnson put it long ago, "The oneness of a thousand whites is verbal. The unit is a creation of language."[49]

Is it, however, mere caprice? Occasionally, some good explanation can be found. For example: Eskimos do not see one single white in the world around them, as has often been pointed out. In their speech they distinguish many shades and qualities, for the obvious reason that they must think and communicate accurately about snow and ice; just as Arabs, so we are told, have a dozen words and more for types of sandy desert. It may be the same with the describing of affective variety: salience will be awarded, now to this feeling among this people, now to some other among another. Particular social values may be reflected in the strength and common occurrence of an emotion, hence in language. The point was made long ago by James, "...each race of men having found names for some shade of feeling which other races of men have left undiscriminated."[50]

At work in a group or individual, thoughts-and-feelings constitute the ultimate target for historical reconstruction; for of course they govern action. Hidden from us though this interior life may seem to be, nevertheless it has in fact been entered and explored ten thousand times. What allows entrance and yields more or less acceptable findings is the degree of commonality among cultures: the existence of basic emotions to be found among people everywhere. It is this that allows translation through the use of scenarios, pointed out just above.

Hardwiring of the most often reported feelings, into specific parts of the mammalian nervous system, together with the uniform manner of their display in facial gesture, affirm our common nature, whatever society we may belong to. The conclusion could be questioned, once;[51] but, in time, specialists in the relevant "-ologies" began to listen to each other, and doubts have given way to a very broad consensus, which the preceding first Section tried to make plain.

Of basic emotions, then, anger, happiness, sadness, fear, and disgust make up Damasio's list, with shades or variants, euphoria or ecstasy, wistfulness or melancholy, and so forth; and he would distinguish these from biological drives — the drive to conform or to preserve one's life — however much these may express themselves in feelings. Other authorities would add dependency and surprise, guilt and shame.[52] Among those used in cross-cultural study, it is natural to find choices located toward the high-arousal end of Russell's circumplex, "where the action is," so to speak. Here, there are various possibilities; yet none so striking as anger. It governs, for example, the choice of feelings to be entered in Russell's circumplex. It governs also a similar one devised by White.[53]

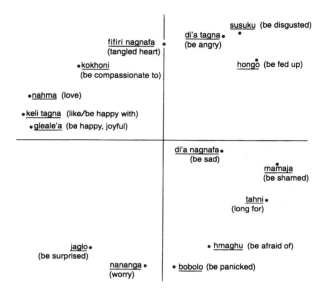

Fig. 2: White's circumplex

The people studied were the Cheke Holo on Santa Isabel in the Solomon Islands. Here, White sifted out by questionnaire the most common terms for feelings, which he then grouped according to their closeness of meaning to each other; and this resulted in the set of fifteen seen here, where the horizontal axis is evaluative, positive or negative, and the vertical axis shows strength or activity (comparable to arousal in Russell's circumplex). White like other anthropologists had no great difficulty with the differentness of his subjects. He could easily find basic emotions, in Cheke Holo terms. This is the point of presenting Figs. 1 and 2: to illustrate the universalist assumption at work — not to attempt any detailed consideration of them. Quite evidently, differences of language as well as of emotional processes may be surmounted, to get at the thoughts and feelings of remote societies.

In the testing of the universalist against the constructionist approach — the one insisting on what all humans feel in common, the other looking for the varieties of feelings invented, so it would seem, by their societies — anger itself has offered a challenge. For one thing, it is aroused by different stimuli in different societies, according to the prevailing sense of the need to respond.[54] In a classic study, Margaret Mead found it virtually absent among Samoans (though her findings suffered harsh attack much later). It must never find violent expression, among the Ifaluk; is pretty well trained out of children of the Lohorung Rai in Nepal; and absent among Tahitians, too.[55] "These people do not get angry," at all, or "anger is rare." So also among Utku Eskimos, though it can hardly be said they are entirely at peace with everything around them: they do sulk, they beat their animals, and so forth; they have words for many shades of feeling close neighbors to anger.[56] They stand out particularly against the West, America above all, where anger is so prominent and often remarked on.[57] To the extent these Utku villagers or Tahitians are different from most of our common species, socially enforced regulation is the most obvious explanation; or, as Zajonc says, "Emotions are above all social."[58]

Samoans distinguish types of anger that are permissible according to age and sex. It is proper and accepted that young males will be overcome by it, though they must also be helped to see that it is controllable. With maturity, different conduct will be expected.[59] Feeling grateful for Tamils in South India is something sincere and ordinary; but its expression makes it appear almost non-existent, so hedged about it is with considerations of status and respect dictated by the moral code. It is not an individual but "a fundamentally social emotion."[60]

It may be that the actual feelings of sadness are modified by the desirability, and hence, the teaching to children, of repression of the display, as the English (though less than formerly) value a "stiff upper lip;" and if this is the case, then other societies must feel all the more, where displays are allowed or encouraged.[61] The same would be true of anger, it has been suggested: equally, expression or repression has inner consequences. Certainly the most common type of anger, indignation, will respond in its inner reality to different stimuli in different cultures, since it results from the sense of wrongful hurt to oneself or others, undeserved according to accepted views on what is fair or just. They will determine whether it is felt or not. This same prediction was made by Aristotle.[62]

And shame, likewise. It is induced by the expectation of our fellows' disapproval. Such disapproval in turn will be directed at different targets according to prevailing norms. What would be shameful in one culture will not be in some other; and the same is true of pride and of guilt (the expectation of punishment).[63] All three emotions are aroused by the stimuli that society determines properly should have that very effect; in this sense they may be called social constructs; yet at the same time they count as basic. They are hardwired, the area of the brain where they are controlled is identifiable, we even share them with other social animals. For example, in a group of macaques, if the subordinate males are given access to females to copulate in the absence of the dominant male, when he is returned to the group, their behavior will be more than usually submissive.[64] He didn't catch them at it, to be sure, but they well know what are approved standards in their community, and what he would have every right to think of them — if only he knew. Accordingly, they act out their acknowledgement of the disapproval their conduct invites. As we do, too, ashamed.

The pendulum of consensus has tic-tocked back and forth over the preceding half-century. Are not emotions for the most part, in strength and expression and direction, "historically shaped sociocultural constructions?"[65] Per contra, it takes a deal of courage to speak of human *nature*. To do so is almost too determinist; but it may be dared. Indeed, societies of very different behavior and norms can be shown to include much deviance — of course — and, at a level below the conscious, a detectable degree of identity; hence the term for it, "pancultural".[66]

To measure universalist against constructionist theory, in recent decades, a great deal of work of interest to historians has been done of a comparative sort. It has, for example, found expression in the journal of the Society of Psychological Anthropology, *Ethos*, since 1973; in the *Journal of Cross-Cultural Psychology* — published since 1971 and offering some thousands of articles (but only two of them diachronic, of small value for historians) — along with many other forums for discussion. They are all underpinned by common assumptions: that basic emotions do exist, appear even at birth, are hardwired and of the species, and dominate the behavior of children; but that adults are different. Adults in their emotional processes display also the effects of regulation determined by the values of the society around them.[67] To that extent, incidentally, the argument is strengthened for emotions being conceptual constructs — for their being thoughts-and-feelings in combination.

Whether in children or adults, emotional responses will always be subject to modification according to individual temperament; but individual discrepancies disappear when groups are studied as such. Then uniformity within a given culture emerges.[68] Even across the great expanse of Western societies, at least in contrast to Asian societies, feelings resemble each other to a surprising degree.[69] It is silently assumed by psychologists in their testing of their indispensable college students, surely the best known population in mankind's history. Where uniformity only appears to be defied, it will be by known and tolerated (or sufficiently resistant) groups, and then, more in the display of emotions than in inner reality.

Differences according to sex are easily demonstrated. At many junctures in Western history, irrationality, meaning the tendency to feel and express and be governed by emotions, has been attributed especially to women, and in no respect more than in crying.[70] This is the very wide finding in the modern world, and a variety of illustrations from past times may be added in the next chapter.

Of course, differences are discoverable also according to class. An instance, above, was the feeling of gratitude in a South Indian population. In a society like the Indonesian, where stratification is expressed with unusual force and clarity, display of emotions is correspondingly modified by social rank; but there is a less obvious illustration to be found among the Wolof of Senegal. "Emotional dispositions are directly

associated with status....Thus, nobility is solid, 'heavy', lethar-
gic, bland, and controlled. The lower-caste people are 'light-
weight', volatile, and excitable. And these are not stereotypes
but normative emotional dispositions, seen in everyday behavior" — reflected in their lexicon.[71] By the same token, among
peoples of long ago, historians must expect to find (as we
judge) almost untranslatable peculiarities. The *indignatio* asserted by a medieval king, his serfs can hardly claim nor, surely, did
they actually feel anything quite of the sort.

Constructionism we would expect to find supported by
some Darwinian logic: the display of emotions should serve
the purposes of survival of the group, just as the experiencing of emotions has been shown, in Section 1, to do so for
individuals. In fact a variety of phenomena touched on in
these last pages are useful, quite obviously. They constitute a
means of sharing openly what is experienced inwardly, and
offering them to the reaction of others. Reaction modifies
them, it shapes them, and the shape of each and all together
will define a way of life. Only by the external signs of anger,
of resentment, of concupiscence, or of whatever else the
members of a society establish as undesirable feelings, can that
society judge of inner impulses, so as to reward or punish
them before they are acted out; but they will certainly be regulated; for, "If expressions have an adaptive value because they
broadcast internal states among conspecifics, then the presence of conspecifics must have at least a modulating effect on
all aspects of the emotion process" (Zajonc).[72] The reason
underlying controls is plain. "I would guess," adds D'Andrade,
"that the information conveyed by emotional expression is
crucial in maintaining group loyalties, and in determining
what others are really likely to do, so that groups deprived of
this channel would be transient and uncoordinated."[73]

Group character, the focus of ethnopsychology, as it distinguishes a community, a society, a nation, arises thus from
the most familiar circumstances. Adults, being in agreement
on what makes a good person, raise their children accordingly and, among other lessons, teach them when to cry, when
to smile, when to lash out; so a type becomes prevalent. True,

regulated behavior is on the outside, feelings on the inside; and there is no way to measure the degree of approximation between the two, so as to be able to say that among one people there is actually and truly more or less of some feeling than among some other, to judge only from external patterns. Nevertheless, researchers do not doubt that there is some correspondence; and, in any case, behavior in itself constitutes a fact of personality, of the persona on display, however much it may be the consequence of suppression.

Ethnopsychologists thus look at individuals both as departures from and expressions of the ethos of the people, and at the ethos in an over-arching way, as if the people were a person. So long ago as the 1950s that could be defined as "'the expression of a culturally standardized system of organization of the instincts and emotions of individuals.' Or, more briefly, ethos refers to the dominant emotional emphases, attitudes, and modes of expression of the culture as a whole.... [I]t is culturally expected that a person feel a certain way and adapt a certain affective posture and expressive style in relation to particular events. One may even be evaluated as a person in part according to the manner and to the degree that he or she does so. A culture's ethos is thus not only a characterization of a style of feeling and behavior but also a model for it."[74]

And another author writes, "The ethnopsychological structure of the Baining [of Papua New Guinea]... is not culturally distinct from their sociocultural structure." Their preferred or necessary routines of the day, the established chapters of their life, give rise to characteristic feelings — shame, loneliness, at moments even disorientation.[75]

The external control a people apply to their own daily creation explains their "peculiar habits..., creates opinions, engenders sentiments, suggests the ordinary practices of life, and modifies whatever it does not produce." (It is Toqueville who speaks here as a reminder that ethnopsychology has long roots into the heart of history, too.)[76]

★★★★★★★★★★★★★★★★★★★★★

Reviewing these two sections, to draw out the findings useful to historiography, the most striking thing is the very general indifference of the scientific community to the subject of human emotions except such as are available for live study. Quite understandably, where science is the object, laboratory conditions are required, or at least approximated by quantification of questionnaires. Studies that reach beyond these contemporary boundaries are very few, and best left to the next chapter.

Science prefers, too, the individual, or very small groups, to be put under the microscope. How else can any tolerable sort of accuracy be expected, or results verified? The masses that make events of any historical significance, today as in other times, are beyond this reach. In consequence, scientific or social-scientific discussion can be and generally is conducted without a word about the past — however much the living are outnumbered by even that minute part of the dead whose lives are in some slight way known to historical sources. It is as if these latter had never existed.

Yet science quite comfortably moves from a conclusion about "913 college students," to the world at large, that is, to humankind without qualification (though in Anglophone discussions, of course, really speaking only of the West, or of some smaller unit of population). There is hardly a sign that researchers know they are doing this. It just comes out that way.

Historians should take heart. If the assumption in science will stand up, then they may be allowed to apply findings about 913 college students to 913 Persians at Thermopylae. Reasoning across time, they may be allowed to assume that the basic nature of emotional processes has changed not at all over the course of only two or three millennia.

From what is "basic," each society in the past, as each across the globe today, creates it own patterns and preferences. Of course — and these, no historian can disregard. In proof of their importance, I need only recall the prevalence in the Roman record of terms like *amicitia, gratia, beneficia, fides, clientelae, pietas, dignitas, contumeliae, maiestas*. It must be allowed to historians to understand these, if ethnolinguists are allowed to understand *aime, amae, rulatjarra*, or *musu*. In science, then, historians may find much of at least heuristic value.

Further: I instance Whissell's work in compiling a dictionary of some 4000 English words given a rating on the two axes of the circumplexes shown above, that is, along a line of pleasantness-unpleasantness, and arousing-not arousing. Historians could use the rated words to measure the effect on a reader of some sample passage, for example, I Corinthians 1.13.1f., so resonant and well known; but any sort of document could be analyzed. In the study of the relation between group action and motivational literature, this or a similar dictionary could add some extra firmness to historical interpretation.[77]

And again: it is useful in understanding political events of long ago, as of today, to know that "a unique function of the experience of anger is that of mobilizing and sustaining energy at high levels.... No other emotion can equal the consistency and vigor of anger in increasing and sustaining extremely high levels of motor activity."[78] The psychologists drawing attention to these qualities illustrated it in use among football coaches, but historians might raise their sights a bit.

As to the equation with which my first chapter ended and to which the present chapter is addressed, emotion=motivation: this can be seen to stand up not too badly, although necessarily to be hedged about with warnings and definitions. The terms and images that *energize*, as they may be summoned from memory, come forward in the color of some feeling. They are inseparable from color. Beyond that, even cool cognition invoked for means not for ends owes its rapidity and smoothness to colors: those as tags that identify good or bad. Investors or adventurers, then, with nothing but some

mathematical formula for their ambition in mind, and a target for ambition with no affective quality added from experience or culture, appear not to exist. Among moderns, this
was a truth on which the historian Marc Bloch insisted, so
long ago as the 1940s.[79]

CHAPTER 3:
MODERN HISTORY

BY the science reviewed in the preceding chapter, we are advised to put some trust in empathy, just as common sense would recommend; to take account of background moods and emotional dispositions in whole groups of people; to expect a specially energizing power in anger, among various common feelings; to listen for the emotional overtones of debates and moments of decision-making — all these and other matters, just as the Classical historians understood them (and indeed science bestows a great deal of up-to-date respectability on their operating assumptions).

But Thucydides or Nikolaos arrived at their assumptions about human nature in their own way; its students today, quite differently. Students today work most often in the laboratory, with one-on-one interrogation by questionnaire or interview. Each subject in a study is counted as an individual, however wide the embrace of the investigator's summing up. What most resembles these methods of study among historians is biography. This then, as I turn to their craft in our own era, ought to be the focus of my discussion: the discussion promised in my preface, of historiography of "the better documented" sort.

Perhaps. But historians also pursue the understanding of behavior en masse, of group norms, institutions, and decisions. These too are their study, quite as much as individual lives; and on these and their historiography, rather than on biography, I choose to focus in the present chapter.

For two reasons. In the first place, science makes clear that the emotional life of individuals is to a large degree shaped by the norms and institutions around them. Indeed, we hardly need science to tell us this. No single life in its affectual flow can be understood in isolation.

In the second place, individuals singly (except as a mere illustration and representative of many) lack historical significance. Emerson or Garibaldi must have had impact on others in order really to count. Without followers there can be no leaders — as, without chains to the rudder and the rudder itself, the helm only turns idly.

The drama, the human interest of the individual life will always retain its hold on the general public; the possibilities for nuance and insight that exist in the record of more recent centuries, even for psychoanalysis, will always draw in readers. But even psychohistory (and the doubter may ask, what is it but Plutarch with a PhD?) cannot raise the claims of biography to the heights. Historians will demand larger views.

In illustration, and surely the best that can be found: the French school of the *Annales*, given wholly to the study of masses, communities, groups, strata, trends, "mentalities". It was to introduce this tradition that I concluded the last chapter with the name of Marc Bloch.

1. IN FRANCE

Marc Bloch's is a natural name to usher in a chapter on modern historiography; for, among historians in the West, to the extent they have looked beyond the boundaries of their own country, the leadership of France has been acknowledged in the course of the last half of the twentieth century; and Bloch has been especially admired. With Lucien Febvre, he defined historiographical ambitions of a new sort, and together they launched the *Annales* to assert its claims. The journal began its run in 1929, a decade before *The Roman Revolution*; it too was not at first valued as it was to be, later.

Born under the title "Annals of Social History," then "Mélanges of Social History," then "Annals: Economies, Societies, Civilizations," it later reverted to its birth-days as "History, Social Sciences." Regardless of how it was called, it always favored two instruments of understanding: quantification and the social sciences.

As to the first of these: for the purposes of any inquiry or debate, the virtue of quantification lies in its finality. If disputants can count, and represent their thought in numbers, one will appear the winner. Inquiry and debate can then move on to something else.[1] This constitutes progress in the strictest sense. Or one may say, agreement, which is accepted as truth, has been made to embrace more territory.

As to the social sciences and their methods — the various "–ologies" which contribute to our understanding of emotions — they appear capable of bringing history closer to those exact sciences that provide our best models. Psychology, anthropology, ethnology, and sociology — especially this last, and its perfect exemplification in the once-celebrated works of Pitrim Sorokin — delighted students of the past, from the 1930s on, stimulated all sorts of hopes and interpretational adventures, and were imported wholesale into the new French historiography.[2]

I am aware of speaking quickly and loosely about a large subject matter, simply to open it up. Within it, however, my interest is quite limited: limited to modern historians' consideration of feelings. Thus I need expand only a little on what I have said so far, sampling studies of the seventeenth and eighteenth centuries and not much more. There, much of earlier *Annales* work was concentrated.

In the style of such work, the first thing that may strike the eye is the use of graphs, charts, and tables, in which a prodigious variety of phenomena can be quantified. This feature is so prominent, it has been tellingly if a little mischievously used to describe how the *Annales* itself became established and the center of a didactic structure.[3]

According to its teachings, quantification may be used to provide exactitude (sometimes, of course, quite deceptive) — an air of the laboratory. It may serve also the very important purpose of allowing statements to be made about masses of individuals through aggregation. The individuals as such are too little understood and appear too little in sources for anything to be said about them; but as contributors to a total, they and their actions can be counted. Their sheer numbers in censuses and their dates in cemeteries constitute demography; their wages, economics; their decease in epidemics and their expenditure on pills and doctors, the history of medicine; the number of books published, a measure of literacy; and so forth. Historians may thus break free of the tyranny of political narrative and Great Men, to embrace the whole of life in the past as it was lived by the many.

Even matters quite of the spirit can be counted at least indirectly: religiosity, through bequests to pay for remembrance in masses; diminished belief in church teachings, through a rise in illegitimate births; and so forth. Echoes of Sorokin! The numbers devotedly totted up derive from, and therefore express, some certain mind-set, some disposition, a belief, what's taken for granted by the whole or most of a community: in a word, a *mentalité*.[4] Bloch made use of both the idea and the term in his *Feudal Society* of 1934; a little later, so did Febvre. The two historians didn't see them in quite the same way and they have given rise to much discussion.[5] There is no dispute, however, that *mentalités* offer a view into men's very souls, without loss of scientific rigor in the reporting.

Yet the promise of science is illusory. Operations and productions of the soul — urges and ideas and judgements all entangled in feelings, as the previous chapter made plain — hardly lend themselves to expression in numbers. Externals do, but only externals — meaning, actions and whatever else an observer could note who might have been present at the historical moment. Anything more requires the actor's own words of self-description; anything more without self-description can only be guesswork based on the assumption that people back then acted in such-and-such a way out of the same impulses that would make you and me act in the same fashion, today; and we know what our own feelings would be.[6] Therefore .... So to describe the realities of the reasoning is not, of course, entirely to discount its findings. By no means.

Bloch and Febvre, however, and their properly self-disciplined descendants as well, have in fact remarkably little to say about *feelings*, even in the midst of their discussions of *mentalités*. They certainly attempt no estimate of the *force* of feelings, which would be essential to an understanding of causation; and they seem seldom or never to explore mixed motives. For this they are occasionally criticized.

Readers may be deceived, perhaps writers as well. Bloch writes,

> Accustomed to danger, the knight found in war yet another attraction: it offered a remedy for boredom. For these men whose culture long remained rudimentary and who... were seldom occupied by very heavy administrative cares, everyday life easily slipped into a grey monotony. Thus was born an appetite for diversions which, when one's native soil failed to afford the means to gratify it, sought satisfaction in distant lands.[7]

The interpretation certainly sounds perfectly acceptable. It helps to explain things. But just how does the writer know what he tells us? In arriving at what may be judged a valuable insight, he uses no science, only imagination.

Empathy, intuition, *Einfühlung*, had long roots in French historiography, going back at least to Hippolyte Taine. That great practitioner of his art in the 1850s could be heard asserting the value of immersion in the acknowledged cream of a people's literature because almost by definition it must encapsulate their spirit, *la psychologie* (with his italics); and again in the 1870s, writing to Dumas, he says of his progress through his own monumental study of modern France, "We are trying at the moment to do in history something similar to what you do in writing for the theater: I mean, *applied psychology.*" Once more, his italics; and he goes on to add, appearing to anticipate the *Annales*, "in sum, the instrumentality of ideas and feelings, '*sentiments*', is the true cause of human action, while the parading about of politics is quite secondary."[8] No one, however, in the later school would generalize about social structure in the terms Taine chooses, from his own or humanity's common experience: "Man feels compassion for the ills suffered that he himself witnesses..., the heart is touched when the eye observes them..., one can hardly remain cool in the face of the agony of the poor." And so on, drawing on and quoting contemporary comments.[9]

The *Annalistes* only appear to follow in this tradition: at the beginning, Bloch. For him, "everything is psychology" and "historical facts are in essence psychological facts;" and he goes on to protest that historians, too, are "no strangers to the passions." No, they have a passion *to understand*. But is that all? Just curiosity? His sense of the meaning of psychology he reveals better in saying of the Black Death that its spread must be explained psychologically, because the key factors were "certain social conditions, these, themselves, being mental," i. e. *mentalités*, "in their roots." The very choice of his subject was that of an economic historian.[10] And Febvre chimes in, that everything in history "is the history of ideas... economic facts are, like all other social facts, facts of belief and opinion; and wealth itself, and labor and money are perhaps nothing more than ideas."[11] In all of which there is nothing of Taine and *Einfühlung.*

The reasoning instead runs: if it's true that we think about what we do, then everything we do originates in the mind. Well, who would dispute that? It is added, that all sorts of habits which amount to institutions and belief-systems lodge in our heads (and that's true, too) so that *mentalités* can subsume these "structures" as they are termed. There is indeed a place for broad and subtle understanding of the past through such perceptions; but no reservation for our feelings.

A fair test of meaning may be had in an early work (1932) of Georges Lefebvre's. For years a colleague of Bloch and

Febvre at Strasbourg, a lifetime friend thereafter, ready to acknowledge his special debt to Bloch, a regular contributor to the *Annales* from its birth to his death, Lefebvre was of that school though not quite at its center. He writes about the wave of panic that swept across France with uncanny speed in 1789. Here should be a perfect instance to examine if one were interested in the operation of affective currents upon a population. He does indeed examine them in great detail and with great common sense, concluding with every reason that people acted out of the most pressing anxiety, ready to pick up and pass on with a tremor in their voices every rumor of danger. Fear is what he finds, fear and violence in a hundred incidents.[12]

But missing in *La grande peur* is an empathy that would sense and convey to the reader the *force* of feelings at work. This, our understanding of the period requires. As we all know, the Revolution is replete with incidents of pathological politics, as it may be called; meaning, in a word, barbarism. About this, "there is an abundance to be said and shrieked," in Carlyle's words; or more coolly, "a phenomenon well known to historians of *mentalités*."[13] A contrast in historiographical temperature confronts us. According to the French observer, active participants in larger episodes are best studied through tables quantifying income, age, literacy, occupation, mobility, etc., etc.[14] Besides, where they begin to resemble a mob, they can be dismissed as a mere mass in the grip of the irrational.[15] Such episodes, however, include the bearing aloft of the guts torn from a victim and paraded about in the city to the cry, "Offal, offal, who wants fresh offal?" Is this a picture the meaning of which is easily to be rendered numerically? Is it best studied in such exquisitely detached terms as "phenomenon"? Paraded bits and parts of people — here, a heart; there, a pair of hands; elsewhere, a head or two; and so forth — turn up in reports from many towns and cities.[16] They amount to much more than fear and its consequent behavior; and they are not merely sensational, either. Carlyle hit the truth: "there is an abundance to be said." Non-*Annaliste* analysis discovers profound historical significance in the savage passions on display here in their extreme form, thus: whatever explanation one chooses for shows of violence, "in any case, it is of the initial opening acts that Terror was born," "it is the manifestation of terrorist violence which brought forth the political system of the Terror," "'without the September massacres,' as a friend of Robespierre later remarked, 'there never would have been a Mountain.'"

In my attempt to suggest the quality of the French school, the way historians treat violence suggests itself as a point to have considered first; for violence displays emotions so obviously at work, they can hardly be ignored or given only a bare mention here and there. In fact, however, emotions beyond their external manifestations seem to hold no interest for the school in question. Witness *Annaliste* treatments of savage killings and so forth, Revolutionary or Frondiste or other; witness also treatment of various other phenomena treated as *mentalités* in the modern French manner. They have been indicated already, mostly in the notes.[17] In my text, to have spread out one example after another would have been too tedious — though to relegate them to the end of the book .... A fair appraisal of such a great company of scholars over decades of their work is certainly not easy.

Still, their tendency may emerge a little more clearly through their treatment of other impulses at work in the past. What they show would once have been called the history of taste (now, "emotions studies"), including the permissibility or desirability of displaying this or that that one felt.

For example, anger, the several varieties of which give most, and most long-lasting, force to our actions. The *Annalistes* with their openness to psychology and anthropology might be expected to show an interest in the history, the changes across time, of such obvious elements in human behavior. Both Bloch and Febvre were indeed much struck by what Huizinga had to say regarding displays of this passion in the medieval and early modern world (above, n. 7). Medieval rulers with their *ira regia* made history. Whatever kings felt had effect. It turned into law. Grassotti draws illustrations from Spain showing its operation, or more accurately, the operation of one of its varieties; for the instances he collects have a particular character. What they show might better be called indignation — that particular passion arising from the withholding or violation of what a society has endorsed.[18] The endorsement itself is a value, a moral norm, a *mentalité* that determines the reaction, the feeling, whether by an individual or a community. In different societies of course people will get angry about different things. A constructionist point of view fits very well within an *Annaliste*.[19]

The poverty of European languages in distinguishing indignation or other kinds of anger can be brought out by comparison with the richness of description available to Australian aborigines (above, chapter 2) when they speak of grief. They recognize different inducements, then different feelings, thus a need for different words. Where, instead, an adequate choice of words doesn't exist, analysis cannot go far enough.

"Autre temps, autres moeurs:" Poseidonius was struck by the sudden outbreaks of rage he heard of at Gallic dinner-parties; Gregory of Tours in this same land describes scenes of revenge of such infantile barbarity, they verge on the comical. Then we come to civilized times, with which the *Annalistes* are concerned, and see French anger of one sort partially repressed, taking on more elaborate ceremony, turning into duels, until eventually duels are outlawed.[20]

Anger at a blow cannot be always expressed, if one is too low on the totem pole. Servants, kicked, in past times must not kick back. Imagine one challenging to a duel! "A poor man has no honor," as Johnson once said — who had known what it was to be poor, and was no stranger to pride. Aristotle indeed supposed that "no one grows angry with a person on whom there is no prospect of taking vengeance, and we feel comparatively little anger, or none at all, with those who are much our superiors in power."[21] What can he have been thinking of? Perhaps of his own and his friends' slaves? — who appeared so equable?

In those civilized times in France, underlings of various sorts did what they will always do, that is, protested so far as they could without provoking punishment. Class differences show up in the expression of resentment, hatred, rage: among the lower, by aping and making fun of their betters.[22] As an instance, two teenage printing-apprentices in Paris: one is Contat, the other, young Wide-awake, Léveillé, "our cut-up," *notre drôle*.[23] He has a genius for mimicry and loves an audience, even to the point of ridiculing his like (not the journeymen, above him, though they are his audience, too). Angry at the meanness of the Master's wife for never giving them a square meal, the two lads kill her beloved cat and with their fellows go on to a general chase and slaughter of any others they light on, executing one with the fullest court ceremonies before the delighted shop-crew. "All the journeymen," recalls Contat of the story, years later, "are united against the Masters, one need only speak ill of them to earn the admiration of the whole Typographical crowd. M. Léveillé was one who could do that...." And the mistress complains, too: "These wicked fellows can't kill the Masters, so they've killed my kitty." Quite right.

The cruelty of Contat and Léveillé anyone can understand who has passed through not too hygienic a childhood and early adolescence, especially one where boys go off into the woods or back-alleys; or one has heard of this. And they experiment with frogs or dogs or each other, to see what happens; or in a play-yard, torture by derision.[24] An incident of this order is, in Contat's account of the trade in which he was raised, only a very minor bit of spice among his otherwise quite businesslike recollections. For the historian, however, it is an illustration *with feelings* (and that is the value) of class difference. Parallels may be had in the recollections of another son of a church family, young Seabury apprenticed in New York to a furniture-maker, and still bitter, years later, about the "roasting" and mockery he got: "The degradation to which I was continually subjected was horrible." Should he, for a goods-delivery, submit to the humiliation of a tip, a *pourboire*? "I made some demur to this habit, but was soon laughed out of my feelings or rather into a suppression of them... occasional mortifications of pride were more easily endured than the incessant gibes of ridicule."[25]

The Paris printer's employes express their anger at the humiliations of their place through laughter with an edge to it. It is meant to requite their pain. But at a very different rank of society, too, a man "chokes with rage" in recollecting the honors paid by the king to a person the observer judges unworthy, while people entering the court without the sort of credentials its residents judged adequate would, on a particular occasion, be made to feel that "all the duchesses saw this as so awful that they [the intruders] never dared come again."[26]

The indignation can be felt; its colors may be supplied to make more vivid what is unsaid when one man must get off his horse on encountering another, who does not dismount; must check, and offer a greeting, not returned; must deliver a more ceremonious "Good morning" than he receives. It is insult offered by strength to weakness; insult endured, and endured; and remembered. The strong, on the other hand, enjoy having the upper hand in such exchanges. Taine in explaining social structure on the eve of the Revolution retails the complaint of someone at the village level in the church, inflamed by the arrogance of his superiors recruited from the nobility. The poor man is obliged,

> as they pass, to throw himself close against the embankment to get out of the way of their horses' hooves and the splashed-up mud, and the wheels, perhaps even the whip of an insolent coachman; then, all dirty, his wretched stick in one hand and such a hat as he has in the other, humbly to salute, and quickly, too, through the window of the closed-in, gilded coach, that pretended holy officer snoring away on the wool of the flock that the curé tends and of which nothing is left for him but the dung and the grease.[27]

For what other reason than an emotional one would a person of the nobility impose purely symbolic demands on those lower than he? — demanding his own pew in the local church (which he doesn't ever attend), priority of mention in prayers and offerings, and various other "droits honorifiques," for the number and exaction of which, the local people burnt down his chateau (and served him right).[28]

To finish off: in the same period of the Ancient Régime up to the 1770s from which all these matters of behavior, high or low, are drawn (except the American), and generally from works of *Annaliste* flavor (except Taine), without their ever bothering to examine the evidence for its usefulness, I offer a number of advisory booklets on how to sign off at the end of a letter. The problem they address, an American may remember with trembling from his school-day lessons: "Veuillez agréer...," and then, what follows? In the eighteenth century, what might follow are any of several scores of polite formulations, such as, "Je suis, Monsieur, très parfaitement à vous," "I am quite completely yours," or, "... entirely," or, "devotedly, *inviolablement*," or, "your most humble servant," or, "obedient", to be calibrated according to the recipient's rank as a village priest, a civil official, someone of noble blood, or any degree or mixture of such important things, on which a great deal depended.[29] Such booklets sold like hotcakes. With a copy in his hand, a purchaser could compare a letter he had received so as to learn just what his correspondents thought of his position in the world. One can imagine this. It is a kind of fact in social history.

To learn one's place, to know and to defend it had nothing about it of material or in any real sense rational calculation. It was a matter of feelings. Were they generally strong, then class boundaries held firm, with consequences that historians must take seriously, and thereby justify their claim to be psychologists or sociologists. Otherwise, not. It will not do, to ignore what Elias calls "the affective life." So, to convey the meaning of class lines and of the different lives lived on either side, Elias chooses a moment from the 1770s: a particular encounter, and the very words of the principal participant — who happened to be the young Werther: "I gnash my teeth." To read these words in the 1930s, like Elias, as to read them today, is, one's self, to experience at least some of Werther's rage and isolation. Which is why Elias used a page to recall the scene, where his intent was not particular but general, across an entire society.[30]

French epistolary manuals offer evidence of a quite different order: without express affect. By themselves they paint no scene. Moreover, they and village church pews set aside for the nobility give us the past on a very small scale. Micro-history, however, in the 1980s came in for its fashion. The tale of the cat massacre will be offered as exemplary. In it, one confronts "the otherness," much emphasized, of other times and peoples. It is quite mysterious, the modern observer "just doesn't get it."[31] His difficulty may be in fact nothing insurmountable: let historians enter into and compassionate with whatever their subject requires of them, using their whole selves and imagination; but, this said, such obscure moments as micro-history makes use of can be illuminating. They are especially valuable if their affective content is considered. It may indeed be better found in unguarded interchange and among people of no account than in the formal documents of the grand.

From outrage and resentment and other varieties of anger, to crying: the history of this latter is much less likely to affect events. Among people of no account, however, it leaves its own signs of a quality and force that can characterize a period. In the letters written to the author of *Héloïse* (1761), a variety of social types and classes send their thanks to Rousseau for the delicious chokes and sobs and moral improvement elicited in them by their reading of his novel. In the same style, MacKenzie's *Man of Feeling* (1771) and Goethe's *Werther* (1774), too, but above all Sterne's *Tristram Shandy* (1759-) and *Sentimental Journey* (1768), met and marvelously shaped the tastes of Europe and America alike. The fact, in good *Annaliste* fashion, can be quantified.[32] Precursors in England must include Hume, surprisingly;[33] in France, the so-called "theater of tears" and its best-known champion, Chaussée in the 1730s up to mid-century, enjoying a large audience. It was, however, from the 1760s onward that change in manners became really widespread. The letters to Rousseau in their scores constitute an especially good base of data on which to found an understanding of this striking phenomenon: the open enjoyment of tears. Enjoyment is not merely to be inferred from our own reactions to the same stimuli, the same *Héloïse* or *Man of Feeling*; it is spelt out also by readers who report on it at the time. They cannot reveal their feelings too much; for these were, by fashion, call it, or more grandly, by society, licensed and approved and expressed in literature. From novelistic scenes of ready crying, to real-life scenes of the sort, was a natural progression. It is, however, rarely looked for or noted.[34]

Then sensibility passed; its history was over. Endings for historians are always less interesting than beginnings, but equally a challenge. In a letter of 1826, an elderly woman tells her correspondent that she had been recently asked to share some book aloud with her friends. Her choice fell on *The Man of Feeling*.

> I, who was the reader, had not seen it for several years, the rest did not know it at all. I am afraid I perceived a sad change in it, or in myself — which was worse; and the effect failed. Nobody cried, and at some of the passages, the touches that I used to think so exquisite — Oh Dear! They laughed.... Yet I remember so well its first publication, my mother and sister crying over it, dwelling upon it with rapture. And when I read it, as I was a girl of fourteen not yet versed in sentiment, I had a secret dread I should not cry enough to gain the credit of proper sensibility.

And she goes on to wonder, "What makes [young people of a different era] judge so differently?"[35]

"A history of feelings as distinct from a history of the theory of feelings, still remains to be written," in 1983; and still today.[36] A reason is suggested by letters like the one above, or those about *Héloise* to Rousseau. Where a particular emotion is intended as the chief reward in the reading of some style of literature, then the literature itself will provide what historians need to work with. And, of "sensibility" as it was called, a great deal existed, and much survives to be described and analyzed. For other emotions, no comparable data-base is available.

Exceptions which are really not very exceptional suggest themselves. Regarding sloth and apathy in combination, and an associated indifference to one's spiritual state, called *accidie*, defined by the church as a particular moral challenge, there was a good deal of discussion by medieval authorities.[37] Melancholy was written about in the same period, too, so we can know about it.[38] And horror could be instanced. As a source of pleasure it made its appearance in works of literature of about the same period as the pleasure in tears. In English, Collins' *Ode to Fear* (1747) leads into Grainger's *Solitude*, with "nodding towers" and "the desert's trackless gloom" to rhyme (of course) with "the yawning tomb" (1753); and on to Walpole's much-imitated *Castle of Otranto* (1764).[39] None of these feelings took hold of an audience on anything like the scale of sensibility.

There is always love between man and woman, whether or not it is best called erotic. Surely that has been much studied; surely the affective side of domestic relations is discussed. But no, not to my knowledge. The forms and externals, yes; the institutions and roles; but intimate feelings underlying them are little explored, or they are explored quite indirectly through inferences from the physical conditions of living together.[40] Inferences from institutions to emotions, sometimes ventured, are easily challenged.[41] There is surprisingly little use made of scenes in fiction like Balzac's with their emotional coloring.[42]

It is vain, too, to look for so much as the words "longing" or "indignation" or "guilt" in the tens of thousands of pages of *Annales*-volumes of recent decades. Old fashions never find a place there. Taine, long prior, and Huizinga, so much admired by Bloch and Febvre, with Norbert Elias as his work came to be known, after long delay, had once used these very words; had once directed attention to the affective elements in people's behavior; had acknowledged the fact that people loved, lost their tempers, and so forth, and merited description in so doing. Some interest (if not very much) in the color of the past — color, which is also so much a part of the motivating energy of action — could be seen in French historiography of the 1930s, still. It was not wholly absent from Bloch's early work (above, n. 17). In the journal and its school, however, it was to yield before long to a preference for the appearance of exactitude such as can be gained through dealing with a subject in numerical terms. Thus the outside of things would be better displayed; but the inside, much worse, or not at all. For, notice, the inside of *groups* as opposed to individuals is particularly difficult to penetrate; and it was groups, classes, communities as blocks in which *Annalistes* showed most interest rather than in individuals. It was Bloch himself who had set the style.[43]

In his last work of historiography he undertook the examination of just such large blocks. Most of what he had to say fitted within a familiar genre: a war memoir by someone not in the highest rank detailing and deploring the sheer stupidity of those above him, by whom all was lost. The "hardening of the mental arteries," *la sclérose*," among the elderly professionals in the higher commands projected its faults on everyone and everything beneath.[44] But here and there in his narrative, and with care in a concluding chapter, he engages himself more analytically in the resulting, fateful patterns of thought and behavior that characterized the French government, civil population, political parties, age-cadres, classes, centers of training and education, the press, and of course the army, as he knew these various communities over the course of his own adult years from 1914 to 1940.

His approach is sociological in the ordinary sense of the word, belonging thus to the historiographical tradition he helped to establish; but he dispenses with statistics or any pretensions of the laboratory. Then, too, the academic naturally deplores the laziness (by which he means, and sometimes specifies, the mental laziness) that can turn every community inward, selfishly and shortsightedly; but he shows a deep respect for qualities and impulses that are not intellectual at all. He discovers affective causes for behavior far more often than economic or material causes, to explain everyday working relationships within groups, on up to major, difficult, personal decisions. In evidence, he instances his own decisions (and in time might have instanced those also that led him to his death at the hands of the Gestapo). *Soul* and *heart* he uses in his discussion without apology; conscience and sense of duty he presents as his ideal and answer.[45] Indeed, if the perdition of his country was its laziness, its salvation he sees in a compound of feelings that amount to love of *la patrie*.[46] A few passages may give the sense of this, the first, comparing

lazy selfish instincts which, side by side with those of a more noble potential, lie sleeping in the depths of the human heart. These enthusiasts [for surrender], though many of them were personally courageous, unconsciously labored to make others, cowards. So true it is, that virtue unaccompanied by the sharpest controls of intelligence is ever in danger of turning in against its most cherished objectives.... In May of 1940 the spirit of their first mobilization was not dead; over the men who made it their rallying-song, the *Marseillaise* still with its wonted inspiration breathed a devotion to country and a detestation of despotism.... There are two types of Frenchmen who will never understand France's history: those who cannot thrill to the memory of the Kings' consecration at Rheims, and those who can read without emotion an account of the Festival of Federation... [And now let a new generation rebuild the country on a new basis:] They will discover for themselves the best lines of it in the depths of their minds and their hearts.

This last, at the very end of his work. Yet Bloch (since candor invites ridicule) nowhere risks a discussion of feelings, his own or those that he lovingly attributes to so many of his countrymen. "Let us move past the region of the emotions," he says at one point, quickly. It is as if, in the study of that period of the past which he knew most intimately and had thought about most deeply, the historian preferred to keep the key to its understanding in his pocket. And to this as to his apostasy in any other regard in what was his final work, the school of which he was a founder paid no attention.

In the very face of the *Annales*, however, Paul Veyne in 1971 published a grand essay about the writing of history. He challenged the prevailing fashions head-on, without disloyalty — rather, by returning — to Marc Bloch.[47] He went on (1976) to show what sort of history would result from the

views he had propounded, taking as his subject the willing-
ness of rich Greeks and Romans freely to support their cities
and states with their money and services: euergetism. What
was taken for granted in their societies by rich and poor alike
was a set of expectations. This did more than anything else to
create their civilization. In these two books, like Bloch, Veyne
assumes that his or any observer's understanding can indeed
penetrate groups, to the motives that control them. But not
by counting.

How is this to be done? For illustration, this passage from
the second of the two works (1976), explaining a certain gift
to Rome, a piece of ancient "magnificence" of an almost
Florentine style:

> The Column [of Trajan] is no more propaganda than
> the Gothic cathedrals were visual catechisms. It is
> ornamented with reliefs showing figures because, being
> a monument, it could not exist without speaking or
> speak without saying something. It therefore contains
> a message; it tells in detail of Trajan's campaigns so as to
> express his glory, but this detail seems to have interest-
> ed the sculptor himself more than it interests the
> passers-by. It is with Imperial majesty as with the star-
> strewn sky that expresses the glory of God. What is
> more expressive than the sky? But in order to perceive
> its expression we do not need to itemize the stars one
> by one.... The ruling power obtained additional pres-
> tige from the very irrationality of its expressions, which
> spoke for themselves, and were proudly indifferent to
> their audience. Grandiloquent nonsense has always
> been the privilege and sign of gods, oracles, and 'boss-
> es'.[48]

Readers here are told just what went on in the donor's
mind. It can be entered and understood to operate just as
other people's do, who are in fact momentarily glimpsed in
the sources. Their behavior may be taken all together to show
a texture of influence and routine and expectation — which
is assumed to have enclosed Trajan as it did everyone else. So
the individual instance can be presented without particular

evidence. Bloch offers similar explanations naked, so to speak, like Veyne's. No reader protests (nor do I), "The explanation has no clothes." It is enough if the given motives fit with whatever else challengers might know of the civilization and period, and better than anything else they can suggest. What weighs the most is the historian's good judgement, good sense.[49] No mystery about it — until one gets to national character, where the distinguishing traits make up so complicated a whole, explanations are indeed ineffable.[50]

Veyne's contribution, in most respects irrelevant to my own interest, is nevertheless important to my purpose; for motivation is his continual concern. Why did various groups, or individuals as illustrative of groups, act as they did? How did they relate to each other? His curiosity is directed continually at the reasons for action; and in the reasons, as he is well aware, emotions play their part. So much, he makes clear by occasionally touching on duty, shame, the love of the subject for the ruler, sense of entitlement, competition for applause, and the like; but the feelings are mentioned without examination or evocation; so the reader doesn't internalize them.[51] Besides, useful as unsupported intuitions may be, and more than useful if they derive from the historian's deep familiarity with the scene he describes, what is unsupported must be ever open to challenge.

Consider a quite different passage on euergetism, this one by a contemporary, John Chrysostom. It too explains a huge gift to some city; whereupon,

> the theater fills, and the whole citizenry is seated up there, presenting the most brilliant spectacle made up of so many faces, that the very topmost gallery and its covering is blocked out by men's bodies.... Upon the entrance of that benefactor who brought them together, they leap to their feet, uttering a salute as from a single mouth, with one voice calling him guardian and leader of their common city. They stretch forth their arms; then at intervals they compare him to the greatest of all rivers; they liken the grandeur and flow of his civic generosity, in its abundance, to the waters of the Nile, and they call

him a very Nile of gifts, himself; and some who flatter
still more, declaring the comparison with the Nile too
mean, set aside rivers and seas and bring in Ocean, and
say that is what he is, as Ocean among waters, so he in
his gifts. They omit no term of praise.... He himself
bows to them, and by this pays his respects, and so he
seats himself amid the blessing of all, who, every one,
pray to be such as he — and then to die.[52]

Between the two explanations, Veyne's and Chrysostom's,
I see a great difference. Veyne's is bold and right and clears
away considerable nonsense which could once and can still
be found in learned books. It is *interesting*; that is, we hadn't
thought of the matter in just his way, and now see it much
more clearly. The irrational of the past which cannot be
quantified, but yet makes people behave as they undeniably
did, has been confronted in terms beyond the powers of the
Annales, with welcome success.

The scene in the theater, however, is not merely interesting: as Taine would have said, "the heart is touched" (and
what *Annaliste* would dream of *this* as a thing to aim for?).
John Chrysostom moves us to a point beyond such cognition
as would enable us to answer a question in an exam on
ancient history; he moves us to empathy in the most literal
sense. By language intended to arouse feelings, and used with
passion or with art, like the complaint of the humiliated curé
on the roadside, above, or by the tricks that earned John the
nickname "Golden-mouth," readers in their emotional selves
become the man described so as to experience what he experienced; and in that full sense they understand what is more
than interesting: they understand a felt truth that can move a
person to behave in some certain way.

Use of contemporary sources not only vivifies, whatever
this may add to the pleasures as well as to the instruction of
reading history; it not only supplies the *enargeia* of which
much was made in my first chapter. Beyond such benefits, it
gives title to the historian to explain the inner man in terms
for which he can adduce testimony; and it incidentally supports the equation earlier proposed, emotion=motivation.

2. IN AMERICA: THE ANTISLAVERY CAUSE IN PRINT

Annalistes practices and approaches seem not to have traveled very well to the United States. At any rate, imitators on this side of the ocean have been few and far between and not very successful in establishing a school.[53] Perhaps the trouble has been a focus on particular persons to which American readers of history are so happily habituated. From the French journal under all of its various titles, clearly the close study of individuals was to be excluded. So much can be seen in any of its volumes one cares to open. That wonderful reification of *Annaliste* methods, Braudel's study of the Mediterranean world, only in a final volume turns to conventional narrative and to the familiar run of kings, popes, admirals, ministers, and so forth, and does so, then, without much connection or carry-over from the more general volumes. The two seem somehow as immiscible as oil and water.

And for all its mentions of individuals, the final volume very rarely dips into the feelings at play in the past.[54] Strange; for emotions are and can be known only through what is revealed by a specific someone from within himself. *Known*, however, is different from *guessed at*. Perhaps the fact explains why an *Annaliste* might feel uncomfortable with any affective element in history. Certainly historians of all methods *infer* feelings from actions, just as juries are expected to do in courts of law; and the results are accepted as reasonable. Mention of this altogether familiar practice was made, above, in my second chapter. Still, it fits ill with the social-scientific exactitude that *Annalistes* aspire to. They cannot be happy with so low a level of demonstration.

In consequence, a loss; for "by showing how cultural tensions and contradictions may be internalized, struggled with, and resolved within actual individuals, [biography] offers the most promising key to the synthesis of culture and history."[55]

This, an opinion acceptable back in the 1960s growing out of a study of the antislavery movement.

It is surely acceptable today; for D. B. Davis' thought, here quoted, is representative of that body of serious work intermediate between the American tradition of local history, so often amateur, and of biographical narrative so often unreflecting, for which latter there has always been a great readership and a corresponding place in commercial as opposed to scholarly publishing. With results well known: "They have their reward."

Challenge to the "peculiar institution," long a focus of Davis' interest, is not chosen for mention here at random. Though it is all a twice-told tale, and though my discussion aims at nothing new, nevertheless there is for consideration the sheer magnitude of antislavery's place in the nation's history, igniting the flame, one may say, beneath the cauldron which was before very long to boil over into a great war. The martyr Lovejoy's name as well as any draws us into the stream of cause and effect.[56] Moreover, the early decades of the abolition movement can provide a natural view into the operation of the affective element in shaping our past — for this reason, too, they suit my purpose. Still further, they satisfy the limitations confessed to in my preface, which confine me to some few generations toward the mid-point in the American story. And within that period my purpose — again, indicated in my preface — requires at least a visit to some area where the historian confronts, not too little, but almost too much to work with. Antislavery feelings in the 1820s and 1830s indeed gave rise to a Noah's flood of ink on paper.

My understanding of the difference between the two proportions of evidence and the difficulty each presents dates to a summer many years ago when I lodged in a university town ill-equipped, as it turned out, in its library; so I had to commute daily to a huge research collection not too far away. My ride for this was offered by a friend working on a major topic in modern U. S. history (myself, at the time, in the classical world). On arrival at our place of work, as we parted company each morning, assistants would be already wheeling up my friend's diurnal diet of primary sources by the cartload, and when we met again at the end of the day's reading, he would have finished his great pile of type-written note-pages, to my five or six handwritten five-by-eight-inch cards — reflecting the ratio of ten thousand to one in the materials available to each of the two of us.

In that inky mid-point in American history to which I now turn, a huge flow of words on the page, hand-written or published, was both a determinant and a characteristic. It determined the methods of the anti-slavery movement, requiring as it did a setting such as America was at the time, of very widespread literacy, reliable mails, and news media; and however ephemeral these latter may have been, individually, yet they were as common as the weather and much more interesting to talk about. Moreover, while the American movement gathered force, its development was so abundantly marked in the written word, this latter characteristic encouraged accounts of the lives of its principals: accounts revealing of their subjects' inner selves and based on their very words surviving in floods, of Adams as a Congressman, of William Lloyd Garrison, Theodore Dwight Weld, the Tappans, and many not-so-important figures, or of figures who were only partially given to the cause, such as Lydia Child, the Grimké sisters, Whittier, Mott, Stanton, or Marks.[57]

In the background to these figures could be seen the prior history of antislavery in England. There, to reach very large audiences, techniques had been developed that suited American conditions equally well, and could be learned from. At first they had had as their focus the trade in slaves, understood by reformers as a manageable preliminary to total abolition. Then they moved on to slavery in its very self, pervading the West Indies. Active in both phases of the long campaign, and convenient to represent the example that Britain set, was Henry Brougham. Others — Clarkson, Wilberforce, George Thompson — were more obviously associated with the cause, but none more eloquent.

And eloquence must do the job, where the job was to change public opinion.

Brougham helped to found and contributed enormously to the *Edinburgh Review*, where American abolitionists could find articles of interest to themselves, giving a view on the cause in Britain. In the same year of the journal's founding (1803), he also published a serious study of colonial history. It established him as a useful young coadjutor in the campaign that Wilberforce headed. He contributed other writings from an early date. He thus served the cause in quantity; but in quality, even more. He had a way of saying things that gave them irresistible force.[58]

For example: "Tell me not," was his protest in a debate on abolition, looking back to the triumphs against the slave trade twenty years earlier and more, and in the language that the times most admired,

tell me not of rights — talk not of the property of the planter in his slaves. I deny the right — I acknowledge not the property. The principles, the feelings of our common nature, rise in rebellion against it. Be the appeal made to the understanding or to the heart, the sentence is the same that rejects it. In vain you tell me of laws which sanction such a claim! There is a law above all the enactments of human codes — the same throughout the world, the same at all times — such as it was before the daring genius of Columbus pierced the night of ages, and opened to one world the sources of power, wealth, and knowledge; to another, all unutterable woes; — such as it is at this day: it is the law written by the finger of God on the heart of man; and by that law, unchangeable and eternal, while men despise fraud, and loathe rapine, and abhor blood, they shall reject with indignation the wild and guilty fantasy that man can hold property in man. In vain you appeal to treaties, to covenants between nations. The covenants of the Almighty, whether the old or the new, denounce such unholy pretensions. To those laws did they of old refer, who maintained the African trade.... Yet, in despite of law and treaties, that infernal traffic is now destroyed, and its votaries put to death like other

pirates. How came this to pass? Not assuredly by parliament leading the way; but the country at length
awoke; the indignation of the people was kindled; it
descended in thunder, and smote the traffic, and scattered its guilty profits to the wind.[59]

The protest, so framed, today retains its power, it still thun-
ders; and it especially suited a cause so closely identified with
church direction and participation, deriving as it did the central image of its thought from Scripture (Dan. 5.5). This must
appeal to American readers, who quote it in turn, as William
Lloyd Garrison was wont to do.

For Brougham to have joined Wilberforce was, incidentally, a silly thing to do: the young man being from the little-
regarded North, without money or connections, and yet keen
to rise in the world. Wilberforce and antislavery wouldn't help
him. He made the choice out of his nature, which detested
cruelty and oppression. It was a choice from indignation.

Many lessons in America could be learned from Britain's
course: from 1806 forward, lessons in the notion of slavery's
intolerability, the pressing of this upon the half-opened mind
of fellow-citizens by an accumulation of evidence, so as to
change theology and philosophy; all this served by the energies of a denominational community.[60] In the end, indeed
"the indignation of the people was kindled." But to change
public opinion was a labor of decades.

A representative instrument was an Englishwoman's pamphlet of 1824, later republished and widely circulated from
Boston in 1838: Elizabeth Heyricks' *Immediate, Not Gradual
Abolition*. Among other topics which she took up was the
slave insurrection in Demerara, Jamaica, and its consequences
to the losers: a flogging of a thousand strokes (where 39 were
the standard of severity).[61]

What was the offence which brought down this frightening vengeance on the heads of these devoted victims?
What horrible crimes could have instigated man to
sentence his fellow man to a punishment so tremendous? — to doom his brother to undergo the pro-
tracted torture of A THOUSAND LASHES? — to have his

quivering flesh mangled and torn from his living body?
— and to labour through his life under the galling and
ignominious weight of chains! It was insurrection. But
in what cause did they become insurgents? Was it not
in that cause, which, of all others, can best *excuse*, if it
cannot *justify* insurrection? Was it not the cause of self-
defence from the most degrading, intolerable oppression? But what was the immediate occasion of this
insurrection? What goaded these poor wretches on to
brave the dreadful hazards of rebellion? One of them,
now hanging in chains at Demerara, was sold and separated from his wife and ten children, after a marriage
of eighteen years, and thereby made a rebel. Another ...
whose wife ... was torn from his bosom and forced to
become the mistress of an overseer....

And she elaborated further on such cruelties. The force of her
work swung Wilberforce from gradual to immediate abolition, toward which he and Brougham and those others with
him thereafter worked until they had achieved their full success by 1838.

Among other tributes to this final triumph was a cele-
bratory pamphlet published by the American Anti-Slavery
Society (AASS) in a hundred thousand copies for distribution everywhere. It was anticipated that a half might be sold,
the rest, manufactured at $12\frac{1}{2}$ cents each, subsidized and
offered free.[62] Such distribution-figures (with more to follow) bring home the nature of the effort on both sides of the
ocean: to change many people's minds — to break them out
of one certain taken-for-granted, out of one certain way of
thinking, into another that was altogether different. Since
physical means availed nothing, success depended on effec-
tiveness of argument and its reaching to a great number of
readers and listeners.

As an instance: the happy report from an English Quaker,
wife of an abolitionist member of parliament, to her
American friend Angelina Grimké, that "our ladies' petition
measures $2\frac{1}{4}$ miles."[63] This was a way to make legislators listen, if the job could be done at all.

Legislators in the American Congress had been the target of this form of appeal from the later 1820s, focused on the slave trade in the Capital district itself. There, Northerners, visiting or lodging on business, could not avoid a view of realities they had no knowledge of back in Vermont or New York; and, since the city was felt to belong to everyone, everyone felt entitled to a share in the determining of its ordinances and usages. So they spoke out to their government. In time, by the mid-1830s, John Quincy Adams offered himself as champion of their protests on the very floor of the House, cool and determined and not to be silenced. As he insisted, Southern representatives must not be allowed totally to disregard or still the voice of the citizenry on any question, no matter how infuriating; while outside, pressing in the results of their efforts by the wagon-load, were earnest throngs to reify the challenge: not only from the AASS but its local equivalents, town- and city-societies dedicated to the cause, over a thousand of them nationwide by this date, energizing in New York state some 20,000 members; in Ohio, 15,000; in Massachusetts, 8,000 — from whom flowed, as early as 1828 when their numbers were vastly smaller, 2,352 names on a single list, and a decade later, one with over 130,000.[64]

Other aspects of slavery were by this date also the targets of petitions (as also some public questions not related to it at all). Through all such activity, driven by the consideration of slavery more than anything else, a most remarkable dose of education was administered, in the duties and possibilities of citizenship, and quite remarkable numbers of persons were obliged, being pressed for their signature, to read what was before their eyes, so worded as to encapsulate a controversy of general interest, and then to decide where they stood.

Carrying forms around one's town, perhaps as they were written by the local society or perhaps by the national, and soliciting signatures, was from the start a job in which women took a principal part, and their names were in time as numerous as men's on the petitions they circulated: above two million by 1840. In this way as in others, the British model served to help. An increasing number of antislavery societies were formed, too, entirely of women, speaking their convictions in their own voice. "Suffer us, we pray you," one petition for the District read as women wrote it, "with the sympathies which we are constrained to feel as wives, as mothers, and as daughters, to plead with you" against the sufferings inflicted on slave families.[65] It was a form that invited in its signatories their identification with the objects of its care: in short, it invited feelings.

The same societies circulated newsheets, weekly or monthly or occasional, and in large numbers. Mostly *gratis*, these went out to sister societies in exchange, and to editors, judges, lawyers, legislators, to postmasters for local distribution, and especially to ministers for the dissemination of antislavery ideas among their congregations. They could bring a sharp focus to events of special interest. Tributes to Elijah Lovejoy the martyred publicist, for example, appeared in hundreds of newspapers, as one of them (*The Emancipator*) noted at the time (November 1837). The AASS detailed the events which led to Lovejoy's death in its publication *Human Rights*, and ran off an extra 40,000 copies; similar news-items were picked up for republication in quite non-partisan media, too, which needed something for their columns; and there were other antislavery publications to draw from: Benjamin Lundy's *The Genius of Universal Emancipation* from 1821, *The Philanthropist* which James Birney founded in Kentucky in 1833, *The African Repository* representing proponents of Afro-American colonization, and so forth. In local societies, information and interpretation fed in from the editorial desks of state and national organizations was read aloud and discussed, and members wrote about it to their friends.[66]

The Tappan brothers in New York constituted a particular center of energy in the cause: Arthur, wonderfully rich and devoted and generous, and Lewis, a planner and organizer who also wrote occasional advocacy-pieces, with the *Emancipator* which was their child and the voice of the AASS. Theirs was an important role. A testimonial to the one of them was afforded by an Alabama woman particularly respected in her town, declaring to her minister "that she could 'cut Arthur Tappan's throat from ear to ear.'" The remark was remembered in Weld's all-famous pamphlet, *American Slavery As It Is*.[67]

The object of her interest was himself a passionate man, but hid it better. The quality appears only occasionally in his letters: "It is more painful to me than I have words to express to contemplate any suspension in this [the funding for the AASS] and similar efforts when so much is to be done" (1828), or again (1833), "What! Shall eight or nine millions of 'pale-faced' human beings arrogate to themselves the right to trample under foot their fellow-men, because the color of their skin is different?"[68] For a most devoted, successful, punctilious, buttoned-up businessman to excite himself so, and endure searing headaches for most of his life, over the plight of slaves, made no sense; but within him burnt the well-banked-down fires of indignation, evidently.

More hated in the South even than Arthur Tappan, many times more hated, was Garrison up in Boston and his instrument of persuasion, *The Liberator*. It was in the later 1820s that he exclaimed of his antislavery state of mind, "The detestation of feeling, the fire of moral indignation and the agony of soul which I have felt kindling and swelling within me reach the acme of intensity;" and again in 1832, "I protest against the system [of slavery], as the most flagrant violation of every principle of justice and humanity. I NEVER WILL DESERT THE CAUSE.... I NEVER WILL DESIST FROM THIS BLESSED WORK."[69] And he never did. The reaction to his ceaseless loud ardent excoriation of slaveholders, first, and of all temporizers, second, was reflected in the remark of a New Jersey lady in 1839, mistress of a slave-holding house: "I would help to tar and feather him."[70] He was the target of death threats and bounties offered for his production in a Southern court of law, or preferably before resorts of more summary justice; and he was jailed and mobbed, like others — without the least effect on his activities.

In all the flood of ink poured out on at least the northern states (though the southern refused it entry), Garrison's part was the most highly colored. By far: what he wrote every

week made tremendous reading. The color and scalding quality of it, which earned him such enemies in such numbers,
Howard Zinn has defended, quoting the man himself:
answering the friendly question, "Why are you all on fire?"
— "Brother [Samuel] May," replied Garrison, "I have need to
be all on fire, for I have mountains of ice about me to melt."[71]

In contrast to eloquence and quite as effectual in the story
were plain facts, the incontestable truth. So very much against
slavery could be said, after all, in any kind of impassioned ful-
mination you might please, and just as easily denied. Facts
alone could break through the generally serene acceptance or
(as needed when provoked) the angry defense of an institution to be found, after all, without condemnation in both
Testaments and at the present time prevailing over half the
country — there in the South, perfectly lawful, and subject
only to the occasional abuses that could be found in any custom or relationship. What, then, were all the abolitionists so
excited about?

Pamphlets describing slavery in hostile terms dated at least
from the year of Lexington and Concord, with Thomas
Paine's; but the series really picked up again only in the 1830s
with John Rankin's *Letters* ...(1833), containing "some most
appalling facts... *Facts* will always produce an effect, at least on
pious minds. You can easily possess yourself of *facts, the bare
recital of which will make the heart bleed.* These facts must be pro-
claimed" — and here, the bona-fides of the author were clear
from the title of his work, showing his connection with
Virginia.[72] Two years later came Maria Child's (she didn't care
for her real first name, Lydia), *Authentic Anecdotes of American
Slavery*, followed by her *Evils of Slavery* and *Appeal* ... (both,
1836),[73] in the first of which she made plain her method: "The
FACTS stated in these sheets are capable of satisfactory and
legal proof," to be provided on request at such-and-such an
address. In the other of the two and further writings, she followed through. And before as after these works, Garrison
published in his newspapers (especially *The Liberator*, from
1831) weekly glimpses of horrible things suffered by slaves as
reported to him by good witnesses: facts, again.[74]

But it was Theodore Weld who brought the art of authentication to its height, in 1839, with his *Antislavery As It Is*: a very bible for abolitionists from that date forward, ready to hand in the libraries of all the antislavery societies, admired and read in Britain, quoted all over, and given, in much of its substance, a renewed and enormously vibrant form in *Uncle Tom's Cabin*.[75] Hundreds of thousands of copies of Weld's book were printed in its opening years, a hundred thousand in the first alone.

He had collected unchallengeable evidence for years, prior, as an aid to his own and his friends' lecturing; had encouraged his associates to add to his collection whatever they could; and, with AASS-funding, assembled a team to help him more systematically. So: much work; but still, the amount of it astonished even the workers. A quick count of the newspapers in the office-attic from which the team had clipped items was given up after they had reached the twenty-thousandth.

The work paid off. The major part of the antislavery indictment could be offered in the printed words of the Southern states themselves, showing the casual and common mutilation of slaves, permanent scarring from flogging or other punishment, breaking up of families, pursuit of fugitives either to capture or kill them, light penalties or none for the torture or killing of slaves, harsh penalties for the education of slaves, spiritual or other, and so forth, just such as any Southern newspaper would not hesitate to offer to the interest of its subscribers; in addition to which, Southerners by name were cited (for one, Weld's wife, Angela Grimké, born of a slaveholding family) as the source for reports along the same lines.[76] The value of such witnesses and materials, Weld knew better than anyone. He knew it through the testing of them on thousands of audiences himself, *viva voce*, across the whole of the country that would let him speak in the earlier 1830s, until his voice broke down, and thereafter, through his correspondence with brothers in the field. His letters make plain that he reflected on what they and he observed, and on what strategies they should pursue to win over their listeners.

3. THE ANTISLAVERY CAUSE IN SPOKEN FORM

To turn now to the spoken word, after my survey of advocacy in printed form: Weld offers the most natural introduction to that army of speakers, himself by far the best known, which served the cause of abolition throughout the 1820s and 1830s: men of extraordinary devotion and energy, whose thousands of miles of travels brought them and their message to thousands of towns across the border states and the northeast, from Missouri to Maine.

And, to begin with, their recruitment. Where did they come from? Why did they ever set out on an ill-paid, most demanding, often dangerous path?

Though the army included a few doubters (in their later years, Garrison, Wright ...), it was essentially and markedly church-born and church-driven; and the church was evangelical. As to these two points, there is general agreement.[77] In religion arose the impulse to change opinion, from the revivals of the Second Great Awakening — and had it not been for these, what other source or locus of energy in the nation could have proved adequate to make history as in the end it was made? Revivals inspired feelings of reforming urgency both on one's own behalf and on others'.

First, on one's own behalf, there were the realities of damnation and salvation to be pondered and talked about. For a period of a generation at the start of the nineteenth century, the nation of the Second Awakening dwelt on these as it had not done for a half-century. Whatever the causes of this rise in anxiety, it troubled the mind. In diaries and letters of the time, it is common to find the writer engaged in obsessive self-examination, worried and "weeping", or at other times convinced of salvation assured, which "filled my soul with peace and joy" (the adolescent David Marks in 1816); "very miserable" over her conduct and inadequate piety, often in tears, "wept bitterly," "trembled as he [her minister] portrayed her doom, and wept bitterly," "loaded down with iniquity," and much more of the same from Sarah Grimké, periodically ill from such preoccupations (1813-1818); or again, "Has *no sin* any dominion over you?... Are you digging your way *deeper* and *deeper* into the dust?" (Weld to Finney in 1828, to urge him into more moral introspection, following up these challenges with a sermon!).[78]

In this manner a group of young men, friends from Yale, corresponded after they had moved on, some of them, to one or another theological seminary, and they lamented or rejoiced as the season or their temperament moves them: Leonard Bacon to say, with that self-satisfaction that carried him to eminence as a divine, "I am sure that I have rarely enjoyed more of the presence of God or felt more devotedness to him than I have during the past month. I have been examining anew my affections and motions and principles of action; and though the examination was painful I trust it was beneficial" (1822) — while the friend he addressed gloomily admitted, "I am exceedingly worldly at present, indeed I ever am; yet peculiarly so now. I am persuaded that to slight prayer, to go over it as a task, to recur to it with pain is perhaps the most dangerous sin we can commit.... I have ever neglected the seasons of prayer which I established when I first hoped myself religious," that is, first felt some conviction of being saved, "yet I have most seriously lapsed into a neglect of the essence of it."[79]

A third member of the same group gives us a glimpse beyond individual agony, into a sphere and a religious phenomenon closely observed, their college itself under the presidency of Day: "The revival I think does continue. Instances of conversion appear now and then and there may be many of which we are ignorant. Great solemnity at one time appeared... Many professing Christians," that is, coming forward with declarations of repentance, "seem to be animated and zealous in the good cause. But is there not danger that those who have deeply at heart the interests of pure religion may sometimes injure the cause that they love by neglecting their proper duties, for religious meetings? I think that I can see this in some individuals. Meetings are multiplied without number and many attend almost any meeting they hear of. Is this not religious dissipation?"[80]

The grip of feelings shown in these latter excerpts confines us within a particular circle of the young. For a wider sense of the Awakening we can turn to descriptions of its effects among quite various groups and classes, the accounts to be found singly in church media, or bound together as collections in a volume, or as illustrations to works on revivalism. The subject was of the greatest interest at the time and a rich source for anecdotes; for there were above 1,300 revivals reported in the towns of New York state over the course of the decade from 1825 on, to suggest what other regions also were experiencing.[81] Softened up, so to speak, by the home missionary societies of the time and their production of many scores of millions of tracts addressed to every sect and opinion,[82] communities would be encouraged by the local minister or an itinerant preacher to look within, with the hope and object of discovering a heartfelt sense of sin, of the penalty in store for them, and of a responsive repentance that longed to find public expression.

Individual reactions naturally varied, from the little-troubled to the quite overwhelmed. The little-troubled yielded to personal reflection over time, to accumulated instruction, nameless ministers; in sum, to change without drama. This, according to their temperament, had surely been the style of conversion among the buttoned-up like Arthur Tappan; this, Lucretia Mott, a Hicksite Quaker respectful of the traditions of that sect, knew and preferred.[83] Of something more, there were many experiences recorded. Sarah Grimké's confessions to her diary were quoted above. She could find no peace until she stepped clear of the quieter services that she was used to, and tested those of a neighboring Methodist church, "and under their loud and alarming preaching, together with associating with some truly spiritual minds I became revived from the state in which I was," that is, an introverted depression. Her much younger sister Angelina likewise responded to a dose of unfamiliar preaching, "communications," she says, which "were sent so powerfully to my heart that I was at times exhausted with weeping." It was a revelation, "for I had been accustomed to nothing but moral discourse."[84]

Of this more designedly and radically emotional re-making of life that evangelicalism aimed at, Lyman Beecher had been the first real hero. In his own life, he knew religion as deeply moving; deeply moving was its communication, too. He recalled a moment when his conversion to deeper faith was still recent, and he was recently engaged. "About this time I became troubled as to the defence of religious views between myself and Roxana [Foote, fiancée]. I went over to [her home in Connecticut at] Nutplains on purpose to converse with her, and, if the disagreement was too great, to relinquish the engagement. I explained my views, and laid open before her the great plan of redemption. As I went on, her bosom heaved, her tears flowed, he heart melted, and mine melted too; and I never told her to her dying day what I came for."[85]

From the pulpit, also, tears of a truly feeling penitence, or at least not doctrine in any detail or dissection, were always Beecher's concern. His message was a new teaching but a simple one: salvation was in one's own choice; but one must confront one's own sinfulness, come forward to talk it out, join with one's fellows in this affirmation and the rejoicing of the moment, and then, from that moment on, prove it true by working for the moral improvement of one's society.[86] Conversion-experiences of themselves were nothing without follow-up — without "benevolence". The word recurs and recurs in this period.

To bring his listeners to a change of heart he used what, to one of his listeners, recalled the powers and techniques of the theater; or what Beecher himself called the "thunder and lightning" of proper sermon-delivery.[87] The sense of theater struck other observers, one remarking on the coming forward of congregation members to the "anxious bench" in front, there to be individually urged and harangued: it was a "movement always more or less theatrical.... The pulpit is transformed more or less into a stage." This was fully accepted by Beecher: a preacher must so "throw himself into the spirit and meaning of the writer, as to adopt his sentiments, make them his own, feel them, embody them, throw them out upon the audience as a living reality."[88] He was by the 1820s very widely known and admired for the particular effect of his services.

As his were not the first services of this sort, so they were not unique in his own day and after. Preachers both itinerant and resident counted as evangelicals, in all of the major sects and across all the states of interest to my subject. In Maine, an account of 1817 speaks of a "flood of penitent grief;" and, like a misbehaving child who cries at the forfeit of his parent's love and at the pain of punishment to come, sinners wept in a New Hampshire church. "Many were scarcely able to leave the house where weeping, and sighs and prayers abounded," in a revival town of Delaware; they "groaned and trembled," again in Maine.[89] They were "all classes of citizens" in "complete despair," "sighing and sobbing," "almost every part of the city became more or less the theatre of illustrious displays of divine power and grace. Publick assemblies were crowded...." "Children and servants have been so overwhelmed with distress, that they have been heard in their secret retirements, to cry out for God, amid the dark watches of the night, to save their sinking souls." Such and similar reports from a scattering of preachers across all of the 'teens of the nineteenth century when Beecher was on his rise are matched by others with shrieks, bedlam, hysteria, suicides; instances of settled depression; people jerking about, falling to the floor or into the arms of friends, or leaping and rejoicing at the top of their lungs; "cries, 'Lord have mercy!..., Lord save or I shall perish! I shall die!'"[90]

Of a school of preaching more demanding of its audience than Beecher's and more likely to produce such extreme reactions as the above, Finney was the best known expositor. He was a generation younger and so, active from 1825 on in upstate New York, first.[91] He is described by Henry Stanton:

His sermons were usually an hour long, but on some occasions I have known an audience which packed every part of the house and filled the aisles to listen to him without the movement of a foot for two hours and a half. In his loftiest moods, and in the higher passages of a discourse on a theme of transcendent importance, he was the impersonation of majesty and power. While depicting the glories or the terrors of the world to come, he trod the pulpit like a giant. His action was dramatic. He painted in vivid colors. He gave his imagination full play.... As he would stand with his face toward the gallery, and then involuntarily wheel around, all the audience in that part of the house toward which he threw an arm would dodge as if he were hurling something at them.[92]

Or described by another admirer, Finney in a typical moment is "surrounded by anxious sinners, in such distress as to make every nerve tremble, some overcome with emotion and lying on the floor,... others shrieking out as if they were going to hell." At the height of his fame, when he came to lecture on his art and achievements, he emphasized the absolute necessity of "excitement" and "intensity" of feeling shared in groups.[93]

These somatic manifestations, this play of feelings across communities large and small, one suspects, might have something to do with the fact that in the one year 1825 — when, as it happened, Finney began his swing of sermonizing through New York state — the American Tract Society and the American Sunday School Union were founded as national organizations, and in the next year the American Home Missionary Society and the Society for the Promotion of Temperance and the American Peace Society; as, in 1816, the American Bible Society was founded. This latter was the year, too, when a proposal was published to form a national antislavery society.[94]

No, not all coincidental, these developments of a decade — one suspects. The Great Awakening felt in homes and churches made its mark also institutionally and socially. The deep engagements of what contemporaries called their souls or "hearts" — the latter word so regularly appearing in the words of the various speakers quoted here in recent pages — were registered with all their force in the speakers' emotional memory and there made a part and coloring of their ideas of "sin", of "duty", of "salvation", of everything that constituted a good man or woman; for the teaching was clear, that those experiencing a change of heart must act out the change in benevolence. First, one's self; then, a life "tending to the complete moral renovation of the world. This result is to be accomplished... by their [revivals' converts'] direct influence, in elevating the intellectual, spiritual, and social condition of men."[95]

The emotional dynamic of antislavery across the 1820s and 1830s is, however, my proper interest, not the general reforming nature of the period. Enough to recall it only as background to the zeal shown by many abolitionists, Tappan or Weld or others, for other causes earlier in their careers: for temperance, or home-missionizing, or the relief and counseling of prostitutes and unwed mothers. I must recall, too, what was said about emotion and motivation in earlier pages, these two being one. For the equation, the reminder of Weld may serve, when he was recruiting itinerant antislavery lecturers: "If your hearts ache and bleed, we want you, you will help us; but," he warned them, "if you merely adopt our principles as dry theories, do let us alone."[96]

Theodore Weld's role in the development of an antislavery movement dated really to 1831. An itinerant lecturer, then convert of Finney's, he like others of the same loyalty had earlier enrolled part-time in a New York state theological seminary, from which he broke away from time to time for preaching, and in that year first added abolition to his message. Over the next two years, invitations from back East and generous funding from Arthur Tappan resulted in the transfer from the older seminary of all its students to a site near Cincinnati, Weld along with them, and the resuscitation there of a struggling institution, the Lane Seminary, now to be presided over by the Reverend Lyman Beecher.[97] In his mind though not in Tappan's, the object of the enterprise was of a general evangelical sort, not abolitionist at all. Like many other church leaders from Boston or like Leonard Bacon in

New Haven, the new president saw slaveholding as a dark sin, indeed, but his views on its victims were detached and chilly. He and his like inclined to the notion of shipping at least the free African Americans back where they came from or where their ancestors came from, where they would doubtless be as happy as the day is long. Colonization, it was called. For a time in the mid-1830s it was the dominant message of anti-slavery advocates.

The fifty-odd Lane students were all very committed evangelical types in their twenties and early thirties, and much under Weld's spell. His convictions he increasingly shared with them, and so over the course of many months brought them round to a debate, whether to favor immediate abolition or colonization — this, coming to a head in the spring of 1834. It lasted through eighteen nights of candid, temperate confession, argument, and prayer. Beecher's daughter Harriet attended to represent him, in his own absence East. At the end, all but a tiny handful had come round to "eventual abolition immediately begun," as it was sometimes defined. They formed an abolitionist society. They were signally assisted in their thinking by the contribution of those among them who came from the South, such as James Birney, who could supply "facts." "Facts are the great instrument of conviction in this question," as one of the converts wrote at the time.[98]

When the seminary re-convened in the fall, it was in the president's continued absence and under the trustees' ban of the new Society and of any further mentions of abolition. The students rebelled and walked out. In their defense, to a spokesmen for the cause of suppression, Weld answered in a public letter widely disseminated and worth sampling to illustrate his eloquence. It was a match for Brougham's:

> Why, I ask, should not students examine into the subject of slavery? Is it not the business of theological seminaries to educate the *heart* as well as the head? to mellow the sympathies, and deepen the emotions, as well as to provide the means of knowledge? If not, then give Lucifer a professorship. He is a prodigy of intellect, and

an encyclopedia of learning. Whom does it behoove to keep his heart in contact with the woes and guilt of a perishing world, if not the student who is preparing for the ministry? What fitter employment for such a one, than gathering facts, and analyzing principles, and tracing the practical relations of the prominent sins and evils and all-whelming sorrows of his age.... Sir, you have mistaken alike the cause, the age, and the men [of the insurrection] if you think to intimidate by threats, or to silence by clamor, or shame by sneers, or put down by authority, or discourage by opposition, or appal by danger, those who have put their hands to this work.[99]

And to Lewis Tappan, a little later: "the sin of slavery in this country is omnipresent.... The thieves, the man stealers, the whore mongers, must be thrust out with headlong haste and in holy horror, that God may come in."[100]

Within another two years, royally funded by the Tappans and the AASS, the Lane students had fanned out, lecturing and founding other new abolitionist societies for all of Ohio, for western Pennsylvania, and elsewhere; and their numbers were augmented to a notional team of Seventy (never in fact so many, but two score at their most), seen as a special band under Weld's direction, by the fall of 1836.[101] The idea of such a group was no novelty. At the 1833 National Anti-Slavery Convention in Philadelphia it had been resolved that "We shall organize antislavery societies if possible in every city, town, and village in the land. We shall send forth agents to lift up the voice of remonstrance, of warning, of entreaty, of rebuke."[102] Much had in fact been done. But the Seventy were new in the almost military manner of their organization, with the Scriptural model on top of that and almost too close to their situation to be comfortable (Luke 10.1ff., "I send you forth as lambs among wolves").

With the Seventy my narrative returns to the questions put some pages past, regarding the agents for the propagation of antislavery arguments: "Where did they come from? Why did they ever set out on an ill-paid, most demanding, often dangerous path?" They came from the experience and teachings of evangelicalism, nourished on the force of its feelings, and prepared to carry their chosen message everywhere in the face of whatever opposition. They were Birney, Wendell Phillips, Orange Scott, Miller McKim, the future husband of Harriet Beecher, Calvin Stowe — a host of energetic and dedicated young men in whose final training and inspiration Weld was above all others engaged, before they scattered to their journeys. Over the course of three weeks of nine-hour days he advised them how to meet every argument or cavil, every distraction or falsification, every show of contempt or violence that might be offered. These were the last words of his failing voice. He never again spoke in public; but he remained in charge of them all, at his desk in New York.

In his audience in that November of 1836 had been the Grimké sisters. With additional coaching from Weld, they spoke to antislavery groups around New York where the meeting had been held, and in January of 1837 went on to a Massachusetts tour. They addressed at least 88 meetings in the course of the summer, in scores of towns, to a total audience that cannot have been less than 40,000.[103] Angelina addressed a special committee of the Massachusetts legislature, reducing its chairman to tears.[104] All these events excited a very great deal of attention and controversy. Of course the sisters could be dismissed as "two fanatical women."[105] This was a judgement centered on their ideas. But beyond that, for a woman to stand unguarded before an audience of men, or containing many men, and display her thoughts and, inevitably, her person to them all, was considered unchaste, to say nothing of its being presumptuous. A remark of Leonard Bacon in a speech to a pro-colonization society in Boston, that Sarah Grimké "had not yet, in her Quaker fanaticism, walked naked through the streets," illustrates the gallant reception she or others must expect.[106] There could be no reply to him.

Nor a reply possible to riotous interruption, to shouted threats and insults. Abby Kelley Foster had endured all this, just short of bodily attack, in New York and later in Connecticut lecturing on abolition. She was a Quaker, like the Grimkés. Maria Chapman, president of the Massachusetts Female Anti-Slavery Society, had protected and hidden Garrison when, in a Boston lecture hall in 1835, he was sought by seriously dangerous crowds; and, as one of the women said to their face, "If this is the last bulwark of freedom, we may as well die here as anywhere."[107] The intrepidity and readiness for sacrifice shown by these women were responses only to exaggerated challenges that others were not called on to face, but might have done if they had had to; instead of which, they risked less but still much: being talked about and against, and disliked and ostracized. The question why they came forward for such treatment can be put aside for a moment.

The matter of a woman's right to be heard at all can be put aside, too, however great a part abolitionism played in that area, or arena. Enough was said earlier, in regard to the generating and circulating of advocacy documents including petitions, to justify the general belief today that women made absolutely crucial progress toward equality through their work in Female Anti-Slavery Societies and other agencies of campaigning in the 1820s and on.[108] But what counts for my own discussion is no more than an understanding of the barriers to a hearing that women lecturers had to get over, with heavy cost and struggles.

Men had an even harder time. About this, there is a mountain of evidence. Antislavery papers of course gave it full coverage: 157 instances of mob action reported in only the three years from 1834 to 1837 over all of the North, though worst in Connecticut. Over a longer period and wider area in his career of advocacy Stanton was a target, it was estimated, at least two hundred times; Connecticut and Rhode Island were his special field of action.[109] Garrison in the earlier 1830s was attacked as he spoke in Willimantic in Connecticut, and in Maine, Ohio, New York, Michigan, Rhode Island; most notoriously in Boston, where he was lucky to get out alive.[110] Weld's correspondence of the early 1830s is filled with mentions of the rotten eggs, brickbats, and stones, not to mention abuse thrown at himself or his fellow lecturers on the platform or through hall-windows. He was called "the most mobbed man in the United States."[111]

Mob acts may be taken as an index of the prevailing hostility to the ideas and provocations of antislavery agents, which was great; also, as an indirect index of the extent of the agents' activities. They well understood they would provoke. Printed propaganda provoked the destruction of presses, Lundy's and Lovejoy's among them, again and again; the spoken message succeeded in part because its content was equally of a character to stir feelings and be talked about. This was what brought in its audiences. As Elizur Wright made clear, speaking for the national antislavery convention of 1833, "We want a number of faithful agents ... who will electrify the mass wherever they move." "Electrify" turns up in many accounts of the spoken cause.[112] Just this effect was intended by Amos Phelps when he "brandished about in the sacred desk [the pulpit] the slave driver's whip such as had 'lacerated the back of a woman'."[113]

Lecturers and preachers and, in time, the Seventy, well understood the reaction they invited and its attendant risks. They indicate their understanding in terms of martyrdom. Anticipating Martin Luther King's best known moment of eloquence, Garrison replied to death threats,

As for myself, whatever may be my fate — whether I fall in the spring-time of manhood by the hand of the assassin, or be immured in a Georgia cell, or be permitted to live to a ripe old age — I know that the success of the [abolitionist] cause depends nothing upon my existence. I am but as a drop in the ocean, which, if it be separated, cannot be missed. My own faith is strong — my vision, clear — my consolation, great. "Who art thou, O great mountain? Before Zerubbabel thou shalt become plain: and he shall bring forth the headstone thereof with shoutings, crying, 'Grace, grace unto it.'"[114]

Zerubabbel! With warlike music of this order, in a limitless supply thanks to the language of King James' day (Zech. 4.7), Garrison hardly had need of his own. He was a great quoter of the Bible.

4. VIVIDNESS

The Seventy like the antislavery agents before them or under different auspices all behaved irrationally, one might say. Indeed it was said and believed, hence the term flung at them, "fanatics". But of course they are not to be dismissed so easily from the historical record. They were acting rather under a compulsion of a different sort which they themselves occasionally compared to Martin Luther's: "I can do nothing else, Ich kann nicht anders."

What brought them to their individual decisions is a matter as important as the effects that flowed from it.

To begin with, they found themselves surrounded by hostility in the South, from which those who were Southerners themselves withdrew, or fled: the Grimkés, Birney, Stanton, and many others. As to the Northerners, while their advocacy indeed provoked intense reactions at times, the chief enemy they perceived was "so much apathy."[115] Such was Ralph Gurley's view of the times, to which he added what more impatient observers of slavery also had to say, "that it is idle to talk of abolition without making the South feel strongly on the subject." Birney agreed: "we of the South have so long been accustomed to degrade and rob and despise the Slaves, that nothing short of the most intense sympathy for them, on your parts, can rouse it for them, in any degree with us. We will despise them, as long as there remains in your breasts any sympathy for their sufferings that is unexcited."[116] Passion thus was recognized as key.

There was passion of a sort on the other side, of course, explaining (with some help from local editorials, and some application to the nearest tavern) angry crowds of anti-abolitionists. The arguments they might have offered are of no concern, here, with perhaps the exception of plain bigotry — the conviction that African Americans were a race, and one inherently inferior, to be "despised" in Birney's word, nor ever to be raised up or trusted. In the city of the Tappans and the AASS, even among the enlightened, this conviction could be found; in the city of Garrison it could be found, expounded by Leonard Bacon on behalf of the colonizationists;[117] and it was acknowledged so as to be challenged head-on by Rankin (1833) or Harriet Beecher Stowe in their publications.[118]

The distance perceived between the races relieved slaveholders from some of the restraints of humanity. Humanity belonged within one's own kind. Whoever did not share that kindness had no claim on it, according to a rule of behavior that has not changed in human history; and sensibilities where they might perhaps be felt could be denied. Exactly like Roman slaveholders of old, so Southerners gave over their misbehaving slaves to a place apart and to agents removed from their sight, to be flogged, tortured, or killed.[119] That was at least the practice of the more fastidious. So they could shield their sympathies from provocation. Bolder cruelty behaved differently, as Weld's chief publication and others' made clear through cases. But it was also discovered by Northerners becoming slaveholders (or married to such) that they could themselves become easily habituated to what was once disgusting, just as the more tenderhearted or thoughtful or philosophic Romans could enjoy gladiatorial exhibitions, if they gave themselves to watching.[120] That too is human across the centuries.

In contrast, for many, a sense of shock in confronting slavery for the first time. Innocents, their sympathies lacked any shield. Their reactions constitute a part of the dossier of converts to the cause whom I want to explain. One, a Northerner who visited Mt. Vernon, spoke subsequently to an antislavery society, where the subject of chattel slavery and the idea of property in another human being had arisen. He recalled his visit to Washington's tomb. There he had noticed and spoken to an African American.

He was a *man*, Mr. President, not a *thing*, a man with a black face. His head was whiter than any one's in this audience. I was not then an abolitionist, not even a colonizationist. I asked the man if he were a slave. He said he was — was Washington's slave. But, I said, I thought Washington liberated all his slaves. He retorted, "I guess

if he had, I should have known it. No, he only liberated his household slaves. His field slaves descended with
the farm; I was a field slave." I inquired, have you any
children? "I have had ten." Ten — where are they? "I
don't know. They were taken to a southern market and
sold...." While I gazed on that poor old man, my vow
went up to heaven that I would be an abolitionist.[121]

Or the scene of enlightenment might be in Wheeling,
West Virginia, with the first sight of a train of slaves passing
through that common routing-point in winter on the way to
buyers further south: "droves of a dozen or twenty ragged
men, chained together and driven through the streets, *bare-
headed* and *bare-footed, in mud and snow*, by the remorseless
'SOUL SELLERS,' with horse whips and bludgeons in their
hands."[122] The witness, he too, "made a solemn vow."

And a third instance from 1839, returning the story to the
Capital. The city was mentioned above as a place of exhibition of slavery. Here James Giddings turned up, recently
elected to the Congress, he too seeing for the first time a
"coffle of about sixty slaves" driven by a man on horseback
"with a huge bullwhip." He saw much more, many holding-
prisons for slaves included. He stepped aside into an auction;
he tried to shame the auctioneer, in vain; particularly he
noticed a free black man there who had been kidnapped and
who watched, and "as the bidders one after another raised the
price of their fellowmen, his eyes followed them and the deep
horror and agony of his soul was portrayed in the contortions
of his countenance."[123] Giddings heard shrieks of pain, too, of
beaten slaves, such as Northerners were not used to hearing.
Vivid facts.

Occasional Northerners remembered their months or
years spent on visits deeper into the South, or in other settings where they had become closely acquainted with African
Americans and their situation. Through acquaintance they
might be made friends and defenders. Or instead, they might
be confirmed in their distance from an alien race. Weld drew
closer to the free black community in Cincinnati; Bacon, further apart, as his pastoral work drew him into contact with

those around Boston. Temperament or powers of imagination and empathy made the difference between the two men.[124]

And it may be said here that such individual differences in the origins of abolitionist sympathies should naturally be taken into account, while broad generalizing explanations of a psychological sort should be looked at critically.[125]

With Weld, a childhood scene counted for something: "When seven years old [in Hampton, Connecticut] I begged the privilege of sitting on the 'nigger seat' at school with a little colored boy, who was hissed and trodden by scholars and teachers."[126] Why did he do this? From a sense of fair play? A seven-year-old can know what this is without having to understand much higher-sounding principles, and he can act it out, too, if he is willing to take a chance and go against others, as Weld proved himself willing to feel and do, life-long. But first, he asked permission! The disciplining of his rebellious impulses fits with his declaration much later, "I am *constitutionally*, as far as emotions are concerned, a quivering mass of intensities kept in subjection only by the *rod of iron* in the strong hand of conscience and reason."[127]

Henry Stanton, if memory served a very old man, was turned to his career by his Connecticut childhood experience, listening to "a negro slave whose voice was attuned to the sweetest cadence. Many a time did she lull me to slumber by singing this touching lament [for a Narragansett leader, betrayed by a Mohican to the whites]. It sank deep into my breast, and moulded my advancing years. Before I reached manhood I resolved that I would become the champion of the oppressed colored races of my country. I have kept my vow."[128] His recollection is of a piece with the line or trajectory of the man, life-long; which is not to say that the experience did more than contribute to a course toward which Stanton's whole temperament inclined him.

There were converts to antislavery made through facts they had read or heard about. Such a one was David Marks, first through reading, then listening to the celebrated English antislavery agitator, George Thompson, whose appeals "overpowered his feelings to a degree that almost produced suffocation, and it was often with difficulty that he could get power to breathe."[129] Another who read was Angelina Grimké; others, Orange Scott and Miller McKim.[130] There were converts enlightened or talked around by a friend or spouse;[131] and some in retrospect assigned the moment of conviction to the hearing of some particular lecture, and being then "so much affected as to be moved to tears by it," like Samuel Fessenden, thereafter long a useful adherent to the cause; or Samuel May, like Fessenden listening to Garrison at his best, and declaring, "Never before was I so affected by the speech of man.... That night my soul was baptized in his spirit, and ever since I have been a disciple and fellow-laborer."[132]

An openness to feelings obviously characterizes these many individuals. They confess as much; they appeal to the same capacity in others, who must be and are addressed through their emotions. Identification with the plight and feelings of slaves is taught or stimulated.[133] "What, my brother, would be more distressing to you, than to have the yoke of slavery put upon your neck or that of your little daughter?" "Every man knows that slavery is a curse. Whoever denies this, his lips libel his heart. Try him; clank the chains in his ears, and tell him they are for *him*. Give him an hour to prepare his wife and children for a life of slavery. Bid him make haste and get ready their necks for yoke, and their wrists for the coffle chains...." He must be made to feel he and his *are* the due objects of a rescuing pity. And let Garrison sum it up: "This, sirs, is a cause that would be dishonored and betrayed if I contented myself with appealing only to the understanding. It is too cold, and its processes are too slow for the occasion."

Exactly this was the purpose of facts, facts, and more facts on which antislavery advocates laid so much stress. These were to be as much as possible detailed and contextualized, so as to bring believable images to the mind — in a word borrowed from my first chapter, *enargeia*. They included bits of dialogue, so as to be still more lifelike, often with woodcuts added to assist the mind's eye.[134] And such devices shade off into fiction, with the publication of various antislavery novelettes, a melo-drama, vignettes, sketches, didactic dialogues for children.[135] All these possibilities were seen but not fully realized until, in the first year of its publication, *Uncle Tom's Cabin* sold 300,000 copies. That well known story, however, is a dozen years down the road from the one of my telling.

Last among the causes of a change of heart, the excitement that might be aroused by combat itself. It drew in bystanders. As an illustration, consider what happened in November of 1837, when news of the shooting of the newspaper editor Lovejoy in Alton, Illinois, reached Western Reserve College in Ohio, and the president galloped about the community on his horse to spread the word and call a meeting in a convenient church; at which, in a famous moment two days later, an eye-witness to the violent drama in Alton gave his account, broken by tears, and John Brown in the audience rose at the end to say the one sentence, "Here, before God, in the presence of these witnesses, I consecrate my life to the destruction of slavery."[136]

Not only is the church setting suited to a summary point in my chapter, and the emotions among the partici-pants, but there is here, also, the energizing role of indigna-tion on display.

Here were persons quite representative of what was at the time a very broad regional response to the headlines from Alton. They had never met Lovejoy but reacted to his death as exemplary. They grieved deeply. Whoever he was, he was a brave man doing a good thing. Tears, then, were natural enough. But Brown's reaction points to something further. What evidently struck home to him, as to the college presi-dent and the other people swept into the occasion, was the contrast between the goodness of the martyr and his reward. Lovejoy had, in simple terms, obeyed the rules of right and wrong, and still lost. His death was not deserved — not condign. Indignant must be the reaction, then, of those who held to right and wrong in their hearts, wherever the event was reported.[137] The world must be set right!

The same cause and effect attended the many scores of mob attacks that have been reviewed. They won the victims

friends; for, in the moral terms people held to, what provoked
the attacks hadn't justified them. Contrast between a just
expectation and its harsh denial roused anger, an indignation
that must express itself at least in partisanship, perhaps in
active combat.[138] That was how Brown felt; and it was the
reaction likewise of a perfect nonentity, Seth Hunt, teenage
clerk for Arthur Tappan, in a much milder way for a much
smaller reason. At the time of the New York riots which
threatened Tappan's whole business, Hunt's landlord told him
to leave the building. "I asked the reason, or if I had done
anything amiss. He said, 'No; but the other boarders declared
they would not have a clerk of that d-----d abolitionist,
Arthur Tappan.'.... I paid my bill and went to board at 21
Broadway.... I took a kind of boy's oath against slavery, and
whatever I have done since or left undone, that oath has been
fulfilled. I came, when a lad, from Vermont, thinking little, and
at the time caring less, on the subject; and yet here I was
turned out of a hotel for being a clerk to an abolitionist! In
less than a week from that time, 'Jim,' the colored waiter, and
I helped one slave to run off to Canada."[139]

★★

Young Hunt and old rich Tappan bring out some of the
range of differences among people sympathetic to emancipation. Types like Hunt could be a little further illuminated, and
in a way perhaps they should be, constituting as they did the
body of the movement. There are their letters to be used; there
is contemporary fiction too little used to read the mind of
times past.[140] But it is among the better known like the
Tappans that the more self-revealing records are to be found.
Through these persons the forces of change must be discovered — these, who have been quoted in their own words. At
too great length, readers may object. Yet it will not be too
much, if readers find in what is quoted the material for the
evocation in themselves of the feelings that governed the past.
    The cast of actors in a primary role, that is, initiating a
course of events, was never large. Anecdotes and details of

their lives therefore take on some broad explanatory force. They were hundreds, after all, not thousands, who were moved to send off letters and address church groups and travel about in any weather an incalculable number of miles — reckoning all the itinerant lecturers together as a group. Some also or principally wrote for the cause. Their selfless sincerity had no particular claim on a friendly reception; more often, the reverse. No matter, they were in the grip of impelling emotions, emotions of a "primary" role that was distinguished in the ancient historians (above, Chap. 1); theirs, a choice made against the grain, to which they invited others to come forward, equally against the grain. In whatever communities they touched, they left behind local action-societies to raise consciousness and money and to multiply their effect. Force of feeling attested among the scores of the better known agents — a force adequate to stir them out of their ordinary lives and thoughts — can be assumed of the less known as well. The assumption seems necessary. A relative abundance of surviving evidence for a significant group thus makes the problem of historical understanding manageable — manageable for anyone at least who is open to the vividness of the record: its *enargeia*.

It remains to be said, however, that the force of feeling was not only greater or less in different people, but aroused by different aspects of the thing called slavery. For some, it arose out of the image before them of sin; for others, out of the image of liberty; for still others, out of kinship through identification with suffering. It had no one common origin; it rather brought energy to a common focus, which is no doubt how significant changes and events ordinarily do take their rise.

They generate in turn, in their society at large, a response of the same sort but less strong, or of the same sort but participant in other impulses as well, pre-existing or arising out of the situation created by change itself. Thucydides especially in his Corcyrean pages explored this level of feelings which I called, for convenience, "secondary". It is not likely to register so clearly in the sources — in memoirs or the like — as the "primary". Certainly in the records of the antislavery movement the most active agent-figures are the most easily read and understood, while the mixed emotions they aroused in others, the less well defined sympathies, the semi-conversions or mere slackening of resistance, may go unreported and can only be inferred indirectly from actions or probabilities. Herein, modern historians seem to find what interests them most. It is material that is less highly colored. In Ronald Syme's term of preference, it is "cool".

By the close of the 1830s, the energy that made the antislavery movement, without diminishing, underwent a great shift of focus from Awakening to still more vigorous petitioning; from lecturing to politicking; from church to Congress; from Boston and New York to Washington. Here in this year or so of change is a natural point at which to break off my account.

The account was in any case meant only to serve my argument. I repeat from my Preface: the early story of abolitionism does no more than illustrate how emotions can be found in the modern record underlying events, and how later readers of that record (if I have done it justice) cannot escape the replication of those emotions within themselves. Replication *is* understanding.

CHAPTER 4:
CONCLUSION

"NAÏVE idealism" might be the verdict on my version of abolitionism in the 1820s and 1830s (or, for that matter, of Augustus in the 40s BC in my first chapter) — idealism to be avoided if at all possible, equally with "reductive materialism."

The two descriptive phrases are borrowed from Thomas Bender in his collection of interpretive essays on antislavery by David Davis and others. These offer perhaps as good a point of entrance as any to a great body of books and articles on the subject from the mid-eighteenth century to the 1830s, largely in Europe but also as it is seen in the United States.[1]

What moved the abolitionist? This is their central question. Only in passing, Davis indeed mentions "the cultivation of empathy" in the period. It was touched on in the first section of the preceding chapter ("sensibility"). It exerted some effect; and he can see "moral consciousness" at work, and he concedes that antislavery was "largely religious and philosophical in origin;" but he goes on to say, "I have repeatedly insisted that I have little interest in individual motivation."[2] Rather, it is collective intentions that count for his purposes, especially the underlying "unconscious" ones. Explanation proceeds best in terms of these, and of abstract ideas (philosophy, ideology, abstractions like discipline of the labor force, various '-isms'). Accordingly in Davis' analysis, hardly a word of self-revelations by individuals finds a place in any sort of broader treatment. Rather, "The paramount question, which subsumes the others, is how antislavery reinforced or legitimized such hegemony" as "the dominant social class" enjoyed. And one of Davis' critics in the collection agrees: "To explain humanitarianism, then, what matters in the capitalist substructure is not a new class so much as the market, and what links the capitalist market to a new sensibility is not class interest so much as the power of market discipline to inculcate altered perceptions of causation in human affairs."[3]

Of feelings, close to nothing in the ongoing debate; of *force* of feelings, less still. Of any invitation to readers to think like anyone else outside of themselves, likewise, nothing. Instead, ideas, philosophy, ideology, abstractions, various '-isms held to by actors in the past. But it is one argument of my second chapter that all these are in fact invested with emotions, or may more truly be said to *be* emotions, deriving motivational force from their emotional nature; and a second argument, that distance in space, time, or culture need not preclude our understanding of such irrational forces in the past, however difficult the attempt. All of which obviously runs quite counter to the style of serious historical interpretation of antislavery prevailing nowadays.

What the better alternative might be, and how ready to hand it actually is, I may suggest through a recollection. My novelist friend Maxwell in his later years had leisure to return to his favorite books again and again; but he found himself unable to re-read *War and Peace*. He said it hurt too much. What hurt most was what happened to Petya Rostov, who adored the Tsar, longed to go to war, joined up; and the war killed him, just a boy.

A reminder, here, of the effect on the reader which historical narrative may achieve if its author chooses. As Flaubert in writing of Madame Bovary found the tears rolling down his face while he summoned up "both the emotion in the idea, and phrases to express it," or as Dickens wept while he wrote of Tiny Tim, so too did Tolstoy of Petya and other

scenes; so too, to move an audience, should ancient court-
room orators address a jury.[4]

And to move an audience may also serve to inform it.
Through Petya's death as Tolstoy sets it before us we understand how the casualties of war must touch the survivors and
so affect the will to fight. We are reminded of other important matters: how eager to serve in war young men may be,
and how much the Tsar was cherished by his people. Petya
makes the fact clear — a fact and an illustration of that submissive gratitude amounting to a sort of love for the ruler
that is of our species.[5]

Anyone who wants can of course find just such facts in
proper history books, along with various other aspects of the
war-scene: recruitment demographics, civilian morale, trans-
port-capacity, food supply, munitions, unity of command, and
so forth. All can be taken in through cognition in the most
common cool simple sense of that word.

But the form of communication controls the form of the
resulting knowledge. By the merely factual, which yields this
simple cognition, we are interested; by the other, we are
brought to feel that we could have acted in the same way as
Petya or lads like him in the past. We understand within ourselves the *force* of what was in their minds and so governed
their acts; for motivation is emotion — the equivalence was
proposed in my first chapter.

It is in this way that history in its grand movements, such
as we find through examples brought to life in *War and Peace*,
can be most fully understood. But micro-history, too, is not
beyond Tolstoy or his like (if not his match). Who that reads
can then forget the account of the governor of Moscow in
the final hours of its freedom, just before the French entered,
and how in that moment the frenzied Rostopchin gave
orders to his guardsmen, "Saber him!" to dispatch the
wretched Vereschagin? And how the crowd joined in the
madness of the man's death, and then repented, and were a
different animal? The "otherness" of their conduct is just such
as anthropologists encounter. Novelists can make it vivid,
almost penetrable.[6]

Theirs is the art to explain an emotion of any sort, first by inducing it in themselves, then by choosing the words and images that best express it. Denotation cannot do the job; for in the cause of a kiss, of a fist shaken, of a tear, there can be at first no more than interest. Fellow-feeling hardly comes on first sight. It requires a lingering look, the slower turning of the page, the recollection of matching experiences before the right connections can be made; and art can help to induce and direct this process — as a result of which, there may be an increase in knowledge through that emotionally involved process that was recognized in my second chapter.

There, it was made plain in the findings of science that the distinction between mind and heart, in layman's terms, or between intellect and emotion, or even reason and impulse, cannot in truth be supported. The materials of mind, intellect, reason are wrapped in or half-composed of feelings; and necessarily so, for the survival of the species.

Of this, the first historians took account: Thucydides and others among his direct successors, and many historians in much more recent centuries, too. They could well sense the truth through their experience of human affairs around them, though perhaps they could not quite explain it. They could convey it through art: through well conceived verisimilitude, *enargeia*, as my first chapter tried to demonstrate. Where, in contrast, modern periods afford an adequate view into the affect, the hearts, of the actors in the past, it may be enough to present the evidence almost by itself, in the form of people's own words, to convey a novelistic degree of lively insights. Witness, in my third chapter, a crucial period in the American antislavery movement, as just one illustration.

There, too, but also through Thucydides, the distinction may be discovered between those emotions of a force to open up some quite new path of action, and those others only in response among a more or less passive community, or perhaps as a more or less unintended consequence, at work "unconsciously". To the latter, Cliometrics are applied and similar imitations of science within the historian's art, where rational calculation about ways and means and details may take over, and all decisive feelings may be somehow lost.

Over-all, what I suggest is a certain way of reading the record — nothing new, but only long out of fashion: a way of searching out the emotions that determined behavior; and entering into them, ourselves; and representing them in all their colors, so as *more accurately* to reveal the past, or re-feel it, and so to understand it.

NOTES
CHAPTER 1

1. Burckhardt (1979) p. 52.
2. "Political scientist" Orwin (1994) pp. 3f.; Oost (1975) p. 186, "modern scholars speak repeatedly of Thucydides' 'rationalism' or 'intellectualism';" or of his "désir de se retirer de son histoire, d'en être seulement l'ordonnateur, de laisser parler les faits avec une rigueur toute scientifique," Romilly (1956) pp. 86f., cf. e.g. p. 242, "rationalisme constructif de Thucydide;" Salmon (1990) p. 25, Thucydides "s'efface devant les documents et atteint à une explication totalement rationelle;" and Syme (1962) p. 55. Rood (1998) p. 3 in detecting some recent cracks in the façade of Thucydides' rationality can instance only Connor (1977, cited below) and a study by Brunt that brings out the excitement in the text, its dramaticness — which is not what I am talking about.
3. Strasburger (1977) p. 9, "An Präzision und Kraft der Darstellung, an Tiefsinn und Hintersinn des Geschichtsverständnisses hat das Werk des Thukydides in der Tat wohl nicht seinesgleichen;" and Romilly (1956) p. 32, "il tend aussi à l'interprétation la plus en profondeur" — but it needs "les lecteurs plus attentifs," p. 89.
4. Thuc. 5.111.2, οὐ πανταπάπασιν οὕτως ἀλόγως θρασυνόμεθα. But to the Athenians it is indeed ἀλογία.
5. Thuc. 2.89.6, "we are feared more for what is beyond reason, οὐκ εἰκότι, than by what we undertake in good reason, κατὰ λόγον.
6. Woodman (1988) pp. 25, 27 (Aeschylus, Euripides...), with previous scholars' assent; Edmunds (1975) p. 6, seeing that Thucydides is "both detached and compassionate, his work both rational and tragic;" Rood (1998) p. 3, citing the Plutarch-passage, without drawing out its significance; Connor (1985) pp. 10f. also on the Plutarch text, recognizing a shift among critics toward accepting Thucydides' own "involvement" and, still more, through his mastery of the techniques of *enargeia*, his readers' involvement; Strasburger (1977) p. 27, that Dionysius sees the historian only in a rhetorician's terms.
7. Connor (1977) p. 289 cites earlier writers like Hans-Peter Stahl (e.g., in 1973) who saw this side of the author; also Weil (1967) p. 201, that Stahl sees Thucydides as "un adepte de l'irrationel; il substitue la passion au calcul, la souffrance tragique à l'analyse politique, et une philosophie sceptique ou angoissée à la confiance dans l'intelligence humaine," to which Weil com-

ments, "La thèse est sûrement excessive," and requires correction: Thucydides "no doubt has a sense of the tragic" but "masters his feelings." A collection of passages, some, also noted by Weil, is offered by Cobet (1986) p. 12, to show a sensibility to the tragic in wartime calamities which "give occasion for some sympathy with the victims;" but more often, he finds bare statements of the facts; with persistence in the contrary view by Connor (1984) pp. 32, 232 (quoted) and (1985) pp. 3, 10f., 13ff.

8. Here as elsewhere, unless otherwise indicated, the translation is my own. For a difficulty in the text, see Connor (1984) p. 205 n. 53.

9. Orwin (1994) pp. 8, 294, the abandonment of the view that Thucydides was an ethical positivist; Rood (1998) p. 185 on the sincerity of Thucydides' portrait.

10. Robinson (1985) p. 21; and Connor (1985) pp. 1ff. squarely addresses the need to understand what goes on in our minds as we read Thucydides, asking that we believe in order to penetrate the ancient scene. No belief, no penetration.

11. Connor (1984) p. 98 n. 44.

12. Thuc. 3.53.1; 3.58.3, cf. 4.97.2; Krentz (2002) pp. 26, 33, and passim.

13. Thuc. 3.82 passim, and especially 3.82.8, with πλεονεξία, φιλοτιμία, and φιλονικεῖν (here omitting the αἴτιον of most texts).

14. Hope, e.g. 5.103, cf. 4.108.4; shame, αἰσχύνη (5.104), with Elster (1999) p. 148 quoting Dover on 8.27.2f.; and shame's other self, desire for good repute (3.57.1); friendship, φιλία, of the citizens of one state for another (or sometimes for a leader), e.g. 3.12.1, 7.57.10, or εὔνοια, 6.88.1; gratitude, of the Corcyreans, above; and pity, often evoked, e.g. 3.98.4, 3.113.5f., 7.75.3f.

15. Provocation often seen as ὕβρις, examples just cited in the text, or 3.45.4; the common ὀργή used for "indignation," e.g. ibid., 3.36.2, 4.122.5, 4.123.2, perhaps 5.28.3 or 5.62.2, where just expectations are not met; as also at, e.g., 3.39.2, 5.42.2, without the specific term; reflections on "the Greek conception of [all!] war as arising from insult," in Lendon (2004), these quoted words from near his note 22; but ὀργαί to mean all rough passions however aroused, e.g. 2.65.1, 3.85.1, cf. Edmunds (1975) pp. 9f.; and "aggrieved" as an alternative, ἐχαλέπαινον, 8.86.4. Sometimes ἀγανακτεῖν, "to be irritated," is used to mean almost "to be indignant," "resent" or "be angry," in e.g. Dem. XXI 123 or Plat., Rep. 563d; sometimes also νεμεσᾶν/νέμεσις, with, however, a range of other meanings and rare in historians (no occurrences in Thuc., only twice in Polyb., only to mean divine wrath).

16. Hatreds, ἔχθραι, e.g. 4.24.2, 4.57.4, 7.57.9; μῖσος, 5.27.2; revenge, e.g. by Corinth, 1.55.2.

17. Despair, e.g. 8.1.2 and Stahl (1973) pp. 72ff., 76; Romilly (1956) pp. 36f. and Connor (1985) p. 13, on Athenian morale at a certain point, a crucial factor; or eagerness, προθυμία, detected in the actors, or enthusiasm, ἐπιθυμία, often.

18. Fornara (1983) p. 32.

19. Strasburger (1977) pp. 12ff.

20. Strasburger (1977) p. 12, among 32 Greek historical works of known size,

Poseidonius' second only to Agatharchides' with 59 Books (Polybius and Diodorus with 40 each); for the principal series, Gabba (1984) p. 51, or Malitz (1983) p. 411. Caprice not what we would value in a history often resulted in survival through selections, markedly, of Poseidonius through Athenaeus (with an interest in dining scenes) or of Polybius through the Constantinian collection with its interest, *De legationibus*, cf. L. Thompson (1985) p. 120.

21. Pédech (1964) p. 437 on Timaeus.

22. Noted by Fornara (1983) p. 35.

23. Walbank (1938) pp. 61f.; Pédech (1964) p. 224, on the θυμικόν and ἄλογον in Philip; governed by ὁρμαί, Polyb. 7.11.2f.

24. Polyb. 3.8.1, correcting Fabius' attribution of the war to Hasdrubal's πλεονεξία and φιλαρχία, added to indignation at unjust dealings, ἀδίκημα, where rather it was Hamilcar's θυμός (3.10.5) combined with the Carthaginians' ὁργή and "urge for vengeance, ἀμύνασθαι σπεύδοντες, for the defeat over Sicily" (2.36.6), beyond their being more recently resentful, βαρυνόμενοι, at the loss of Sardinia. Hannibal, sworn to enmity against Rome by his father (3.11f.), in the early irritant — the Saguntum affair — acts out nothing but "unreasoning fury," καθόλου δ'ἦν πλήρης ἀλογίας καὶ θυμοῦ βιαίου (3.15.9); cf. later, a particularly cruel slaughter of captured Romans, "due to his [Hannibal's] pre-existing inbred hatred of the Romans" (3.86.11).

25. On Queen Teuta's rage, Polyb. 2.8.12; on Demetrius of Pharos, 3.19.9; cf. the policy-choice of Scerdilaidas dictated by indignation, ὁργή, at unfairly shared booty (4.29.7).

26. Polyb. 4.3.5, 9f.; 4.4.2, 4, and 8f.

27. Μεγαλοψυχία (I recall an old-fashioned translation of the term from Werner Jaeger), at 29.24.13ff., for example, being joined there to φιλανθρωπία and εὐεργεσία; or another illustration of good will, 16.26.7; and discussion of the word by Veyne (1976) p. 339.

28. Polyb. 1.13.12; 1.64.5, μεγαλοψυχία; but Carthaginians' ἔμφυτον Φοίνιξι πλεονεξία καὶ φιλαρχία, 9.4.2; Aetolians' ὁργή, etc., 3.3.3, 3.7.1f. (labeled the cause of war with Antiochus), and 4.6.11f.; Spartans, 4.27.7, 5.106.4; Cretans, 4.53.5.

29. For army mood, often aroused by a general's eloquence before an engagement, see e.g. 1.27.1, 1.45.2f., 1.49.10f., or 3.44.10ff. The Achaean Terror is described at 38.16.5-7, with people throwing themselves down wells, fleeing blindly, and so forth. The Carthaginian senate is angry at harsh peace conditions and determined to answer only in a manly and noble way (1.31.7f.); the Achaean assembly is guided by considerations of high honor (2.47.1, 2.50.11) or at another time by anger (38.12f.), as the Acarnanians, by "their fervor to be avenged and do a hurt to the Aetolians" (5.6.1); later, guided "partly by a general despondency, their hopes benumbed, partly by their fury" (9.40.4); and the Roman senate shapes its decisions according to its mood of the moment (1.20.1, "joy and elation" lead to larger war aims; indignation and passion, ditto, 2.8.13; 2.19.9f.; 30.31.17, ὁργή).

30. Polyb. 10.17.1, in the context of praising the Roman military system of distributing booty; cf. 2.19.3, the savage Gauls "through their greed over what

they had taken mostly destroyed both their booty and their force." Harmand (1967) says nothing about Roman soldiers' motivation, though (pp. 468ff.) he covers money awards; and Harris (1971) is likewise silent, though (p. 1385) he says much about greedy commanders, while quoting three passages from Polybius to show the (rare) noble indifference of some of them. The Plautus-passage he also quotes may be, as he suggests, real Roman or borrowed Greek comedy; it shows a recruit eager for booty.

31. Polyb. 2.47.1, the Achaeans pursue τὸ κάλλιστον; Eckstein (1995) pp. 65, 241.

32. Polyb. 6.55.4, ὁρμή καὶ φιλοτομία πρὸς τὰ καλὰ τῶν ἔργων.

33. Polyb. 21.23.9, τὸ καλὸν καὶ πρὸς ἔπαινον καὶ τιμὴν... ἀξιοδόξη.

34. Polyb. 1.7.8f., 12: πίστις is at stake.

35. Pédech (1964) p. 429, comparing the conversation with other documents (n. 113) to conclude that "les traits de la mentalité romaine ... sont ... frappants" (!); Hölkeskamp (1987) pp. 206f.

36. Polyb. 31.23f., 31.24.5ff., obligation to the Cornelian οἰκία and πρόγονοι; 31.28.9 and 33.12.3f., φιλοδοξεῖν; concern for δόξα, 31.24.10 and elsewhere; and the triple objective of σωφροσύνη, ἀνδρεία, and μεγαλοψυχία, 31.25.9, 31.27.8ff., 31.29.10f. Note that some of Scipio's generous acts, so admirable in his teacher's eyes, were "quite amazing" — read, "absurd", to many of his audience — while his training in sport had to be begun in the Macedonian royal preserves with royal beaters, 31.29.3ff.

37. Notes 21, 23, and the character of Demetrius of Pharos or of the demagogue Critolaus in Achaea, 38.12f.

38. Among many passages in support, a good one is the discussion of generalship at 9.12-20, echoed in connection with Scipio, 10.2.5f.; cf. Pédech (1964) pp. 214-16, 224f.; answered at length by Eckstein (1995) pp. 29 and passim; and Fornara (1983) p. 67 notices Polybius' openness to "human interest."

39. Above, n. 37; Eckstein (1995) passim; emphasizing "the basic drives of human character" (p. 238); and quoted, p. 241, with emphasis on φύσει τῶν ἀνθρώπων.

40. Eckstein (1995) p. 52.

41. For the pillorying of Phylarchus, see 2.56.6ff., where Polybius would instead confine his account to "legitimate pity or suitable anger" (2.56.13); comment in, e.g., Walsh (1961) pp. 22, 25f. or Wiseman (1994) p. 19; a similar attack and argument against Timaeus, 12.23-28. For Polybius' ample use of the extraordinary to excite, astonish, or appall, see e.g. the story of a plot (8.15-21), ending in what is totally unexpected, παράδοξος (the same term and quality often, e.g. 1.2.1, 1.24.1, 2.37.7, 12.26b.5, 26c.1).

42. Polyb. 23.16.11, on τὰ πρέποντα; Pédech (1964) p. 258, on frequent use of term ἐνάργεια, and of invention, for "un air de vérité;" and consensus, on authenticity.

43. Walsh (1961) p. 22.

44. Gabba (1981) p. 52, Polybius in Poseidonius; Walsh (1961) p. 29 and Fornara (1983) p. 69, Sempronius Asellio reflects Polybian influence in insisting on analysis of causation, which (pp. 32, 139) Cicero shows also in several

passages; Diodorus in various passages draws on Polybius, Walsh p. 210 and Pédech (1964) p. 429; Dionysius of Halicarnassus read and reacted to Polybius, cf. Sacks (1983) p. 73; and Sallust, too, cf. Fornara p. 86 — to say nothing of Livy's debt. On Dionysius' choice of a terminus ad quem, Fromentin (1998) 1 p. xxv.

45. Walbank (1938); Gabba (1981) pp. 52ff.

46. Malitz (1983) pp. 3off., work on the *Histories* extended into his late life; unmentioned by Dionysius, Diodorus, and others, pp. 37, 43; travels, 138-41, 169ff.; style and thought, 410ff.; life-sketch, Kidd (1999) pp. 4f.

47. "Beyond doubt...Caesar read and used Poseidonius," Kidd (1988) 1 p. 308, but doesn't merely rehash the work; cf. Malitz (1983) p. 170; on enemies' heads, quoted, trans. Kidd (1999) p. 347.

48. Trans. Kidd (1999) p. 231, of the Galen-passage where Poseidonius is the source; pp. 20f. on the *Emotions*-treatise.

49. Kidd (1999) pp. 89f. on ἐπιθυμία and θυμός, and relations with κρίσεις; p. 234 on the physiology of affects.

50. Elster (1999) pp. 52-75 on Aristotle's *Nicomachean Ethics* and especially his *Rhetoric*, "the earliest systematic discussion of human psychology" (p. 53); Diog. Laert. on Theophrastus' lost Περὶ παθῶν; Fortenbaugh et al. (1992) 2 pp. 264ff., on Theophrastus' treatment of ὀργή, θυμός, etc.; Brennan (1998) pp. 31ff. and passim on Stoic thought regarding emotions, without any mention in this substantial essay of any historian; and Fowler (1997) pp. 17, 20ff., dismissive of universalists.

51. Fritz (1977) p. 175, "Was ihn [Poseidonius] ausgezeichnet ist die anthropologisch-ethnographische Grundlage, die an die Geschichtschreibung zu geben gesucht hat, sowie die Verbindung von Völkerpsychologie, Massenpsychologie und Individualpsychologie;" p. 179, "especially interesting here is the close connection drawn between descriptions of social and political situations, with the psychology of groups and individuals."

52. Trans. Kidd (1999) pp. 341, 126.

53. Both in Plutarchean excerpts: Kidd (1999) pp. 330f. and (1988) 2 p. 891; (1999) 334ff.

54. Peter (1967) 1 pp. ccliiff., 179-84; Wiseman (1981) p. 376, calling the work *Res Gestae*. Earlier than Asellio, I find nothing in the fragments of Latin historians relevant to my subject, that is, showing an author interested in feelings, motivation, psychology, throughout the ca. 400 pages of Peter (1967), and the 68 writers there gathered — save only a bit of Cato's oratory, ibid. 1 pp. 85f., offering some thoughts on national character or mood affected by favoring circumstances, hence *laetitia, superbia*, not *recto consulendo*, etc.

55. Walsh (1961) p. 29, Polybian echoes in the phrase quoted.

56. The two quotations in Malcovati (1930) 2 pp. 140f., 144 (Cic., *De orat.* 3.56.214).

57. Cic., *De orat.* 2.47.194f., trans. E. W. Sutton; 2.189, an orator must, or at least Antonius always did, feel in himself the very feelings he displays and wishes to arouse in his listeners; and (2.185) must have the skill to affect his hearers, *ut oderint aut diligant, aut invideant... aut horreant aut laetantur aut maereant...; Ad Att.* 4.14.4, a counsel for the defense comes to "a truly eloquent

finale in tears." Cf. Schrijvers (1982) 395ff. on oratorical emotional involvement, and pp. 401ff. on *inventio* in Quintilian's prescriptions; MacMullen
(1980) p. 255, Quintilian and Seneca, too, advocating the orator's production
of tears *de industria*, with other references on Roman crying.

58. Cic., *De orat.* 2.62, assuming the historian will be an orator; 2.63, history
must provide the story, *res gestae* if suitably *magnae*, along with underlying *con-
silia*, and the "how", *quomodo*, and the actor's *sapientia*, *temeritas*, or other oper-
ative characteristics.

59. Cic., *De orat.* 2.59, *delectationis causa*, *cum est otium*.

60. Cic., *De orat.* 2.56.

61. Woodman (1988) pp. 75, 77f., on *De oratore*, dramatic date 91 BC.

62. On the late-4th century Duris and his *Hellenika*, see Diod. Sic. 15.60.6;
Walsh (1961) pp. 24 (Polyb. 2.56.7), 26; or Fornara (1983) pp. 35, 132f.;
Wiseman (1981) p. 386; (1994) p. 19.

63. "Mass audience," Wiseman (1981) pp. 385, 387; quoting Cic., *De fin.*
5.51f., as illustrative, p. 384; "middle-brow," Gabba (1981) p. 53.

64. Cic., *De orat.* 2.63, *ne quid falsi* is the basic rule, and no *gratia* or *simultas*,
either, says Antonius; but besides these *fundamenta*, there must be the *exaedificatio*. On these prescriptions, see Woodman (1988) pp. 70-78, 86-118, passim;
adumbrating Woodman's views in some points, among others is Fornara
(1983) pp. 133f. and elsewhere; the great freedom allowed in
exaedificatio/inventio, cf. Cic., *Brut.* 42, in Wiseman (1981) p. 390.

65. *In Verr.* II 5.147.

66. A clear indication in Cic., *Ad fam.* 5.12.5, quoted in Wheeldon (1989) 60:
"... the regular chronological record of events interests us as little as a catalogue of historical occurrences; but the uncertain... fortunes of a statesman...
give scope for suspense, delight, annoyance, fear and hope; should [these] end
in some striking consummation, the result is a complete satisfaction of mind
which is the most perfect pleasure a reader can enjoy." Cf. also on the passage,
Fornara (1983) p. 134, Woodman (1988) pp. 70ff.

67. On Q. Cicero, Peter (1967) 2 p. xvii and Bardon (1952) 1 p. 249; on
Tubero, Peter (1967) 1 pp. ccclxvi-xxiii and 313-17; on M. Cicero, 2 p. 4; on
Atticus, Nepos, et al., pp. xxff.

68. *De B[ello] G[allico]* 1.2, territory too small "for their numbers and
for their renown of courage and war;" *homines bellandi cupidi*, *magno dolore
adficiebantur*.

69. *BG* 1.33, "Ariovistus gave himself such airs and such arrogance;" again,
1.46, *arrogantia*.

70. *BG* 4.17, *navibus transire*... *neque suae neque populi Romani dignitatis*.

71. *BG* 1.33, what was done, *tanto imperio*, was *turpissimum sibi et rei publicae*;
1.12, national outrages avenged, and a private one as well involving Caesar's
grandfather; cf. 1.30, Rome avenged for past outrages; 1.14, Caesar's indignation "the heavier in that the injury to the Roman people had not been
deserved."

72. *BG* 1.35, *tantum beneficium* and *gratia* offered; 1.43, insult to a *beneficium et
liberalitas sua et senatus*; and recall of *beneficia* to a chieftain and his acknowledgement of being under obligation thereby, yet he betrays Caesar, 5.27.

73. *BG* 1.46; again, 4.14.
74. *BG* 7.80, *neque recte ac turpiter factum celari poterat* [*res*]; 8.28, not to retreat, *pudore cedendi*.
75. *BC* 1.3f., *inimicitiae* for the troops, the same and *dolor repulsae* for Cato (for the consulship of 51 BC), Lentulus rather motivated by debts and hope of riches to relieve them.
76. *BC* 1.7, Pompey *depravatum... invidia*, while Caesar endures *iniuriae*, against which the army declares its readiness to defend him.
77. *BC* 1.35f., 2.5, quoted; 2.13, troops' reaction, *gravius permoti milites ... odio defectionis*, etc.
78. *BC* 2.33, *milites... magno cum dolore infidelitatis suspicionem sustinere viderentur*.
79. On the definition of *dignitas*, see MacMullen (1990) pp. 192ff., 352, with ref. *inter alia* to Cic., *Pro Ligario* 6.18; Kienast (1999) p. 19. For more recent analogies, see Ayto (1998) p. 275, and Vital (1999) p. 270, on students at Breslau and a very few other universities in 1886, to declare *Satisfactionsfähigkeit* against the fraternities and the Verein of German Students.
80. "Modern scholarship tends to make the purely personal motive of Caesar responsible for his crossing of the Rubicon," so, Kienast (1999) p. 18 n. 71 (Syme [1964] p. 118 considers it only an "excuse"); Caesar's *dignitas* and choices seen in their sociocultural context, Wistrand (1978) pp. 29f., emphasizing Caesar's sense of his deserts; undocumented but forceful pages by Meier (1982) pp. 435f., but concerned more with institutional consequences; Büchner (1960) pp. 53, 80; full excellent discussion in Raaflaub (1974) pp. 113f. (Caesar's complaints of all the *contumeliae* he suffered), 119, 150f., 183, 188, and esp. pp. 189, 191; and on the contest for *maiestas* with Pompey, Woodman (1983) p. 64, note to Vell. 2.44.2 (and cf. also 2.33.3, Pompey *neque... quemquam animo parem tulit et, in quibus rebus primus esse debebat, solus esse cupiebat*).
81. Sall., *Cat.* 52.33, 54.3, *Orat. Lep.* 26, *Jug.* 33.3, 41.5; and Catiline's *pristina dignitas*, *Cat.* 35.3, 60.7.
82. *Jug.* 41.5. On Sallust's career, see esp. Dio 43.9.2; evaluation by Syme (1964) pp. 279-84, for the defense; Pasoli (1967) pp. 1-10, 17 (on Horti). Modern topographical works have no difficulty assigning the Horti to the historian.
83. Oniga (1990) p. 7.
84. Polyb. 6.54.1ff., cf. Sall., *Jug.* 4.5ff.; Wheeldon (1989) p. 54; imitation of Thucydides (e.g. Thuc. 1.22.4), Wheeldon p. 53, Walsh (1961) p. 44, Scanlon (1980) passim, Fornara (1983) p. 115, Woodman (1988) p. 127; influence perhaps of Poesidonius, McGushin (1977) p. 9, Paul (1984) p. 10; a rehasher of tropes, Paul pp. 10f., Oniga (1990) p. 7.
85. Syme (1964) p. 245, that Thuc. 3.82, on the Corcyrean revolution, "so captivated Sallust that he put it under contribution a dozen times;" Scanlon (1980) pp. 23, 35, 100, on the same Thuc. passage.
86. So-called *metus Punicus*, cf. Sall., *Cat.* 6.7, *per licentiam insolescere animum humanum,* etc., and 10.2f., *Jug.* 41.3, *metus hostilis*, and esp. *secundis rebus oriri sueta mala, Hist.* 1.11M, in McGushin (1977) pp. 75, 201, instancing the same

views in Livy, e.g. 22.22.19, 28.24.6, 45.31.4f.; cf. also Vell. 2.1.1; also Fornara (1983) p. 86, Bellen (1985) pp. 22, 27, and Kneppe (1994) p. 56 n. 16 (the Kneppe book known to me thanks to C. Galvão-Sobrinho); and contrast with the early Republic, where all were greedy for fame, *Cat.* 7.3
87. *Avaritia* much used by Sallust, at 8.1, 10.4, 13.8, 15.1, 15.5, 16.1, 163f., 27.2, 28.5, 29.1f., 32.1, 32.3f., 33.2, 34.1, 35.10, 37.3, 38.3, 38.6, 85.46, and esp. 41.1ff., with the conclusion quoted at 41.9.
88. Love of the dramatic, passim in this author, e.g. much play with the extraordinary and happenstantial, Fortuna/Tyche, *Cat.* 8.1, 10.1, etc.; or *Jug.* 82.2f., choice of high colors in explanation of conduct, or *Cat.* 22.1, plot sealed by drinking blood; vocabulary, *Jug.* 11.3, *ferox*, or 11.8, *ira et metu anxius*; 18.4, *summae audaciae…, factiosus… quem… mali mores stimulabant*; 20.2, *acer bellicosus, at is quem petebat quietus imbellis placido ingenio*; 23.2, *audacia* and past *scelera*; 27.2, *acer et infestus potentiae nobilitatis*; *Cat.* 5.4, *audax*; 5.6, *ferox*; 43.4, *ferox vehemens manu promptus*; and inflammatory speeches, *Cat.* 20.2ff. or *Jug.* 31.11ff., or the four speeches surviving from the *Historiae*.
89. The corrupt senators are the Bad Guys, the Roman *plebs*, the Good, in the grip of their "indignation", *invidia*, at *Jug.* 25.5, 27.3, 30.1, and elsewhere.
90. *Jug.* 11.3, 6-8, Hiempsal's insults of Jugurtha, and "thus [notice the emphasis on causality] from that time forward, torn by wrath and apprehension, he had nothing in his thoughts but what he might devise and prepare to catch Hiempsal in some trap;" Metellus' taunting of Marius, 64.5, cf. Epstein (1987) p. 140 n. 49 on the sources; resentment and rights denied stimulate anger, *Cat.* 20.7f., *Jug.* 31.17 and 21.
91. *Jug.* 14.7, help against *iniuriae* and *scelus*, and the term and thought repeated, 14.8, to the senate, "your *beneficia*, Senators, have been torn from me, and yourselves treated with contempt through the wrong done to me, the *iniuria*."
92. In 2000 I thought I was the first to use the English neologism as a translation; but I have since seen it in another new book. Corbier (2001) p. 161 rightly says *maiestas* "n'existe que dans une échelle de comparaison" (with bibliog.). In the arena of domestic politics, it amounted to that *principatus* on which Caesar was seen to aspire, Cic., *De off.* 1.26 and above, in the context of his fighting for his *dignitas*.
93. Gundel (1969) pp. 283f. on *maiestas'* frequency in Livy; Livy 2.7.7, *gratum id multitudini spectaculum fuit, summissa sibi esse insignia confessionemque factam populi quam consulis maiestatem vimque maiorem esse*; and 38.11.2, *imperium maiestatemque populi Romani gens Aetolorum conservato*.
94. Longing for *gloria*, e.g. insatiable in the elder Scipio, 28.17.2, 28.40.1, cf. 36.34.3, Flamininus; indignation, *invidia*, 2.23.2ff., with maximum pressure on the reader's sympathies through oratory; *indignatio, contumelia, ignominia*, etc., 2.28.2, 2.58.6, 3.2.6f., 3.62.1, 4.51.f. with *iniuria*, 6.37.1, 32.10.7, 33.39.4, 34.1.5, 36.29.1, 37.49.1f., anger at *insolentia*; 39.23.9 and 39.24.1, 5, indignation/*ira* at unfair share of reward, 39.28.1, 4, and 14, *iniuria*, or against Romans' *avaritia*, 42.25.8; unfair representation of conduct is an insult to the senate, 44.14.13, where Livy in his own person registers his *indignatio*, cf. 37.49.1f.; shame, *ignominia*, 2.52.4f., 39.31.9, *pudor*, or loss of reputation, at

42.60.6f., among soldiers after a reverse; parental love, implied in Sabine fathers' actions, *nihil enim per iram aut cupiditatem*, 1.11.5; gratitude for *beneficia*, 32.19.7, 42.12.1, 42.38.6f.; *amicitia* for past favors, 7.30.3ff., 7.31.2, 32.22.10; pity, 35.34.8.

95. *Temeritas*, 27.33.11; greed for booty, 10.17.1, 3, 6f.; 30.33.10f., 33.11.6, 36.17.14; *libido*, 8.28.2; arrogance and conceit, 33.11.4ff., 42.25.8 (Rome's, accused), 45.31.3; greed, *cupiditas*, 8.72.6.

96. *Amens invidia* from a political slight, 8.30.10, 8.31.2ff., 27.35.7, 29.37.4-17, 38.42.1-7, 38.52.9 and 38.54.2.

97. For example, *contumeliae* at 2.38.2, 3.62.1, or (in this case, nobly endured by a hero in the state's cause) 22.26.5; above, n. 79; quoted, Cornelia the mother of the reformer-brothers Gracchi, Agnes (1977) p. 392, lines which are "dei piu ritenuti autentici" (and Horsfall [1989] p. 42 very cautiously inclines toward trust).

98. Being curious to know more about *inimicitiae*, I urged the topic for a dissertation on a student of mine, with an excellent outcome in Epstein (1987), e.g. on revenge, pp. 9, 24, 44f. (though the focus of the study doesn't extend, beyond the consequences of enmity and feuding, to the nature of the feelings themselves); cf. also Kierdorf (1987) pp. 230f. On perhaps the most historic of Roman *inimicitiae*, that between Pompey and Caesar, see above, n. 79, Raaflaub (1974) pp. 114 (citing Caes., *BC* 1.9.2, *contumeliae inimicorum*), 185 (vengeance), and passim, and Kienast (1999) p. 18.

99. Livy 2.17.2, 2.23.2, 14f.; 2.42.1, 2.43.3, 2.56.14, 3.62.1, 4.32.12, 4.51.6, 6.37.1, 8.32.1, 22.1.8ff., 26.18.6ff., 27.50.2ff., 31.9.5, 34.1.5, 37.12.7f.; Walsh (1961) pp. 169f., 185, 204ff., with a variety of further examples and reff.; and, on one particular emotion, anger, W.V. Harris (2001) pp. 15, 216, finding some hundreds of occurrences of *ira* (*irascor*) in Livy, "a leitmotif... of his history" (with my thanks to the author for drawing his work to my attention, since it opens up adjoining areas so well).

100. Livy 8.28.2f., cf. 21.3.1, 4; 39.8.3-20 and MacMullen (1990) chapter 17 passim and (1991) pp. 429f. Of attitudes toward homosexuality, there has been much discussion in recent decades, much of it selectively learned in the highest degree; but the principals of discussion are at last straightened out by Davidson (2001), esp. pp. 29ff. (Rome).

101. Walsh (1961) p. 170; Woodman (1988) p. 108 n. 82; Walsh (1961) pp. 172, 192f., personal involvement in "thrills and chills;" vividness in detail, p. 176, and lavish use of a vocabulary of feelings, pp. 178, 184ff., and ἐνάργεια, p. 187; esp. interest in crowd psychology and motive, pp. 205f.

102. Characteristic affect-passages in Val. Max., e.g. 4.2.2, *odio ardens*, etc. (and 4.2 passim on *inimicitiae*); 7.2.6, *pertinax odium*; 9.2.1f., Sulla's *inexplebilis feritas, ira, saevitia*; likewise in Vell., cf. Woodman (1983) pp. 22, 25, 36.

103. Syme (1958) 2 p. 624, the closing words of the work.

104. See K. Mel in *Der Neue Pauly Enzyklopädie der Antike* 3 (Stuttgart 1997) col. 593, or earlier, Pauly-Wissowa's s.v. Diodoros col. 690.

105. Diod. Sic. 18.49.1, cf. 11.67.6, outrageous behavior "beyond anything that was right," "and for that reason" and other tyrannous qualities, revolt breaks out and the tyrant exiled, 11.68.1ff.; 11.70.3f., "arrogant" and "unfair"

behavior by Athens toward her allies, "and for that reason" grumbling, conspiring, cf. Sacks (1990) p. 42; 13.111.5f., anger and hatred against a tyrant roused among soldiers by the sight of his victims, innocent free-born youths and maidens; 14.45.5 and 14.46.2, Syracuse determines on war, hating Carthage's arrogant bullying and cruelty, and, 14.77.1, other cities in Sicily share hatred of the harshness of Carthage's rule and join in; 16.41.2, revolt against a Phoenician governor for his outrageous, arrogant rule; and men excluded from government, 11.72.2 and 11.73.1, may be aggrieved, and start a fight; 14.107.1, a ruler himself may be shown disrespect and be outraged and exact vengeance; or feels betrayed, and abandons a war, 20.37.2; and, 16.93-4, a young man gang-raped through a plot, unavenged by his lover, kills the latter; per contra, 11.73.1, kindly treatment as was "only fair" because of an ancestral tie, or, 18.36.6, kindness shown in recollection of favors received, or the desire for "acclaim from all mankind," for one's virtue, 13.22.6.

106. Instances in the preceding note; further, a slaughter of captives avenges a defeat suffered by an ancestor, Diod. Sic. 13.59.5 and 13.62.4; individual's violent or savage character, 11.67.5, 33.14.1; thirst for glory, 13.71.2; the attractions of money determine significant decisions, 16.37.4 or 16.54.4, and Sacks (1990) pp. 20f. on Diodorus' understanding of πλεονεξία and the continual occurrence of this "thematic" word in his account.

107. Diod. Sic. 13.111.5 or 17.36.3f., pity; hope and excitement, 13.2.2, 13.91.4 with 13.92.1, and panic at 20.67.2ff.

108. Diod. Sic. 34-35.33.5f., the "Carthage fear" argument, cf. above at n. 86; or 16.54.4, a king through widespread distribution of gifts, amounting to bribes with a fair name, "by his evil communications corrupted the mores of the common people."

109. Diod. Sic.18.60.1.

110. Sacks (1990) pp. 24f., 43, the historian's emphasis on "moderate behavior," ἐπιείκεια, occurring over 300 times, "his hallmark;" cf. also great emphasis on Chance, p. 38, over 250 times, e.g., 18.41.6 or 18.42.1.

111. Diod. Sic. 197.2ff., trans. R. M. Geer; cf. 20.1.1f., deploring too-long, show-off speeches too frequently inserted in the narrative; but some admixture of drama irresistible to this author, e.g. imitative of Thucydides, 13.15.1, or 17.36.3f., a scene of "tears and compassion" in emotive detail.

112. Diod. Sic. 15.60.5.

113. Fornara (1983) pp. 82, 138f.; Sacks (1983) pp. 73ff.; and above, at note 63.

114. Outrage, Dion. Hal. 11.1.6, ὑβρίζεσθαι; law, 8.8.3, 8.10.10, 10.32.1, cf. above, Hellenic law in Thucydides, or in Sallust's Jug.; and imitation of Thucydides' ruminations on the Corcyrean revolution and consequent changes in moral vocabulary, Dion. Hal. 9.53.6.

115. Dion. Hal. 8.26.1; Ep. Ad Pomp. (Teubner ed., 1 p. 246), recommendation to historians to "examine even the hidden reasons for actions and the motives of their agents, and the feelings in their hearts (which most people do not find it easy to discern), and to reveal all the mysteries of apparent virtue and undetected vice."

116. Wiseman (1981) p. 380; Fromentin (1998) pp. xvif., xxxix; and M. Fox (2001) pp. 81f.

117. Tears, e.g., Dion. Hal. 10.29.1; 9.33.3, a general absolved for loss of life among his men, and "What most moved them [the populace] to pity was the fellow-feeling that showed in the expression of his face, as to those who have suffered or will suffer something awful;" cf. on public crying, MacMullen (1980) 254f.; vengeance in the Coriolanus story, 8.1.2, τιμωρία; 8.33.1, χαλεπαίνεις καὶ ἀγανακτεῖς; and 8.6.4, λάβοιμι παρ᾽ αὐτῶν δίκας; and Peter (1967) 1 p. 32 shows Coriolanus in Fabius Pictor living to a ripe old age, cf. Livy 2.40.10; on the war resulting, "two devastating annual campaigns" in 490–88 BC, see T. J. Cornell in the Cambridge Ancient History, ed. 2, 7 (Cambridge 1989) pp. 287f.

118. It is convenient to use the text of Hall (1923) which has also an English translation (though I supply my own).

119. In confirmation, App., BC 3.2.11(36), Augustus reflects on the terms of Caesar's will, and "thought that to do so [i.e. lie low] and not to avenge Caesar would be disgraceful." Cf. again, not to seek vengeance would be "to wrong Caesar," 3.2.13; and on Augustus'"Sendungsbewusstsein," Kienast (1999) p. 8.

120. Nik. 18, the same word as above, "high deeds," μεγάλα; cf. the same ambition in Vell. 2.60.2; mother Atia's reactions, App., BC 3.2.14(48); the sources unanimous, Vell., App., Nik., cf. Kober (2000) pp. 88, [455=] Table #18; and the verdict of Cic., Ad fam. 12.23.2, "there is nothing, as it is thought, which he [Augustus] will not do for fame and glory."

121. On obligations to family, cf. above, at nn. 35 and 93, on the Scipios; Hölkeskamp (1987) p. 206; App., BC 2.16.112, of M. Brutus, "these and many other similar things set the young man aflame to do the deed done by his forbears," as later, 2.17.122, Cassius and Brutus in turn "exhorted the people [in the Forum] to do as their forebears had done, who brought down the kings;" and Lepidus to Cicero, Ad fam. 10.34a.2, promising meam vitam, studium, diligentiam, fidem superioribus temporibus in re publica administranda quae Lepido digna sunt perspecta habes. On the obligations incurred in receiving beneficia, see Hölkeskamp (1987) p. 212, citing Cic., De off. 1.47, nullum… officium referenda gratia magis necessarium est; or, e.g., Cic., Ad Att. 9.7.4, "I dare not lay myself open to the charge of ingrat," being obligated as he would not be, si illinc beneficium non sit; and Epstein (1987) p. 42.

122. Kienast (1999) pp. 8f., 15, on the risk of ingratia and violation of pietas involved in not seeking revenge; or the dictum, "You have said everything possible against a man when you call him an ingrate," Publilius Syrus quoted in MacMullen (1990) p. 196; or Cic., Ad Att. 9.2a.2, he would support Pompey, for Pompey would be angry if he didn't join him, "which I fear…, for I dread the charge of ingratitude."

123. Nik. 27, inaction would be sacrilegious, ἀνόσιον εἴη περιορᾶν τὸν Καίσαρος φόνον; on the special moral obligation against a parent's enemies, see Epstein (1987) pp. 43, 92, with examples; characterization of the dictator's death as an "abomination", μύσος, App., BC 3.2.12(41); on pietas to Caesar's memory in Augustus' words, cf.Vell. 2.60.2, "he kept saying it would be impious, nefas, that he who was thought worthy of his name by Caesar should, to

himself, seem unworthy;" App., *BC* 3.2.13(47), the assassination was itself done sacrilegiously, by the victim's friends and dependents, ἀθεμιστῶς; and Plut., *Cato mai.* 15.3, quoted, in Epstein (1987) p. 24. On the need for vengeance, Polyb. 1.7.8 and 12, and the deep satisfaction of it, above at n. 97.
124. Cic., *Ad fam.* 8.5.3, *Caesariani*=political supporters of Caesar, as again, *Phil.* 13.29, *Pompeiani*; also at Vell. 2.25.4 and [Caes.], *Bell. Afr.* 13.1; ibid. 53, *Caesariani* (the same, Val. Max., Florus, or App., *BC* 3.13.91 — notice, for Appian I use the old style of numeration, of the Loeb and first Teubner edition, Mendelssohn 1881, not of the 2ⁿᵈ Teubner = Magnino [1993]).
125. Nik. 27, with Lepidus specially firm "to avenge Caesar" (at two points in the text); App., *BC* 2.17.124, that Appian immediately after the Ides sees Antony and Lepidus as impelled by the urge to avenge Caesar, whether from love for the man or obligation to their oaths or desire for political power; and, 2.18.130, when Lepidus, after shedding tears before he can begin his speech, asks the Forum crowd, "'what shall I do?'" "Many shouted out, 'Avenge Caesar.'" The latter a little later (2.20.146) are "out of their minds with fury and grief."
126. App., *BC* 3.3.21(77), Augustus' earlier reaction of anger at ὕβρις offered him by Antony, and further insult from Antony and expressions of anger, too (3.4.28), lead up to the accusation of a plot, to which the populace respond with wrath, "seeing how [Augustus] suffered daily outrage," 3.6.39.
127. Augustus' resentment against Cicero was reported, *Ad fam.* 11.20.1, May 43 BC, "for a *mot* which he attributed to you [Cicero], 'that we should praise the young fellow, exalt him, blow him up…,'" *laudandum, ornandum, tollendum*; and Augustus had no intention of being thus exalted (cf. Vell. 62.6, the joke well known, and Velleius' source likely to be Augustus' autobiography, Hellegouarc'h [1982] 2 p. 211).
128. Vell. 2.62.5; Plut., *Moral.* 207C (Bernadakis 2 p. 97); Syme (1939) p. 433, "his [Augustus'] inhuman composure."
129. Nik. 25, 31. Cf. App., *BC* 2.19.42, the crowd later worked up by Antony, μανιωδῶς ὑπὸ ὀργῆς καὶ λύπης, 2.20.146.
130. Above, n. 123; "faction" regularly in Syme (1939), the misunderstanding clear at, e.g., p. 130. The subject has been much studied, naturally. A good place to begin (but inviting and subsequently receiving modification) would be Premerstein (1937). For "party" misapplied (*partito conservatore, dei grandi*, etc.), but in a work that gives as well as any I know the picture and feel of what happened in the later Republic (and available in an excellent translation), see Ferrero (1907). I notice his work is more often cited in the notes of Kober (2000) than is Syme.
131. Plut., *Cic.* 46.6, the triumvirs' θυμὸς καὶ λύσσης; cf. Vell. 66.1, *furente deinde Antonio*; Plut., *Cic.* 47.6f., Cicero among his villas; 48.5f., manner of death, and hands that wrote the speeches (which I suppose were in fact dictated); Dio 47.8.3f., trans. E. Cary, on the treatment of head and hands, the horrific account not challenged, and used without comment by Jervis (2001) p. 164 n. 32, though Wright (2001) p. 450 is "wary". Jervis in fact offers much material to support its historicity, pp. 39–45, 96, 131–64, esp. p. 138 n. 32.
132. App., *BC* 3.3.26(101), on the ὀργή of the troops (Apr. 43 BC).

133. Cicero's alarm at the invincibility of Caesar in 50 BC, *Ad fam.* 8.14.3; after the Ides, *Ad Att.* 14.1.1, 14.4.1, and 14.6.1 in Boterman (1968) p. 13 n. 3, on the legions in Gaul, to be feared; *Ad Att.* 10.13.3, 10.15.1, and 10.14.2, legions in Spain (49 BC); later, *Ad Att.* 14.6.1-2 (Apr. 44 BC); doubts which tyrannicide they hated the most, *Phil.* 10.7.15; 11.38 (Feb. 43 BC), "What veterans are they whose spirits we fear to offend?... For how long, fellow Senators, shall we offer our views at the bidding of the veterans?;" exchange of rumors about troops' mood of anger, *maxime indignari, Ad fam.* 11.20.1 (May 43); *Ad Att.* 16.8.2.

134. App., *BC* 2.4.30, Pompey's intelligence informs him that "Caesar's army [in Gaul in 50 BC] was worn down by labors of long service" and "would change sides to him as soon as they crossed the Alps;" which proved mere "ignorance". In 49 BC L. Domitius Ahenobarbus could raise troops with a promise of land on a huge scale, but they wouldn't fight for him or his cause, cf. Brunt (1975) p. 619 and Cic., *Ad Att.* 8.6.7, "a powerful army eager for battle," but they surrender, ibid. 8.8.2, and join Caesar's forces, *Cambridge Ancient History* 9 (Cambridge 1932) p. 642; and troops raised to defend the capital wouldn't fight, *a pugnando abhorrentium, Ad Att.* 7.13.2. Later, the false reports believed by the senate, App., *BC* 3.13.93(383) (Nov. 43 BC). For Pompey's boast in 50 BC, see Plut., *Pomp.* 57.5.

135. Cic., *Phil.* 13.33 (Apr. 43 BC): "we did string them along and befuddle them! The Fourth Martian knew no better, the veterans knew no better what they were doing. Those fellows did not support the Senate's authority nor the freedom of the People. They wanted to avenge Caesar's death...."

136. Cic., *Ad fam.* 12.2.1 and Boterman (1968) p. 33.

137. Cic., *Ad fam.* 11.10.4; 10.35.1 (Lepidus, May 43 BC); speeches by Antony or Augustus against each other, at various points; or Lucius Antonius against Augustus, Vell. 2.74.2; Augustus' key speech to the army, Kober (2000) p. 90.

138. Boterman (1968) offers the fullest accounting, e.g. at pp. 12f., 15 n. 4, 30, 36; and notice Nik. 17 and elsewhere, cited above; Trebonius' beheading, above; nn. 132, 134, above; Vell., Nik., and App. in Kober (2000) pp. 96f., 103; Cic., *Phil.* 10.7.15; and Florus 2.17.2.

139. App., *BC* 3.4.29 (112); on gratitude, above, nn. 93, 120f.; and, with shock, emphasis on Caesar's former mercy and kindness to those who were among his assassins, "making them his friends," App., *BC* 4.2.8.

140. App., *BC* 3.4.28(109), the veterans' obligations "to Caesar their commander and benefactor;" and the feeling dramatized in Augustus' speech to his mother about his passion to serve Caesar as a commander, 3.2.13(47).

141. Some degree of affection, where Caesar is described by a friend and officer as *eum quem dilexi,* Cic., *Ad fam.* 11.28.2 (fall 44 BC), cf. *homo amicissimus,* 11.28.3; φιλία, felt by Antony and Lepidus, App., *BC* 2.17.124; to Piso, Caesar "a friend and benefactor," App., *BC* 3.8.57(238); εὔνοια, mild term, at Nik. 16.41, but it is "an extraordinary favor," θαυμαστὴ εὔνοια, Nik. 18.56.

142. App., *BC* 2.4.30, a factor in loyalty to Caesar was expectation of war-end bonuses; and pressure for ratification of his honors and will was a concern, as it included the bonuses, 3.4.28(109); discussion by Veyne (1976) p.

614; and Boterman (1968) pp. 51ff., as 43 BC goes on, between Antony and Augustus, the soldiers' choice is more and more a money matter.

143. App., *BC* 2.17.133; cf. MacMullen (1990) p. 226.

144. Caes., *BG* 7.80; App., *BC* 2.9.60, it's αἰδώς that provokes great bravery, cf. "shame" again, 3.9.67(278), or ἀδοξία at 3.9.69(284); Vell. 55.4, *verecundia magis quam virtute acies restituta*, where Woodman (1983) p. 108 compares Florus 2.13.81, *pudore magis quam virtute acies resistere*; and other texts including Livy in MacMullen (1990) pp. 231ff.

145. Nik. 18.56, noted by Boterman (1968) p. 18 as among *Gefühlsmomente*, the affective impulses that explain the flow of events.

146. Peter (1967) 2 pp. lxxi-vi and 54-64; Manuwald (1979) p. 28; Yavetz (1984) p. 2; Gabba (1984) p. 62; and Kober (2000) p. 21, Nikolaos' version of the autobiography is "recht genau und ohne grossere Aenderungen," though (p. 38 — naturally) an account most favorable toward Augustus which (pp. 92, 243) gives prominence to the Caesar-avenging motif.

147. For Asinius Pollio being a major source for Appian, but a number of others melded in in a careful manner, cf. Hahn (1982) pp. 260ff., 275; Woodman (1983) p. 186; Gowing (1992) p. 40, but other sources used, and the whole (pp. 48, 90) "objective"; Magnino (1993) pp. 525, 538f., 544, 548f.; and, detecting not so much an Augustus-apologetic tendency as an Antonian, Kober (2000) pp. 21, 96f., 103f., and passim (a bias, if actual, not relevant to the matter of affect-history). For Velleius, "steeped in the primary sources," cf. Woodman (1983) p. 115; and Kober (2000), passim, bringing out the many points where Velleius (very much more abbreviated), like Nikolaos and Appian, agrees with them, including points of affect-report (although it is easy to cite passages where this author provides color or detail putting Augustus in a bad light and excusing or explaining the enemies of Caesar, e.g. 2.29.3f., 2.56.1ff., 2.70.4f.). On Dio and some of his sources emphasizing Augustus' aim for the top, see Manuwald (1979) p. 31, and other source-possibilities at pp. 28, 169 (use of Livy), 252.

148. As an indication of the position of Syme among students of Augustus, notice the appearance of 36 of his works in the bibliography of Kienast (1999); his 1939 work "a classic," still worthy of review, Galsterer (1990) pp. 2, 20, and deeper treatment by Loreto (1999), e.g., pp. 55f., 137ff., and passim; "on the nature of the political struggle in the late Republic... the still dominant *Roman Revolution* of Ronald Syme," so, Harris (2001) p. 213; his knighthood and presidency of the international federation of classical studies; many published tributes; and so on. The Anglophone world chiefly built the pedestal, to which the Continent contributed less, cf. Alföldy (1983) pp. 5f., 27ff.

149. Alföldy (1983) p. 20, with illustrations in the dozens. I add others from Syme (1939) pp. 193 (*municipia*), 195; 159 with 15 and 101 (soldiers), and the characterization (p. 120) of those who followed Augustus, "their appetites whetted by the dissemination of propaganda, of promises, of bribes." Cf. also Loreto (1999) p. 77.

150. Alföldy (1983) p. 17, Syme's disregard of the masses noted by all critics; "Roman history is the history of the governing class," Syme (1939) p. 7; and my verse quotation from S. Johnson, *The Vanity of Human Wishes*, line 344.

151. Syme (1939) pp. 31 (Pompeiani); 41 (Caesarians); 201 (Augustus' "faction");198 (tyrannicides' recruits).

152. Syme (1939) pp. 152, 154 (agreeing with Sallust's verdict on *potentia* as the sole objective).

153. "Hatred" of Sextus Pompey against Augustus, p. 228; "grievance" of Ahenobarbus, blocked of high offices, while Bibulus "smarted still beneath the humiliation of authority set at nought," p. 44; "angry" Antony, p. 225; Tiberius' "dearly beloved" wife, whom he nevertheless gives up, p. 416; "fell in love," of Augustus with Livia, but "it was with political advantage," p. 229; "spite and disappointment," of Tiberius, p. 417; "friends" several times, e.g. Augustus' "loyal and unscrupulous friends like Agrippa and Maecenas," p. 234 — these few, I would say, being a majority of all such terms to be found anywhere. For the insight, quoted, p. 337.

154. Syme (1939) pp. 183 and 58, Brutus "firm, upright and loyal;" pp. 6 and 166, Pollio; 179, a minor personage, a suicide, "an honest man," p. 179; the elder Lucullus' "integrity" , etc., p. 21; Sentius, "trusty and competent," p. 398. But "the ambition of generals like Pompey and Caesar provoked civil war," p. 194, Caesar and Cicero "ambitious politicians," p. 29, leading men in the 60s BC, "the *principes* strove for prestige and power," p. 38; Pompey "sinister and ambitious," p. 316, or "ambitious and perfidious," p. 317; and Lepidus, "perfidious and despised," p. 180.

155. On "misrepresentation", deceit, and hollow pretensions in the period from 70 BC on, see Syme (1939) pp. 153f., with further general statements like, "success or failure became the only criterion of wisdom and patriotism" — this, supported illustratively by a Dio-passage on name-calling which recalls Thucydides on Corcyra. But notice, Dio offers this to explain how (as he continues) "Rome's affairs had *then* [43 BC] reached to such a point" — as distinct from political morals and ideals earlier. I waive the similar problem of interpretation in Augustus' later years, where we have reforming legislation, it would appear, from no sincere impulse whatsoever, in Chapter XXIX, e.g. pp. 452f., on "duplicity" and "the strong suspicion of fraud" driving the program.

156. E.g., Augustus a "revolutionary adventurer," pp. 113, 317, cf. 137, 141; demagogue, e.g. 115f., 119; "his ambition implacable," p. 113; and Alföldy (1983) p. 21.

157. "Chill...," p. 191; "rational", p. 177; investment, p. 120; "a cause to champion, the avenging of Caesar, and [Augustus] was ready to exploit every advantage," p. 119; winning of Cicero "not merely the plot of a crafty and unscrupulous youth," p. 143; "cool", p. 122; "more skills," p. 130.

NOTES
CHAPTER 2

1. Only to illustrate what happens without careful explanation of essential terms, notice Nussbaum (2001), in whose earlier chapters "emotion" appears as the chief subject; but the author generally fails to make clear to herself how widely inclusive is her use of the term, rendering her discusssion of the whole congeries confused or indeterminate. By contrast, notice the primacy of definition in Reddy (2001) pp. 8ff., 94, acknowledging the difficulties and proposing his own (though it amounts to a short essay!).

2. "It is extremely difficult to state what lawyers mean when they speak of 'reasonableness'…," and other similar conclusions quoted in *Black* (1999) p. 1272, cf. "reasonable doubt" defined in terms of "a reasonable person," *Guide* (1983) 8 p. 391 (my thanks to Stanton Wheeler for comments on this). For a similar resort to court practices which rely on circumstantial evidence to explain if not to justify similar historical argumentation, cf. Goodspeed (1977) p. 157; and for a close cousin to the law's "reasonable", cf. Geertz's sketch of "commonsensical", engagingly impressionist (Geertz [1983] pp. 84f. and passim). I waive the question, whether the manner of debate common among social historians is in any case suited to the requirements of argument in court, cf. Scott (1999) pp. 169f., as I waive also the argument among philosophers regarding the "truth" of our "understanding" of another's mind — see Kögler and Steuber (2000) passim.

3. Hegel (1956) p. 20, with the modern editor's comment, p. i, that the work "remains the heart and center of Hegel's philosophy [and] has exerted the most profound influence."

4. Zajonc (1998) p. 591. Compare de Sousa (1987) with a different, philosopher's angle of approach, proposing (p. 39) that "emotions control not merely behavior but also the ways that other mental events, states, and dispositions are organized;" and further p. 79, "*emotions motivate but do not determine*" — although, p. 142, "by and large, common sense holds that emotions are typically both subjective and irrational." He can rescue the rationality of emotions only by proposing that (I condense the argument greatly) "rational" is taken to mean "in accordance with the desire," i. e., logical in terms of a foreseen scenario. The upshot of this argument brings de Sousa's *scenario* close to the *appraisal* of psychologists, cf. below, n. 27.

5. Dawes (1998) 1 pp. 498, 509f., allowing only (p. 510) that decision-making may take account of anticipated regret or rejoicing.

6. Loewenstein et al. (2001) p. 267, with my thanks to Robert Shiller for the reference; the latter's remark, quoted, Shiller (1989) p. 2; and compare, e.g., Kahnemann et al. (1999) p. 203, "The economic model of choice is concerned with a rational agent whose preferences obey a tight web of logical rules," which at least this psychologist who comments does not accept.

7. Schumpeter (1934) p. 80, acknowledging the irrationality of the market but at the same time ready to assume and to use a virtual rationality; the "rationality postulate," consensus in neoclassical economics, and aggregation, cf. Blaug (1992) pp. 229ff. or Loasby (1996) pp. 17f.; and good warnings on disregard of emotions in Hochschild (1975) pp. 284f. (with some vulnerability in definition of "rational"). Marc Bloch (1949) in the early 1940s more dismissively wrote (p. 101): "to read certain history books, one might suppose humanity to be made up solely of logicians' intentions, books for which the motives of action have nothing at all obscure about them... which is, again, to repeat while exaggerating the mistake so often held up for correction, of that ancient economic theory. Its *homo economicus* was not an empty shadow only for the reason of imagining him to be solely focused on his interests; worse still, the illusion consisted in believing he could form even so clear a conception of these interests." But Bloch was not likely to be read on The Market.

8. Rogivue (1938) pp. 29ff., 56ff., 120ff., and passim.

9. An early contrarian was Leeper (1970) pp. 153-56, noting how emotions are "misunderstood as disruptive and high-intensity things," but himself asserting the identity between motives and emotions, and the cognitive element there to be found; more recently, Kitayama and Niedenthal (1994) p. 3, quoted, followed by the opening sentences, quoted, of Loewenstein and Lerner (2002), with my thanks to the latter author for a sight of the manuscript; further, Forgas (1991) p. 3, "For the cognitive psychologist, affect was long considered as irrelevant," and therefore not worth studying.

10. Cf. a pair of pronouncements in the press, Lowenstein (2001), "a subversion of the prevailing orthodoxy of the 1980s... accepted economic theory," and Uchitelle (2001) p. 1, correcting the view that economic behavior "responded to change in prices and wages but not to emotions."

11. Cf. e. g. Cornelius (1996) pp. 79, 114f.

12. The two contributions of James (in *Mind* [1884] and in his *Principles of Psychology* [1893]) are conveniently found in Lange and James (1922), with Lange's 1885 article. James' thesis a common starting point for discussions, e.g. Frijda (1986) pp. 125, 177; Damasio (1994) p. 129; Wierzbicka (1994) p. 136; or Berkowitz (2000) p. 3; Jamesianism called "classic" by, e.g., Solomon (1984) p. 238 or Wierzbicka (1994) p. 146; but attacked in the next few decades after publication, Cornelius (1996) pp. 60ff.; and still thought worthy of attack, in a different climate of debate, by most of these researchers.

13. Lange and James (1922) p. 13; emotions without somatic events are unimaginable, p. 17; and what we "feel" as "emotions" are physical changes, so says Lange as well (pp. 64ff.); and subsequent researchers, e.g. Lutz (1988) p. 41 (reff.), Oatley (1982) p. 50, Cornelius (1996) pp. 75ff., Turner (2000) pp. 88f., or many of those cited, below.

14. Damasio (1994) pp. 130f.; Adolphs and Damasio (2001) pp. 28f.
15. Oakley (1992) p. 19.
16. On neuropeptides et sim., Panksepp (2000-a) p. 41; inability to feel, Damasio (1994) passim, esp. pp. 45, 56; on the amygdala, etc., Izard et al. (1984) p. 19; Frijda (1986) pp. 381f. and chap. 7, passim; Ledoux (1994) pp. 218-22; Williams (2000) p. 42; Adolphs and Damasio (2001) pp. 29, 41; other areas of the brain, Leventhal (1982) pp. 127f.; Lutz (1988) p. 41, citing work by Panksepp in *Behavioral and Brain Sciences* 5 (1982); Panksepp (1998) p. 34; Zajonc (1998) pp. 597f. and, on positive and negative emotions, p. 604; Showers (2000) pp. 296f.; Peters and Slovic (2000) pp. 1466f.; and Panksepp (2000) pp. 137f., 140ff.
17. Fox and Davidson (1987) pp. 234f.
18. Russell (1989) p. 96; M. S. Clark (1982) p. 270.
19. Panksepp (2000) pp. 144f., the last, "seeking," "studied for almost half a century."
20. Hyman (1962) pp. 58ff.; Frijda (1986) on universality, pp. 20 (anger), 28 (smiling=friendliness), and 67f. (startle-reflex); Averill (1994) pp. 7f., 12f., with very sensible words on definitional matters; Cornelius (1996) pp. 31, 37, 39f., 133, 186 (some expressions are indeed "constants across cultures," pointing toward "the proposition that human emotions are part of our evolutionary heritage"); Hansen and Hansen (1994) p. 219, cross-cultural identities; Van Bezooijen et al. (1983) p. 388; G. M. White (2000) p. 32; Ortony et al. (1988) p. 7, facial expression a defining constant in emotion; and observed in infants as among adults, Fox and Davidson (1987) p. 234.
21. Leventhal (1982) p. 130.
22. Clore (1994) pp. 103f.; Hansen and Hansen (1994) p. 232; Zajonc (1998) p. 604, quoted, and on the sidedness of facial gesture, cf. also Frijda (1986) p. 400.
23. Zajonc (1980) p. 156; Oatley (1982) p. 54; Izard (1984) p. 18, "the survival of the individual requires that its systems produce actions (sometimes with great rapidity) that adapt it to its environment;" Clore (1994) p. 110; Panksepp (1998) p. 14, "basic emotional states provide efficient ways to mediate categorical types of learned behavioral changes... [and] guide new behaviors by providing simple value-coding mechanisms [=markers] that provide self-referential salience, thereby allowing organisms to categorize world events efficiently so as to control future behaviors;" Branscombe and Cohen (1991) p. 146; and Reddy (2001) pp. 21ff., 31f.
24. Zajonc (1980) p. 165; Loewenstein et al. (2001) p. 271; Bower and Forgas (2001) p. 99; Adolphs and Damasio (2001) p. 34; and, drawing a line to Piaget, Le Breton (1998) p. 96, that there is some affect in every cognitive process, and vice versa, so that "intelligence cannot be imagined without the affective element that fills it."
25. "Vividness, and hence the strength ...," in Loewenstein et al. (2001) p. 275; the example of the "weapons focus effect" in memory, Adolphs and Damasio (2001) p. 34.
26. Dienstbier (1984) p. 486; Scherer (1994) p. 128; Loewenstein et al. (2001) p. 271; Damasio (1994) pp. 172f.; Schwarz (1991) p. 56 (and in an adjoining study, p. 74); Zajonc (1998) p. 591.

27. Damasio (1994) p. 139 on "emotion"; Lowenstein and Lerner (2002) toward the very start of their discussion, offering the illustration of an investor's choice, who considers options and outcomes and wonders "how she would feel under the various scenarios she can envision" (and again, in the section, "Low and moderate levels of intensity," and passim); the process similar to belief+emotion in Frijda et al. (2000) p. 1 and recalling "schemas" in Reddy (2001) pp. 24, 94; a roughly similar sequence to Damasio's outlined by Oatley (1982) pp. 18ff. (appraisal="evaluation"); chief emphasis on appraisal not instant response, reff. in Cornelius (1996) pp. 114f., 128ff. on Zajonc (1980, p. 151 and passim; 1984, p. 117), indicating reconciliation of Zajonc's and the alternative view; Weiner (1982) p. 203, fence-sitting; Elster (1999) p. 270, holding out against "the appraisal theory;" assumption of there being always an appraisal, Thoits (1989) p. 318; contention that there may be no time for appraisal before bodily changes, as in the "startle reflex," Panksepp (1998) p. 33; and appraisal first, then arousal, in Lazarus (1984) p. 124; Ortony et al. (1988) p. 51; Sommers (1988) p. 24; Ellsworth (1994) p. 29; and Kahnemann et al. (1999) pp. 204f. (where "attitude" seems equivalent to appraisal=evaluation). Note the strong view, "the experience of an emotion *is* cognition," quoted to agree by Forgas (2001) p. 5 , or the neologism "cogmotion" supported by Reddy (2001) p. 321, to indicate the inseparability of cognition and emotion.
28. "Complex" in Ortony et al., cit.; Plutchik (1989) p. 6; "integrated", Berkowitz (2000) p. 4; but, Frijda (1986) p. 125, "It is no use quarreling with definition."
29. "Processing structure," Kitayama and Niedenthal (1994) p. 6; "a fuzzy set of component processes," Kitayama and Markus (1994) p. 5; "constructive process," Sommers (1988) p. 24; "a syndrome," Walbott and Scherer (1989) p. 56; and Shweder (1994) p. 38, "The emotion is the whole story, the whole package deal — a kind of somatic event...experienced as a kind of perception...linked to a kind of plan (attack, withdraw...)."
30. Damasio (1994) pp. 45 (quoted), 124, and 167; Loewenstein and Lerner (2002) pp. 619, 633ff.
31. Gambling experiment, Mellers et al. (1999) pp. 332, 335, 340f. On priming, Alloy and Abramson (1979) pp. 441, 478f., and passim, where depression is a factor; Ortony et al. (1988) p. 66; Clore (1994) p. 110; Cornelius (1996) pp. 124f.; reinforcement of an affect by recall of congruent affect, Clore (1992) p. 138, Forgas (2000) p. 5, and Schwarz (2000) p. 433; reinforcement or influence from moods, Mellers (1999) p. 332, with references; Keltner et al. (1993) pp. 749ff., negative mood (anger) yields different judgements/perceptions from negative mood (sadness); and Forgas (2000) p. 5.
32. Schwarz (1991) p. 56; Lowenstein et al. (2001) p. 268 with references.
33. Zajonc (1980) p. 155, quoted; Levy (1984) p. 218; Smith and Kirby (2001) p. 76; Peters and Slovic (2000) p. 1473; and J. H. Turner (2000) p. 139, that we "think" through "emotionally valenced images from past memories."
34. Kahneman et al. (1999) pp. 205, 207, emotional valuation applied to "events...[and] historical figures." Cf. below, chapter 4 n. 5.
35. Lowenstein et al. (2001) p. 271, quoted, agreeing with Frijda (1986);

Levenson (1999) p. 481, quoted, second; Oatley (1982) p. 50; Izard et al. (1984) p. 3; Dienstbier (1984) p. 486; Ellsworth (1994) pp. 24f., with references; Cornelius (1996) p. 118.

36. Levenson (1999) pp. 485f., emotions bring to an action-focus or "orchestrate" a variety of "response tendencies;" Leventhal (1982) p. 124, on variations in fear-level not registered in behavior; and Brehm and Self (1989) pp. 112, 116, 124 (female collaborators).

37. Russell (1980), resumed with discussion in idem (1989); similar differentia proposed by Plutchik (1989) p. 7, i.e. "intensity (e.g., fear vs. panic),... similarity (shame and guilt are more similar than love and disgust)...and polarity (joy is the opposite of sadness)."

38. Ortony (1988) p. 9 and Leventhal (1982) p. 122; Plutchik (1989) pp. 2f.

39. Damasio (1994) p. 143, on "background feelings" like depression; "a crucial distinction between emotion and moods," Forgas (2001) p. 15; but Oatley (1982) p. 23 ranks "moods" as "emotions", though usually weak ones — cf. also Thoits (1989) p. 318 — and Oakley (1992) p. 7 ranks "psychic feelings" without somatic change as a class of "emotions".

40. On social judgments, Branscombe and Cohen (1991) p. 146, Forgas (1991) p. 3, Loewenstein et al. (2001) p. 268, and Bower and Forgas (2001) pp. 97ff.; on emotional markers, ibid.; and Zajonc (1980) p. 153, quoted.

41. Quoted is Agosta (1984) p. 51; empathy hardwired, as regularly inferred from the behavior of tiny infants, but see esp. Vielmetter (2000) pp. 86f.; accuracy generally tested in face-to-face settings, or observers look at images, e.g. Ickes (1993) p. 588; but, with use of an agreed scale of intensity of various emotions, they may look at and evaluate written accounts of a moment, the evaluation checked against self-report by the writer, cf. Duan (2000) pp. 35f.

42. Russell (1989) p. 87; Levy (1984) p. 219; Williams (2000) p. 49, with references.

43. Rosaldo (1980) pp. 22, 27, 28-45 (*liget*), 47 (quoted); Heelas (1986) p. 240; and, on *ker*, Lutz (1988) p. 44.

44. Lutz (1988) pp. 158ff.; Wierzbicka (1994) pp. 137f.

45. In a volume to which C. Galvão-Sobrinho kindly directs my attention, see Lutz (1985) p. 38; Gerber (1985) p. 128.

46. Zajonc (1998) p. 611.

47. On *amae* and derivatives, Morsbach and Tyler (1986) pp. 289f., Kitayama and Markus (1994) p. 12, and Kitayama et al. (2000) pp. 110f.; on *oime*, Ellsworth (1994) p. 38.

48. Wandruska (1986) pp. 130, 133ff.; Ferry (1983) p. 11, reminding us that "feeling" didn't mean "emotion" till Shakespeare, and "emotion", not in its modern meaning till the 17th century; but to pursue the linguistics here would take me too far from my subject.

49. Students under Professor Quine have him to thank for their introduction to this remarkable work of the 1830s, A. B. Johnson (1947) p. 73, quoted, cf. pp. 49f., 54, 173.

50. Quoted in Wierzbicka (1994) p. 136.

51. Doubt that any emotions are basic, Solomon (1984) pp. 250ff.; outright denial, Averill (1986) p. 100; but only a wish to challenge "the current uni-

versalistic, and most biological, perspective on emotion," Kitayama and Markus (1994) p. 2; and a different terminology ("core" emotions) with discussion in G. M. White and Lutz (1986) p. 412.

52. Damasio (1994) pp. 149, 191 (and, on biological urges being not emotions, cf. Izard and Ackerman [2000] p. 259, aggression separable from anger); Van Bezooijen et al. (1983) p. 388; Solomon (1984) p. 242 with references; Cornelius (1996) pp. 32, 39f., 186f.; Reeve (1997) p. 273; J. H. Turner (2000) pp. 67, 70; Plutchik in Williams (2000) p. 43; and above, at n. 16.

53. G. M. White (2000) p. 35.

54. Solomon (1984) p. 240; on anger-stimuli, Kitayama and Markus (1994) p. 8; Ellsworth (1994) p. 33.

55. Ifaluk, Lutz (1985) p. 51; on Mead, cf. e.g. Gerber (1986) p. 122 or Sandall (2001) pp. 62ff.; below, n. 56; on Nepalese, Hardman (1981) pp. 161, 171f.; Solomon (1984) pp. 243f., quoted.

56. Stearns and Stearns (1985) p. 814, citing a study from 1970; Frijda (1986) p. 74; Ellsworth (1994) p. 29; Lazarus (1994) p. 167, doubts about the reliability of the finding that the Inouit experience no anger.

57. Thoits (1989) p. 335, agreeing with Stearns and Stearns (1986); above, on different anger-stimuli, n. 48.

58. Zajonc (1998) p. 604; but notice Konner (1993) p. 178, sceptical about some claims for angerless societies.

59. Middleton (1989) p. 189; above, n. 52.

60. Appadurai (1985) pp. 238ff., 243f., sincere; 236, quoted.

61. Berkowitz (2000) p. 3 on the English; Crespo (1986) p. 215, display-differences in regions of modern Spain and elsewhere; Cornelius (1996) pp. 37, 150; and ready crying either in grief or in joy amounts to proper conduct among the Andaman Islanders, certain South American and Mexican Indians..., cf. Harbsmeier (1987) pp. 91, 94f., 110ff.; Le Breton (1998) pp. 112f., 214-22 (bibliog.).

62. Leighton (1996) p. 208. I mention to disagree with Solomon (1990) who believes indignation is a hard-wired emotion in itself, along with several other emotions like compassion which are involved in and together *teach* rather than learn an idea of (in)justice.

63. Rosaldo (1984) p. 148; Turner (2000) p. 140.

64. Elster (1999) p. 49.

65. Middleton (1989) p. 187, quoted, and introduced, "Our emotional lives, ordered by culture...;" or Le Breton (1998) p. 96, "the emotions active in us and the way they take hold of us derive their force from implied collective norms," with some variation in the individual case, pp. 99, 109, 173.

66. Spiro (1999) pp. 7ff., 11f., seeing (p. 7) the "childhood socialization system" as crucial; below, chap. 3 at note 35, illustrative of pressure on children to conform in their feelings to their culture.

67. To suggest the breadth of agreement, notice, e.g., Izard et al. (1984) p. 8; Shweder (1984) p. 13; Spiro (1984) pp. 323f.; Averill (1986) p. 100; Sommers (1988) pp. 24, 30; Wallbott and Scherer (1989) p. 60; Lazarus (1994) p. 167, broad, very balanced statement; Kitayama and Niedenthal (1994) p. 6; Ellsworth (1994) pp. 24f., with references, in a very good summary statement;

historical sketch of positions in the 1970s-1980s, Rosenwein (1998) pp. 235ff. or Reddy (2001) pp. 35-42; Williams (2000) pp. 45f.; and Damasio (1994) p. 124, "adaptive supraregulations," with (p. 131) a distinction made by others also, between "primary" emotions of childhood and "secondary" of adulthood.

68. Cornelius (1996) p. 156, individual differences; Ortony et al. (1988) p. 3, uniform responses.

69. Ellgring and Rimé (1986) pp. 148 and Appendices 1-8, passim; Scherer (1988) pp. 12ff.; Walbott and Scherer (1989) p. 73; Ellsworth (1994) p. 29; Kitayama et al. (2000) pp. 93ff.

70. Women emotional: e.g., Lutz (1988) p. 54; Brody and Hall (2000) pp. 39, 344ff.; Brody (2000) p. 25; on crying, e.g., Fischer and Manstead (2000) p. 73.

71. Zajonc (1998) p. 620.

72. Zajonc (1998) p. 604.

73. D'Andrade (1981) p. 192; and very good pages in Hess and Kirouac (2000) pp. 369, 374f., showing how to reconcile theories of the role of biology/nature and culture/nurture.

74. Schieffelin (1985) pp. 172f., quoting and expanding on Gregory Bateson's words.

75. Fajans (1985) pp. 367 (quoted) and 376-92, passim.

76. Toqueville (1836-40) 1 p. xiii (and for sentiment's sake I quote from the first edition, a copy of which, once owned by Sir Robert Peel of London fame, was given to my grandfather in recognition of his quoting from the work in a sermon he preached).

77. Whissell (1989) pp. 114, 123f., 127, the rating list including terms of a shading close to the obviously emotive ones, e.g., *demanding, disinterested, indecisive, sociable*.

78. Izard and Ackerman (2000) p. 259.

79. Above, note 7.

NOTES
CHAPTER 3

1. Without quantification, debate must degenerate into a shouting match, or into appeal to authority, or despair dignified in Latin, *de gustibus non est disputandum*. The point must have been made ten thousand times, but as I never saw it in print I thought it worth the ink, long ago (republished, MacMullen [1990] p. 21).

2. "L'anthropologie historique" is the term found, e.g., in Burguière (1995), Chauvaud (1995) p. 11, Oexle (1999) p. 322, or highlighted in the school by Revel (1995) p. 38. Erbe (1984) and other essays in the same volume will suggest how anthropology is made use of in the *Annales*-school — no more, however, than psychology and sociology. On this last, see, e.g., Forster (1999) p. 187; or, in his work of several thousand pages, full of tables and graphs, the conclusion of Sorokin (1937-41) 1 p. 106, that "very Idealistic" (spiritual) Popes between AD 42 and 1930 constituted 0.8% of the list; 1 pp. 428f., quantification of sexiness in Western art, 10th-20th centuries; 2 p. 573, "democratic tendency" in Western law codes decreased from 5.3% to 1.2% between ca. 1790 and 1810; other calculations, passim; and Sorokin (1942) p. 44, pointing out his huge data base, e.g. over 100,000 works of Western art, analyzed under three chief categories.

3. Hexter (1972) pp. 485-96, comparing Dosse (1997) pp. 43, 46f., 102, 126f., graphs etc. to show proportions of "social" as opposed to "cultural" historiography, to the tenth of a per cent. An illustration of the methodological assumptions in the school is Mandrou (1997) p. 335, à propos the analysis of social divisions, saying nothing whatever of the inner person, but recommending a focus only on externals which can be counted: "tax lists and the riches of notarial minutes [which] will give to history the groups, and will give to the exploration of their conflicts, the true *measure*: a dimension which neither the descriptions by contemporaries nor those derived from politico-philosophic systems can provide *with the same precision*" (my italics). Further, S. Clark (1999) p. 238, and Le Roy Ladurie in Hunt (1999) p. 29, "history that is not quantifiable cannot claim to be scientific."

4. For "*mentalités*", "What's taken for granted" is my own equivalence, among a great many offered: *comportement, habitudes mentales,* Tudesq (1973) p. 207; "thought processes or sets of belief," Lloyd (1990) p. 1 (in a book that, despite having "Mentalities" in the title, offers nothing to my purpose); *sensibilità, strumentazione mentale, anima collettiva...,* Pitocco (1996) p. 64, remarking on the

vagueness of the term; the vagueness or ambiguity conceded by Bloch and Le Goff, cf. Mastrogregori (1996) p. 47, Lloyd (1990) p. 4, or Rauzduel (1999) p. 106; criticism and assessment in Burke (1999) passim, with adjoining essays in the same volume. To illustrate an *Annalistic* approach to research on collective "solidarités, sentiments et passions, comportements psycho-professionels," see Mandrou (1997) pp. 288ff., where the data recommended, e.g., social level of pupils in schools (graphed), are almost only such as can be quantified (exception made of religious *obiter dicta* in private correspondences, p. 295). He is not interested in the inner person of the past, nor again, in his earlier work, Mandrou (1976), exception perhaps to be made of a chapter on religiosity, pp. 188ff. Delumeau (1990) passim serves as another illustration, his texts offered as evidence showing delight (p. 10), despair (14), disgust (16), grief (118), fear (323), hatred (473), and countless incitements or condemnations of these and other emotions, but all, didactic and hortatory, i. e., not *revealing* of emotions; and certainly nothing on readers' reactions or the actions induced from them. Similarly, no mention of feelings in Burguière (1995) or elsewhere in the big volume where his essay is a chapter; none in the *Annalistes* generally, Rosenwein (2002) p. 822 n. 4 with bibliography. And to conclude this negative, notice Ricoeur (2000) pp. 739-42, in an essay on social history and its tides, memory, *mentalités*, narrative, and understanding of causation, but with no mention of affect.

5. Burguière (1995) pp. 174f., Febvre in 1928 proposing the term, especially for individuals in history; Bloch, more for groups and masses.

6. The assumption is explicit in Febvre (1973) p. 2, defending study of the "anonymous masses amenable to group psychology which will have to be founded on observation of the present-day masses available for study; the findings then can easily (at least we suppose so) be extended to take in the masses of the past." Cf. Dosse (1997) pp. 79f. Febvre nevertheless goes on (pp. 5f., 8f.) to stress the great differences to be found by any historian, as by anthropologists, in various people's ways of thinking.

7. Bloch (1961) p. 295, with more on "roving disposition," "very restless race of the Normans," "attraction of adventure;" cf. e.g. p. 73, "the emotional stability so characteristic of the feudal era," but "emotionalism" of "the 11th-12th centuries, when moral or social convention did not yet require well-bred people to repress their tears and their raptures. The despairs, the rages, the impulsive acts, the sudden revulsions of feeling present great difficulty to historians, who are instinctively disposed to reconstruct the past in terms of the rational. But the irrational is an important element in all history" — a perception offered in almost identical words in 1938 by Febvre (1973) p. 7, quoting Huizinga (1924), on whom Bloch also draws; cf. S. D. White (1998) p. 122; but neither French historian develops or pursues it. For further thoughts, not very well anchored, on the changing conventions in emotion-display, medieval up to modern European , and their various commentators since Huizinga, see Rosenwein (2002) pp. 827-34.

8. Taine (1905) p. xliii, cf. pp. xiif., "true history arises only when the historian begins to discern, across the interval of time, the living man, in action, endowed with feelings (*passions*), and equipped with his customs;" and con-

tinues, "while his eyes pass over the text, his soul and mind follow the unfold-ing, the changing sequence of emotions and concepts from which the text emerges; he makes out of it *la psychologie.*" Further, quoted, to Dumas, Taine (1902-07) 4 p. 57.

9. Taine (1887) pp. 45, 48ff., and passim.

10. Bloch (1949) p. 72; Mastrogregori (1996) p. 47, quoting a 1942 letter; and Rauzduel (1999) p. 20, Bloch above all a *Cliométriste.*

11. Quoted from a lecture of 1919, in Pitocco (1996) p. 58; cf. Burguière (1995) p. 174.

12. On Lefebvre, A. Soboul in Lefebvre (1963) pp. 4, 19; 406ff.; Salmon (1990) p. 44; Dosse (1997) pp. 23, 48; Rauzduel (1999) pp. 24f., 44; Frigoglitti (1972) passim, Lefebvre's articles and reviews in *Annales* almost annually, 1929-61; and Lefebvre (1973) pp. 11, 15, 17, 55, "fear" or anxiety explain actions; occasionally, hope or despair (pp. 38, 44); but no examination of oper-ative feelings nor more than the inferring of them from prevalent threats. Paret (1988) pp. 124f., remarks on the cool quality of Lefebvre's treatment, its near-total avoidance of psychological analysis, which must all (commendably, says Paret) be supplied by the reader.

13. Carlyle in 1837, near the beginning of Book V; Gueniffey (2000) p. 25, this whole latter work being almost devoid of affect, with a few exceptional lines at p. 65 remarking on "the intensity of political passions" (again, p. 228; ultimate analysis of "le moteur de la dynamique révolutionaire" in terms of *ideas,* p. 230, and of local personal rivalries, pp. 239, 245, with "prudence" dic-tating the conduct of the terrorists, pp. 264ff.). Similarly, cool handling of vio-lence and riots in the Fronde-time, Descimon and Jouhaud (1985) p. 31, where the only "émotions" are those meaning "émeutes", and demagoguery and manipulation, not passions, are the focus; and the documents of grievance for peasant revolts of the preceding century are used by Souriac (1985) pp. 279f. to show causes alleged, not strength of causative feelings.

14. Vovelle (1985) pp. 72f., 76-82, 112-116, 118; a page and a half (pp. 84f.) on savagery, including the "offal" quote from Marseilles ("fraichaille," my translation conjectural, since I find the word in none of the eight or ten multi-volume dictionaries I consulted).

15. Descimon and Jouhaud (1985) p. 31, "la triple image dévalorisante de l''émotion', de l''amas' et de la 'furie'."

16. Lerat (1989) pp. 41, 55, 57, 59, 118f., 131, 218; and his comments (pp. 44, 84, 104) which I go on to quote. It is another non-Annaliste who offers espe-cially interesting pages on the flow of "sensibility" into violence in the Revolution, Reddy (2001) pp. 177-99, ending, "The history of the Revolution cannot be understood without an adequate theory of emotions."

17. Above, notes 4, 8, 10, 12, 13. And yet the founders of the school had the imagination in the fullest measure to see and exploit the value of testimony about emotions, including the violent. I instance Bloch (1939-40) 2 p. 16, where a long troubador quotation introduces a chapter, "La vie noble," with exultation in "the great joy" of battle, and wonderful details of vibrant courage and butchery. Then, discussion of "structures" — and the way was lost.

18. Grassotti (1978) pp. 332, esp. 50f.; but denying the evidence so he may assume always "rational" displays of "the technology of power," S. D. White (1998) supposes royal wrath was only pretended (pp. 145-51); further, Rosenwein (2002) pp. 839ff..

19. Febvre (1973) pp. 5f.; quoted in S. D. White (1998) p. 127; Le Breton (1998) Chap. 4, esp. pp. 173f., on the theoretical plane.

20. Repression of violence, e.g., in Mandrou (1976) pp. 59f.; on dueling, Chartier (2000) pp. 31ff.; suppression not only of angry feelings but of one's thoughts of other sorts, in French court life, pp. 47ff.

21. *Rhet.* 1370b 12f., quoted in Elster (1999) p. 58.

22. Castan (1974) pp. 127, 184; distinction between "laughter that embraces all, and laughter that shuts out," in Clapier-Valladon (1991) pp. 265, 271. Notice, too, in Lundberg (1974) pp. 22f., that "no high level of affective development can be achieved with a low level of cognitive development," that is (as I understand what is not made explicit), the capacity for compassion may be limited according to customs of upbringing, varying by class; and the high level of development belongs to "high social position," i.e. more education and exposure to varieties of points of view. I have not seen this possibility explored by historians.

23. Contat (1980) p. 41, the author imagines himself as "Jérome" in the story who is (p. 64) aged 18, "of brown complexion" (and Contat prints his name as "called LeBrun"), and (p. 62) is looking back three years, i.e. to about age 15. His uncle and guardian is a curé (p. 42), for whose admonitions the lad is "roasted", *on tympanise* for a quarter-hour; notes, there, "la malice, naturelle aux jeunes gens;" Léveillé "our 'cut-up'," p. 51, master-mimic (pp. 52f.), who will repeat his best performances 20 times (p. 53).

24. After being encouraged to see public floggings, brandings, and the like, the boys of a little town in Massachusetts in the 1750s, "very differently from the calculations of their fathers..., would assemble in the rear of the school-house, and inflict upon each other an imitation of the punishments they had just witnessed," accompanied no doubt by as much laugh as shudder, cf. Tappan (1870) p. 27.

25. Seabury (1989) pp. 56 (early 'teens); quoted, pp. 67, 70; disgust at the immorality, coarseness, and targets for laughter of his co-workers, p. 79.

26. Mandrou (1997) p. 326 (a slight exaggeration), the unduly honored being, as Saint-Simon terms him abusively, "this banker;" Saint-Simon (1983-88) 1 p. 45, cf. p. 246, "the upward soaring of the royal bastards caused him [d'Elbeuf, "the compleat courtier"] infinite pain," and provoked a remarkably savage attack. Cf. some (very brief) recognition of the class antagonisms to be measured in Tudesq (1973) p. 207.

27. Taine (1887) p. 98, of 1789.

28. Godechot (1985) pp. 385f.; cf. ibid., p. 384, a curé of another small place accuses the local nobility of petty conceit, prickly insistence on signs of deference, etc., producing a situation that required a judicial inquiry; further, Chauvaud (1995) pp. 14-20, village-level passions vented in humiliations.

29. Rudd (1992) pp. 795-98; "best-seller status," p. 798.

30. Elias (1978) pp. xii, "affective life," 19f., Goethe.

31. For the vogue in a work by C. Ginzburg, another by N. Z. Davis, and Darnton (1985), often cited as a trio, see e.g. Revel (1996) p. 16, Loriga (1996) pp. 226f., M. Cottret in Mandrou (1997) p. 393, or Lepore (2001) p. 133. Darnton (1985), honoring *Annalysis* and subscribing to the historiography of *mentalités* (pp. 3, 257f.), repeats, "doesn't get" and insists on its "otherness", in describing the laughter of the cat-chase and executions (260ff.) — the term, one that anthropologists use, see e.g. Spiro (1999) p. 11, with good comments on it.

32. Recent mentions give access to a huge amount written on the market and influence of these works and their cousins: in Britain, Barker-Benfield (1992) pp. 142ff., 149; in America, Vovelle (1983) pp. 189f. and MacMullen (1997) pp. 35ff., 198f.; in Germany, Sauder (1983) pp. 10f.; in France, Vincent-Buffault (1991) pp. 6, 10ff., passim; *Héloïse*-letters, ibid. pp. 10f. and Darnton (1985) pp. 215-56, passim; 17th century precursors, Bayne (1983) pp. 26f. On the *comédie larmoyante* and Nivelle de la Chaussée, Lanson (1887) pp. 131f., 225, 230-34, passim; Baudot (1978) pp. 95f., 112ff.; *Dictionnaire des littératures de la langue française* (Paris 1994) 1 p. 529. Vovelle (1985) pp. 35ff. is able to count the publications, year by year, that he judges representative of the new style. C. Z. Stearns (1988) p. 41, takes 17th century "greef" to mean grief in the modern sense, sadness, and elsewhere seems to over-interpret her evidence.

33. In Hume's "Of the delicacy of taste and passion" (1742), he approves the study of beauty in all the arts, since they "give a certain elegance of sentiment... . The emotions which they excite are soft and tender... and produce an agreeable melancholy, which, of all dispositions of the mind, is the best suited to love and friendship," cf. Hume (1987) p. 7; further, Toulmin (1990) p. 151, quoting Hume on "the indispensability of feelings as springs of human action," Hume saying, "The Reason is, *and ought to be*, a slave of the passions."

34. I can instance only Baudot (1978) pp. 112f. and a little more of the 1780s in Vincent-Buffault (1991) Chap. 5; but I am no specialist in the matter. For interpretive ideas and references, further, see Reddy (2001) pp. 142, 155ff., with some attempt at empathetic reading, 166f.

35. Partington (1930) p. 273, a reminiscence of Lady Louisa Stuart, bluestocking friend of Sir Walter Scott; by contrast, the impatient, even furious, rejection of sensibility by two leaders of thought in England of the 1790s, cf. Rice (1980) p. 320 on Wilberforce and Coleridge. Lady Stuart's recollection is, incidentally, a good example of society's or convention's influence over the emotions people should show, or even what they feel, a phenomenon much discussed by Stearns and Stearns in their various writings, e.g. (1985) p. 813; but the two do not involve themselves in the effect of emotions on decisions, i. e. on the flow of change.

36. Quoted, Sauder (1983) p. 10.

37. Wenzel (1960) passim; Delumeau (1990) pp. 193, 229ff.; Harré (1986) p. 11.

38. Röcke (2000) pp. 101f., 112f. — not to mention Richard Burton.

39. Bernsen (1996) passim; in the United States, illustration in MacMullen (1997), including both enjoyment (p. 192) and derision (pp. 235, 503).

40. Among rural populations in France, Shorter (1975) pp. 39ff., 58ff.; Flandrin (1979) pp. 95-102, concluding, of overcrowding, "In this warm inti-

macy [of same-sex pairs or two married pairs] in bed, did there not originate, among the members of the peasant family, a relationship as vital and as worthy of our attention as the rituals connected with our bourgeois homes?" Stone (1977) esp. Chaps. 7f. for Britain is the most quoted, perhaps.

41. As an illustration, Boureau (1989) pp. 1494f. rightly criticizing Duby on an inference; Gillis (1988) p. 87, on challenges to the notion of Shorter and Stone "that love was rare before the eighteenth century" (an extraordinary view, to the extent it is actually proposed); and surely account must be taken of class differences in the past as they can certainly be found in the marital and sex relations of today's America, cf. Lundberg (1974) pp. 87f. Non-*Annaliste* discussions of erotic love diachronically indeed exist, e.g. Luhmann (1986) pp. 109-25, with copious use of contemporary fiction in English.

42. By exception, a single line in Tudesq (1973) p. 205; surprisingly absent, e.g., Mandrou (1997) pp. 288f. and passim.

43. Lyon (1999) pp. 202-04, 209.

44. *Sclérose*, Bloch (1957) pp. 70, 71, 161; the aged at fault, pp. 128, 164, and passim; and Bloch's "rage" at their "astonishing resistance, *imperméabilité*, to the lessons of experience," p. 69.

45. E. g., *paresse*, Bloch (1957) p. 189; *coeur*, e.g., pp. 24, 164, 167, 182, 210; *âme*, 164, 211; *la mémoire affective*, p. 160; the effect of feelings on group functioning, e.g., pp. 108f., 110f., or 124ff., *orgueil de caste*; of course also fear, pp. 170, 172f., 176; national *élan* the key, pp. 174, 178; *respect du devoir professionnel, conscience professionnelle*, pp. 58 and 124; decisions to be made by one's emotion, what one thrills to, *vibrer*, p. 210, cf. 23f.

46. Bloch (1957) pp. 174, 176 (need of implacable *héroisme de la patrie en danger*), 178 (sense of fraternity spurs war-efforts), and, 179, the *noblesse* of spirit that can be called on; and, quoted, pp. 184, 179, 210, 220, and 182.

47. Veyne (1971), described by Revel (1995) p. 299 as "an impetuous... case against the scientific credo of the day's historians" — "scientism" , whereas in truth historiography "is at best a literary genre." Veyne's admiration for Bloch's style as well as method is clear, passim, e. g. at pp. 239f., where Bloch is quoted undertaking to read the mind of "le petit paysan," in the abstract or in aggregate, through what may be called a very highly informed intuition.

48. Trans. by B. Pearce, Veyne (1992) p. 381, an illustration of the author's approach of which I made use before (in "The Roman Empire," contributed to *Ancient History: Recent Work and New Directions*, Claremont 1997). Veyne (1971) often reverts to euergetism (e.g. pp. 54f., 124ff., 156, 243f., and elsewhere), which is the theme of his 1976 work, and the Column appears again in Veyne (1971) p. 299; but he is equally ready to say what went on, for example, in the minds of soldiers in WWI (p. 233).

49. "Bon sens" or "jugement", Veyne (1971) pp. 131, 134, 215; reliance on the commonalities in human nature, p. 229; and compare the same in Bloch (1957) passim.

50. Veyne (1971) p. 125.

51. Veyne (1976) contains some dozens of references to people's feelings, in explanation of their acts; but only these, in a very big book. As illustrative, *amour=caritas*, pp. 48, 56; *devoir*, p. 186; *patriotisme*=love of one's home place,

pp. 211, 239f., 342 (the key indication only in a note, "sweetest home town"); *renommé, désire d'être honoré*, pp. 214, 234; shame, but again, the key only in a note, p. 424; and competition with others or with one's ancestors, pp. 197, 195, 238, 274.

52. MacMullen (1990) pp. 20f. The passage is referred to by Veyne (1976) p. 232, though he chose to make little use of it.

53. Among those who write of Europe, Darnton's is one of the names most likely to be brought forward as of the French school; among American historians of America, perhaps Demos (1982; 1986). In his latter volume Demos collects lectures and essays from the 1970s. He acknowledges a particular debt to the teachings of Erik Erikson (1986, p. xii).

54. Braudel (1973), e.g. on the grand visions of Pius V, or (2 p. 910) on the Neopolitan Franciscans joining against the infidel in Africa *con grande animo di far paura a quei cani*; but very little of this sort of thing.

55. Davis (1968) p. 705 — an admirer of Erik Erikson (p. 704); but he does not see his own work as concerned with the affective in history.

56. Cf. Wendell Phillips' assessment, "The gun fired at Lovejoy was like that of Sumter — it scattered a world of dreams," quoted in Dillon (1961) p. 178, with Bartlett (1965) p. 106; or M. Rugoff quoted in Simon (1994) p. 154, "the shots fired in Alton on November 7, 1837, would be... the beginning of the Civil War."

57. All of these men and women have been the subject of at least one Life, but what distinguishes them from others so honored who could be easily named (Lundy, Elizur Wright, Beriah Green, George Bourne, Birney, Orange Scott...) is the particular volume of evidence that I wish to emphasize.

58. References to the *Edinburgh Review*, e. g. Garrison (1932) p. 19, or in the letters of Lucretia Mott, cf. Palmer (2002) p. 65 (1819); on Brougham, D. B. Davis in Bender (1992) pp. 79f.; Hawes (1957) pp. 34ff., 44ff., 69 ("fierce hatred of cruelty"); Barnes and Dumond (1934) 2 p. 560, report from an English abolitionist on Brougham's doings, to an American abolitionist.

59. The passage (of 1830) quoted by Garrison in a letter to a Boston paper of that year, and again in a speech of 1863, see Garrison and Garrison (1885-89) 1 pp. 211, 407; again, Garrison (1832) p. 72; also Barnes (1933) p. 32.

60. Anstey (1980) pp. 35f. ("religious dynamism"); Engerman and Eltis (1980) p. 283; Rice (1980) pp. 319, 322-29 passim; and Barnes (1933) pp. 32ff., 44; recall of Wilberforce in a public letter, *Debate* (1834) p. 16; and Garrison's debt to the British model evident in references, Garrison (1832) pp. 19, 52, 57.

61. Heyrick (1838) p. 31; Dumond (1961) pp. 138ff. on the pamphlet.

62. Barnes and Dumond (1934) 2 p. 623, Weld to Thome in April 1838.

63. Barnes and Dumond (1934) 2 p. 612.

64. Garrison and Garrison (1885-89) 1 pp. 95, estimating AASs at about 130 in 1828; p. 110, the 1828 petition; Barnes (1933) pp. 109-45, passim (122ff. on Adams); Dumond (1961) pp. 236ff., 242-48 (p. 245, the figure of 130,000); Jeffrey (1998) p. 53.

65. Barnes (1933) pp. 141ff.; Van Brockhoven (1994) pp. 180f., the petition quoted by "the Ladies of Massachusetts against slavery in the District of

Columbia," of 1838, matching with its sex-specific appeal another, from the
Mass. Emancipation Society of 1841, "to remember the woes... of the
wretched slave mother as she drags her weary, lacerated limbs to the field after
a sleepless night, with her sick and dying babe" (p. 94 n. 40); and still a third
sex-specific appeal in an 1836 female antislavery society's appeal on behalf of
"captive wives and mothers, sisters and daughters," etc., in Swerdlow (1994)
p. 38; on women's antislavery societies, Jeffrey (1998) pp. 53f.; ibid., p. 88, two
million women had signed abolitionist petitions; and Carwardine (1993)
p. 22.
66. Barnes (1933) pp. 100, 146, 264; Simon (1994) p. 155; precursors, e. g.
Quaker abolitionist propaganda, Needles (1848) p. 30; the quantity of publication an alarming fact to the anti-abolitionists, e.g. *South Vindicated* (1836)
pp. 195f.; *Human Rights* used as a voice on Lovejoy, Dillon (1966) p. 177; republication in neutral media, e.g. Dumond (1939) p. 32; local discussion, e. g.
Jeffrey (1998) pp. 76f.; and private correspondence gives space to abolitionist
literature, e.g. Palmer (2002) pp. 21, 29 (Mott, in 1834).
67. Tappan (1870) and Barnes (1933), passim; Dumond (1961) pp. 286ff.;
Weld (1839) p. 47.
68. Tappan (1870) pp. 79f.; Barnes (1933) p. 20, headaches.
69. Barnes (1933) p. 43, quoted; Garrison (1832) p. 9.
70. The remark quoted in a letter of Grace Williams to Maria Chapman, July
23, 1839, MS A.9.2.12.1, courtesy of the Boston Public Library.
71. Zinn (1965) p. 431, in an essay worth reading a second time, or a third;
and anticipated — that the harsh tone was a necessity, and justified — by
Lucretia Mott in 1839, cf. Palmer (2002) p. 51, "That there may have been, in
some instances, an intemperate zeal exhibited, we admit; — but when we
consider how just is the indignation kindled in the breast of every friend of
humanity, who contemplates American Slavery, with all its concomitant enor-
mities, and atrocities, our surprise is, that Combativeness and Destructiveness
should be so quiescent." For the *Liberator's* enemies, charges that abolitionists
were "fanatics" and "incendiaries" and such-like, weakening their own cause,
etc., see e. g. Barnes (1933) pp. 57ff., 91, and 159ff. (hostile); deploring of ran-
corous accusations by the Lane Seminary trustees in 1834, Henry (1973) p.
196; "fanatical persons... inflammatory publications," in Philip Hones' view
of 1835, Nevins (1927) 1 pp. 170f.; abolitionists "incendiaries," *South
Vindicated* (1836) p. xvii; Catherine Beecher (1937) pp. 14-40, passim, pre-
Liberator, Garrison and Garrison (1885-89) 1 p. 231; James Russell Lowell in
his earlier years (1838, "fanatics"), L. D. Turner (1929) p. 55; and in mid-
century, Wendell Phillips (1863) pp. 107ff.
72. Not to suggest there was a blank between 1775 and 1833. An instance of
something more is George Bourne's *The Book and Slavery Irreconcilable* (1816),
which, after 15 years of neglect, had the deepest effect on Angelina Grimké
as on Garrison, cf. Christie and Dumond (1969) pp. v, 8, 77, 86f.; but there
was no focus on "facts". The quotation in my text comes from the preface to
Bourne's work by Joshua Coffin for the Rhode Island AAS, who adds the
further words also quoted, of Samuel Mills, cf. Rankin (1833) pp. vf., with
Rankin's examples at, e.g., pp. 17-21, 38f.

73. Child (1835) p. 1, No. 1, Preface, quoted; pp. 2ff., picturing of a scene and person of suffering, with verbatim conversation to vivify it all; 3f., young woman flogged to death; pp. 5f., pretty female slave sold to a young man, "I must have that girl!"; No. 2, pp. 1f., separation of families; pp. 3f., desperation of a mother losing her children; etc. Further, heavily documented, anecdotal descriptions in Child (1836) pp. 11-16 (slave trade) and 16-27, horror stories; Rankin (1833) pp. 146f.; praised by Mott in 1834, cf. Palmer (2002) p. 21; and Karcher (1986) pp. 324f. and (1994) pp. 231f.

74. Garrison and Garrison (1885-1889) 1 p. 163; likewise, facts in the Free-will Baptist *Morning Star* from 1834, Marks (1846) pp. 337f.; and scattered in various antislavery periodicals as they were offered, e. g., in *The Genius of Emancipation* of March 1834 p. 40; and items from southern newspapers cited and enlivened by illustrations to show various horrors of slavery by *The Antislavery Almanac*, e. g., of 1840, Dumond (1961) pp. 14f.

75. Weld (1839); Stowe (1853) pp. 16, 40, 42, 44-46, 89, all citing Weld; Barnes (1833) pp. 33 (early fact-gathering), 276 (sales figures); Dumond (1939) p. 42; Meltzer et al. (1982) p. 97.

76. Barnes (1933) pp. 139, 263; Dumond (1938) 1 pp. 138ff. (to Birney in 1834, ending, "I am more and more convinced of the great importance of our procuring fresh facts, well authenticated"), 307, 472; Weld (1839) pp. 24 and 54f. (A. Grimké), and passim.

77. Barnes (1933) p. 62 and passim; Dumond (1939) p. 40; Keller (1942) pp. 44-48; W. R. Cross (1950) passim, esp. pp. 11ff.; Dillon (1961) pp. 25f.; Pease (1969) p. 16; Boles (1976) pp. 23-28; McKivigan (1984) pp. 19ff., 40 (like Barnes, seeing the spoken word as key, not the printed); and Goodheart (1990) p. 9.

78. Marks (1846) pp. 19, 21; Birney (1885) pp. 20f., 30; Barnes and Dumond (1934) 1 p. 14.

79. Woolsey Family Papers, Yale Manuscripts and Archives, ASL Leonard Bacon to Theodore Dwight Woolsey 4/9/1822; Woolsey to Bacon, 8/13/1821, with many similar passages, e. g., to Twining, 11/16/1821, or to Bacon, 12/8/1821, 4/3/1823; similarly, Elizur Wright to Bacon in 1837, Goodheart (1990) p. 37; and for an early instance of the anguished conversa-tion with one's self, cf. Lyman Beecher at Yale (1795-96), B. Cross (1961) 1 pp. 28f.

80. Ibid., Alexander Twining to Weld, 7/20/1821; cf. Keller (1942) p. 46, describing Yale's revival of 1820, "much emotion..., many tears..., outbreak-ing of the agony of the mind... in the expressive look and the half-stifled sigh."

81. On the Second Great Awakening, see such accounts as Gillespie (1985) p. 20; Barkum (1986) p. 23; and above, n. 73.

82. On tracts of 1825-1840, see L. Thompson (1941) pp. 82ff., 91; W. R. Cross (1950) pp. 25f., 108; Dumond (1961) p. 153; Wiebe (1984) p. 231; and Hatch (1989) pp. 144f.

83. Besides Arthur Tappan, leader in the temperance movement before he shifted his energies to abolition, notice as typical his friend William Woolsey, rich and active in organizations like the Bible Society, cf. MacMullen (2001)

pp. 136f., 140, or a third instance of the type, president of the Tract Society, Thompson (1941) p. 83; Brown (1963) p. 59; Speicher (2000) p.105, dislike of "this animal excitement" required, e. g., "among the ignorant coloured people of our city;" and Keller (1942) pp. 46-52, 198ff., on the more restrained Connecticut style.

84. Speicher (2000) pp. 15, 21, on Sarah in 1819 and Angelina in 1824.

85. B. Cross (1961) 1 p. 51.

86. On doctrine's place in the "New School," see Fraser (1985) pp. 50, 56, 95; Marsden (1970) pp. 20, 98; McKivigan (1984) p. 19; Greven (1977) p. 65, of 17th to early 19th-century evangelicals, "The doctrines of original sin and of innate depravity were grounded in the feelings had toward their inner selves;" but, Fraser (1985) p. 51, Beecher did not aim at "emotional wrenching" as Finney did; and on the requirement of active beneficence (always called "benevolence"), see e.g. Jeffrey (1998) p. 17 and 38f., Carwardine (1993) pp. 22, 38f., 48, or Goodheart (1990) p. 9.

87. Fraser (1985) pp. xxii ("thunder", 1805) and 52.

88. Moore (1989) p. 229, quoting an observer of 1842, and Beecher himself in his *Lectures on Revivals of Religion* (1835).

89. From the earliest decade of the Great Awakening, highly emotional scenes, e.g., in Butler (1990) p. 240 (Benjamin Abbot, itinerant Methodist), called "sacred theater" in England; later, W. R. Cross (1950) pp. 9-12, 27, and Boles (1976) pp. 23-28 (Kentucky); quoted, Bradley (1819) pp. viff., 23, 39f.; and 52, 114, 131, 173, and 261; and Dillon (1961) pp. 25f. *Narrative* (1826) p. 20, tears; p. 10, "the spirit of the Lord appeared to come down suddenly in the midst of us..., great distress" (though more often "stillness" and "solemnity").

90. Sprague (1832) pp. 43f., 123, 176f.; Marks (1846) pp. 37f., 43, 81, 261, 311.

91. *Narrative* (1826) p. 44; Barnes and Dumond (1934) p. xxi; Barnes (1933) pp. 10 (quoted) and 13; and Hatch (1989) pp. 196f.

92. Stanton (1886) p. 26.

93. Finney (1835) pp. 10, in the first four pages of his first lecture using the word "excitement" 25 times; further, pp. 16, 30, 34, 96; and Johnson (1978) pp. 97ff.

94. Dumond (1961) p. 153; Benjamin Lundy's proposal of 1816, cf. Dillon (1966) p. 18.

95. Sprague (1832) p. 261; cf. Lundy (1847) p. 22, "the question, 'What can I do?' was the continual response to the impulses of my heart," in 1824; or Dumond (1938) 1 p. 10, Birney's definition of a good reform agent, "His commanding motive must be, *to do good because it is the will of God.*"

96. In the *Emancipator* of July 1836, cf. Barnes (1933) p. 79.

97. Barnes (1933) pp. 13f., 38f.; Henry (1973) pp. 191ff. on Beecher's views of Afro-Americans and abolition.

98. *Debate* (1834) pp. 3ff.; Barnes (1833) Chap. VI, with a quotation from p. 67; Henry (1973) pp. 192f., 196ff.

99. Barnes and Dumond (1934) 1 pp. 143, 146.

100. Barnes and Dumond (1934) 1 p. 244.

101. Barnes (1933) pp. 104f., 196 (Lovejoy's brother joins the Seventy); Dumond (1961) pp. 184ff.; McKivigan (1984) p. 40; on James Miller McKim as one of the Seventy, see Brown (1963) p. 59 and Rose (1965) p. 179; on another, Stowe, cf. Dumond (1939) p. 35; and on a third, Orange Scott, see Mathews (1965) pp. 76f., most effective: "When he spoke, his audience wept with him for the martyred Elijah Lovejoy."

102. Simon (1994) p. 96; and the indication in a note to Lundy (1847) p. 22, that Lundy's on antislavery in 1824 was probably the first public lecture on the subject.

103. Speicher (2000) p. 29

104. Barnes and Dumond (1934) 2 p. 574.

105. Birney (1885) p. 180; the clergy shocked, p. 185; agonizing over the proprieties, Bogin and Yellin (1994) p. 10; ridicule of women's presumption in reasoning like men, Swerdlow (1994) p. 37; and a woman ridiculing another (Maria Chapman) for feeling "she had a mission. Now, if I felt so, I should think I ought to be sent to Bedlam," cf. Meltzer et al. (1982) p. 5.

106. Dumond (1938) 1 p. 478 (and, 479ff., Birney tried to get some satisfaction from the minister, in vain); Bacon's "vitriolic" style in print, too, Karcher (1994) p. 191.

107. Pease (1969) pp. 1f., 26; Wigham (1863) pp. 9ff.; Phillips (1863) p. 220 (some less reliable versions identify the woman as the president, Maria Chapman); mob attacks on the 1838 Anti-Slavery Convention of Women in Philadelphia and the burning of their hall, Bogin and Yellin (1994) p. 16 — not to mention the 1835 jailing and property destruction in New Hampshire to punish Prudence Crandall, cf. Garrison and Garrison (1885-1889) 1 p. 321, Wolf (1952) pp. 50-54, or Karcher (1994) p. 202.

108. Above, note 65; Cross (1950) pp. 29, 38; Jeffrey (1998) pp. 76f., 86ff.; Swerdlow (1994) p. 31. Perhaps the most useful friends women had were Weld, first, then Garrison.

109. Jeffrey (1998) pp. 49f., on the count in the *Liberator, Emancipator,* and *Philanthropist*; Stanton (1886) p. 32 and Dumond (1961) pp. 188f.; ibid., Chap. 26, "Lynch Law," covering the late 1820s on; and Lewis Tappan's house broken into by a mob and ransacked — this, in 1834, cf. Barnes and Dumond (1961) 1 pp. 153f.

110. Simon (1994) p. 72 — all, pre-1837.

111. E. g., Barnes and Dumond (1934) 1 pp. 260, 320 (1836); W. R. Cross (1950) p. 222 on Weld's reputation in 1836; also Dumond (1939) pp. 57ff. on Weld's and Stanton's hundreds of encounters with violence; and Benjamin Lundy brutally beaten in 1827 for published views on slave-traders, Garrison and Garrison (1885-1889) 1 p. 91; Samuel May's lecturing mobbed in Massachusetts, ibid. p. 517; general prevalence of mob action, not always abolition-related, Walters (1978) p. 9.

112. Barnes and Dumond (1934) 1 p. 121, or again, Wright in 1836, 1 p. 270; Stanton's style, Marks (1846) p. 377; and "electric" to describe revivalist moods, Corrigan (2002) p. 227, though of a period somewhat later.

113. Jeffrey (1998) p. 29, New Hampshire in 1833.

114. Garrison and Garrison (1885-1889) 1 pp. 285f., 1832, quoted; Barnes

and Dumond (1934) 1 p. 296, Weld recruits the Seventy with an invitation
that they "yield up their bodies to buffetings;" martyr-thoughts in Angelina
Grimké's diary, Speicher (2000) p. 25, and in Phillips' thoughts of 1841,
Bartlett (1965) p. 104; and considerable fuzzy discussion in Tomkins (1965)
pp. 294ff.
115. Child's complaints of apathy, Meltzer et al. (1982) pp. 90, 173, and elsewhere; or Jeffrey (1998) p. 66; Ralph R. Gurley, ardent for colonization in the
early 1830s, in Dumond (1938) 1 p. 110, leading into his statement by saying,
"The Northern Abolitionists... say slavery never will be abolished in the
Country without a great sensation," i. e., a great surge of feeling; the statement by a character in the drama of 1845, Little (1845) p. 40, "The
respectable, influential part of the Church at the North is with us [Southern
slaveholders];" the declaration of the Old School Presbyterians, "We are a
convention met about doctrine and order — the very quintessence of
Presbyterianism," in Marsden (1970) p. 96 (1836); and a summary statement,
Dumond (1939) p. 12, on "tranquillity..., the paralysis of public morality."
116. Dumond (1938) 1 p. 202 (1835).
117. In NewYork, e. g., MacMullen (1997) pp. 74, 292, 517 (the educated of
the 1820s); Nevins (1927) 2 p. 776, crowds celebrate a court verdict, "such a
mob of all colours, from dirty white to shining blue..., such raising of greasy
hats," in Philip Hone's diary (1846); in Boston and regarding Bacon, H. Davis
(1998) p. 31; and generally, Dumond (1939) pp. 14, 18f.
118. Rankin (1833) pp. 17-21; Stowe (1853) p. 126.
119. Punishment of American slaves was routinely left to "the workhouse,"
cf. Weld (1839) pp. 24, 54f.; Stowe (1853) pp. 89 (Charleston) and 107f.,
110f., 124 (parallels in Roman law), and cruelty thinkable because "the negro
is considered an *inferior animal*" — the same view often expressed, e. g., at
Goodheart (1990) p. 52. Compare, what Stowe could not have known and
what has been barely noticed and never translated, the very interesting documents from Roman Italy, *Année épigraphique* 1971, pp. 37ff., (esp. 39), and De
Martino (1975) p. 213 (Hinard [1995] adds nothing relevant).
120. Child (1836) p. 28 and Weld (1839) pp. 123f.; cf. Alypius in St.
Augustine's *Confessions* and other instances in MacMullen (1990) p. 331; and
the case of a Southerner, Angelina Grimké, whose feelings awoke, seeing a
young woman being dragged into the workhouse for a flogging, Speicher
(2000) p. 25 (diary of 1829, aet. 24).
121. Marks (1846) p. 341, the date, 1835 recalling a visit of about 1832.
122. Dillon (1966) pp. 6f., quoting Lundy of a scene in 1809.
123. Stewart (1999) pp. 173f., with further scenes that horrified Giddings, as
he wrote home to his wife; and for a perfect match, slave auction,
Northerner's reaction, dialogue, and all, see the story in *The Genius* of
Universal Emancipation for Dec. 25, 1829, p. 122.
124. Yellin (1972) pp. 90f. on the author of *Archy Moore* (1936), Richard
Hildreth, in the early 1830s; Dumond (1961) pp. 160f. or Henry (1973) p.
192, Weld and fellows in the black community at Cincinnati in 1833, with
Weld reporting in one letter (1834), "After spending three or four hours
[speaking with families], and getting facts, I was forced to stop from sheer

heart-ache and agony," cf. Barnes and Dumond (1934) 1 p. 135; and Davis (1998) p. 31 on Leonard Bacon in Boston. Abzug (1980) p. 83 quotes only to dismiss Weld's saying he had, in his early lecturing, "seen slavery at home [in the South], and become a radical abolitionist."
125. First, in reading the evidence, one must know what words at the time meant (not always what they mean today, e.g. *interest, intercourse, friend*...), lest one misread it, cf. e.g., Juster (1989) passim or, in 17th century French, Salmon (1990) p. 126. Then, walking past usable evidence, one may conclude that analysis is impossible, as does Wyatt-Brown (1980) pp. 184ff., 188, for "a group as conventional as abolitionists" ("conventional"!). Or one may conclude there is no box in which all abolitionists seem to fit (I agree, but the search must reach beyond socioeconomic or political categories), cf. Pease and Pease (1972) pp. 21f., with bibliography; further bibliography on "emotionology" and psychohistory, Corrigan (2002) pp. 351-55 with notes.
126. Barnes and Dumond (1934) 1 p. 273, recalled in 1836.
127. Barnes and Dumond (1934) 2 p. 560 (1838).
128. Stanton (1886) p. 8 (aet. 80).
129. Marks (1846) pp. 337f. (1835), the editor, as he early explains, using David Marks' exact or almost exact words.
130. Christie and Dumond (1969) p. 8, Grimké reading a certain tract; Matlack (1848) pp. 32f. and Mathews (1965) p. 72, Orange Scott listening and reading over the course of many months (1833); Palmer (2002) pp. 21f. and Rose (1965) pp. 178f., on McKim; the narrator of an experience in *The Genius of Universal Emancipation* of March 1834, on learning of slaves defrauded of emancipation, whereupon "What I have thought and felt, I can never tell to a man — Whether I shall ever sleep again, seems more that I can predict."
131. Karcher (1994) pp. 96f., 175, Child; Bartlett (1965) p. 104, Phillips; L. D. Turner (1929) p. 62, James Russell Lowell.
132. Garrison and Garrison (1885-1889) 1 p. 289 (1832, Fessenden) and 214 (1830, May).
133. Dwelling on mental images of slavery, e.g., Grace Williams to Maria Chapman, in Jeffrey (1998) p. 36; advocacy must be emotional, above at notes 69 (Mills quoted), 92 (Weld), or 110f. (Gurley and Birney); need for "deep personal interest," among women, declared by the Brooklyn (CT) Female ASS (1834), Jeffrey (1998) pp. 39ff., cf. need for "warm hearts," p. 69; above, n. 65, women's empathetic identification; and quotations that follow from Samuel Mills, in Rankin (1833) pp. 20f., from Weld (1839) p. 7, and from Stewart (1992) p. 42, quoting Garrison.
134. Dialogue, above, n. 121 and Child (1835) No. 1 pp. 2f.; illustrations in an early work of 1807, Dumond (1961) pp. 45 and 82; pp. 58, 65, 69, and passim, of the late 1830s-1840; in Garrison's publications, cf. Garrison and Garrison (1885-1889) 1 pp. 163, 231ff., and 304, and in antislavery tracts (and emblematic figurines for sale) objected to by Southerners, *South Vindicated* (1836) p. 197.
135. Better-known examples: Little (1845) passim; Child's *Anti-Slavery Catechism* (1836), cf. Karcher (1994) p. 261; Yellin (1972) pp. 87-120, on Hildreth's *Archy Moore*.

136. Boyer (1973) pp. 313f., and 597f. on the conversion of many at the Lovejoy-news, and on the sources for the meeting, which all authorities count as reliable, give or take a trifle in wording.

137. Above, at n. 66.

138. Instances of converts to the cause at the news or sight of violence: Barnes and Dumond (1934) 1 pp. 253, Utica (NY) in 1835; pp. 260f. and 319, Ohio in 1836; Wyman (1902-1903) p. 547, Concord (NH) in 1842.

139. Tappan (1970) p. 287.

140. Above, nn. 41f.; using fiction, exemplary, Rice (1980) on British views of antislavery; also on other matters than slavery, MacMullen (2001) pp. 6ff. and elsewhere. But I have not happened on more apposite references.

NOTES
Chapter 4

1. Bender (1992) p. 4; and the rejection of the "trap of reductionism and counter-reductionism" by Davis, p. 176, and of "reductionist" treatments by one of the contributing scholars, Thomas Haskell, pp.113, 115, 116, 117, 118 (three times).... The essay-collection contains much bibliography, to which one might add Engerman and Eltis (1980) pp. 272f.

2. Bender (1992) pp. 113, Davis quoted by Haskell; pp. 179 (sensibility, seen as operating mostly on women) and 306, adding, that individual motivation is "a shadowy subject even for the most insightful biographers blessed with the most revealing evidence;" and pp. 70f., on "the paramount question." But compare Dumond (1939) p. 25, "Would that the historian might somehow recover the emotions which surge through men's hearts and alter civilization!" and the comment of A. Schlesinger in the 1959 reprint, p. v., that "the revisionist historians... by refusing to consider slavery a moral issue,... denied themselves the ability to understand the emotions... which *forced* the American Union to its moment of truth" (my italics); and Zinn (1965) p. 426, that "abolitionists were all, in varying degrees, emotional in their response to situations and in the stimuli they projected into the atmosphere. What *is* arguable is the notion that this 'emotionalism' is to be deplored. The intellectual is taken aback by emotional display. It appears to him an attack on that which he most reveres — reason. One of his favorite terms of praise is 'dispassionate'" (as "cool" to Syme, above, Chap. 1).

3. Haskell, in Bender (1992) p. 111.

4. Flaubert (1926) p. 395, cf. (1927) p. 69; on Dickens, the most often cited M. Dickens (1897) pp. 49f., also 54f., and E. Johnson (1952) p. 466 or Ackroyd (1990) p. 564, cf. 318f.; and Tolstoy (1957) pp. 797ff., 1230ff. (Book III i 21; Book IV iii 4-11) — the author in his wife's words "writing, wrought up, the tears starting to his eyes and his heart swelling," p. viii; above, chap. 1 at note 56.

5. Veyne (1971) p. 298, "the Roman emperor or the king of France was wrapped in a charismatic aura... because he was the ruler — because the people's love for the ruler is a feeling that belongs to every time, and because all authority seems more than human."

6. Tolstoy (1957) pp. 1056ff. (Book IV iii 25). There has been much written on the scene and Tolstoy's sources. Ségur (1883) pp. 217f. gives an apologist's version of Rostopchin's part; but there was much more, newspapers and such,

offered to Tolstoy — who preferred an eye-witness he talked with. See the very interesting record of Peterson (1978) 1 pp. 125f., made accessible to me thanks to the kindness of Robert L. Jackson.

BIBLIOGRAPHY

Abzug, R. H., *Passionate Liberator. Theodore Dwight Weld and the Dilemma of Reform*, New York 1980

Ackroyd, P., *Dickens*, London 1990

Adolphs, R., and A. R. Damasio, "The interaction of affect and cognition: a neurobiological perspective," *Handbook of Affect and Social Cognition*, ed. J. P. Forgas, Mahwah (NJ) 2001, pp. 27-49

Agnes, L., *Opere di Cornelio Nepote*, Torino 1977

Agosta, L., "Empathy and intersubjectivity," *Empathy*, eds. J. Lichtenberg et al., Hillsdale (NJ) 1984, 1. pp. 43-61

Alföldy, G., *Sir Ronald Syme, 'Die römische Revolution' und die deutsche Althistorie*, Heidelberg 1983

Alloy, L. B., and L. Y. Abramson, "Judgment of contingency in depressed and nondepressed students: sadder but wiser?" *Journal of Experimental Psychology: General* 108 (1979) pp. 441-85

Anstey, R., "The pattern of British abolitionism in the eighteenth and nineteenth centuries," *Anti-Slavery, Religion, and Reform. Essays in Memory of Roger Anstey*, eds. C. Bolt and S. Drescher, Folkestone (UK) 1980, pp. 19-42

Appadurai, S., "Gratitude as a social mode in S. India," *Ethos* 13 (1985) pp. 236-45

Averill, J. R., "The acquisition of emotions during adulthood," *The Social Construction of Emotions*, ed. R. Harré, Oxford 1986, pp. 98-118

Averill, J. R., "In the eyes of the beholder," *The Nature of Emotion. Fundamental Questions*, eds. P. Ekman and R. J. Davidson, New York 1994, pp. 7-14

Ayto, J., *The Oxford Dictionary of Slang*, Oxford 1998

Bardon, H., *La littérature latine inconnue*, 2 vols., Paris 1952

Barker-Benfield, G. J., *The Culture of Sensibility. Sex and Society in Eighteenth-Century Britain*, Chicago 1992

Barkum, M., *Crucible of the Millennium. The Burned-Over District of New York in the 1840s*, Syracuse 1986

Barnes, G. H., *The Antislavery Impulse 1830-1844*, New York 1933

Barnes, G. H., and D. L. Dumond, *Letters of Theodore Dwight Weld, Angelina Grimké Weld and Sarah Grimké, 1822-1844*, 2 vols., New York 1934

Bartlett, I. H., "The persistence of Wendell Phillips," *The Antislavery Vanguard: New Essays on the Abolitionists*, ed. M. Duberman, Princeton 1965, pp. 102-22

Baudot, M., "Marmontal mémorialiste, reflêt fidèle des mentalités de son temps," *Contributions à l'histoire des mentalités de 1610 à nos jours. Actes du 102ᵉ Congrès national des sociétés savantes, Section d'histoire moderne et contemporaine*, 1, Paris 1978, pp. 95-116

Bayne, S. P., "Le siècle en pleurs: l'émotivité au service de la société," *Das weinende Saeculum. Colloquium der Arbeitsstelle 18. Jahrhundert, Gesamthochschule Wuppertal, Universität Münster... 1981*, Heidelberg 1983, pp. 25-30

Beecher, C. E., *An Essay on Slavery and Abolition with Reference to the Duty of Females*, Philadelphia 1837

Bellen, H., *Metus Gallicus – Metus Punicus. Zum Furchtmotive in der römischen Republik*, Stuttgart 1985

Bender, T., ed., *The Antislavery Debate. Capitalism and Abolitionism as a Problem in Historical Interpretation*, Berkeley 1992

Berkowitz, L., *Causes and Consequences of the Feelings*, Cambridge (UK) 2000

Bernsen, M., *Angst und Schrecken in der Erzähliteratur des französischen und englischen 18. Jahrhunderts*, München 1996

Birney, C. H., *The Grimké Sisters. Sarah and Angelina Grimké, the First Women Advocates of Abolition and Women's Rights*, Boston 1885 [repr. 1969]

Black's Law Dictionary, ed. 2, ed. B. A. Garner, St. Paul 1999

Blaug, M., *The Methodology of Economics, or, How Economists Explain*, ed. 2, Cambridge (UK) 1992

Bloch, M., *La société féodale*, 2 vols., Paris 1939-1940

Bloch, M., *Apologie pour l'histoire, ou, Métier d'historien*, Paris 1949

Bloch, M., *L'étrange défaite. Témoignage écrit en 1940...*, Paris 1957

Bloch, M., *Feudal Society*, trans. L. A. Manyon, Chicago 1961

Bogin, R., and J. F. Yellin, "Introduction," *The Abolitionist Sisterhood. Women's Political Culture in Antebellum America*, eds. J. F. Yellin and J. C. Van Horne, Ithaca 1994, pp. 1-19

Boles, J. B., *Religion in Antebellum Kentucky*, Lexington (KY) 1976

Boterman, H., *Die Soldaten und die römischen Politik in der Zeit von Caesars Tod bis zur Begründung des Zweiten Triumvirats*, München 1968

Boureau, A., "Propositions pour une histoire restreinte des mentalités," *Annales* 44 (1989) pp. 1491-1504

Bower, G. H., and J. P. Forgas, "Mood and social memory," *Handbook of Affect and Social Cognition*, ed. J. P. Forgas, Mahwah (NJ) 2001, pp. 95-120

Boyer, R. O., *The Legend of John Brown. A Biography and a History*, New York 1973

Bradley, J., *Accounts of Religious Revivals in Many Parts of the United States from 1815 to 1818*, Albany 1819

Branscombe, N. R., and B. M. Cohen, "Motivation and complexity levels as determinants of heuristic use in social judgment," *Emotion and Social Judgments*, ed. J. P. Forgas, Oxford 1991, pp. 145-160

Braudel, F., *The Mediterranean and the Mediterranean World in the Age of Philip II*, trans. S. Reynolds, 2 vols., New York 1973

Brehm, J. W., and E. A. Self, "The intensity of motivation," *Annual Review of Psychology* 40 (1989) pp. 109-31

Brennan, T., "The Old Stoic theory of emotions," *The Emotions in Hellenistic Philosophy*, eds. J. Sihvola and T. Engberg-Pedersen, Dordrecht 1998, pp. 21-70

Brody, L. R., "The socialization of gender differences in emotional expression: display rules, infant temperament, and differentiation," *Gender and Emotion. Social Psychological Perspectives*, ed. A. H. Fischer, Cambridge (UK) 2000, pp. 24-47

Brody, L. R., and J. A. Hall, "Gender, emotion, and expression," *Handbook of Emotions*, ed. 2, eds. M. Lewis and J. M. Haviland-Jones, New York 2000, pp. 338-49

Brown, I. V., "Miller McKim and Pennsylvania abolitionism," *Pennsylvania History* 30 (1963) pp. 56-72

Brunt, P. A., "Two great Roman landowners," *Latomus* 34 (1975) pp. 619-35

Büchner, K., *Sallust*, Heidelberg 1960

Burckhardt, J., *Reflections on History*, trans. M. D. Hottinger, Indianapolis 1979

Burguière, A., "L'anthropologie historique," *Histoire et le métier d'historien en France, 1945-1995*, ed. F. Bédarida, Paris 1995, pp. 172-85

Burke, P., "Strengths and weaknesses of the history of mentalities," *The Annales School*, ed. S. Clark, London 1999, 2 pp. 442-56 [orig., 1986]

Butler, J., *Awash in a Sea of Faith. Christianizing the American People*, Cambridge 1990

Carwardine, R. J., *Evangelicals and Politics in Antebellum America*, New Haven 1993

Castan, Y., *Honnêteté et relations sociales en Languedoc (1715-1780)*, Paris 1974

Chartier, R., "Trajectoires et tensions culturelles de l'Ancient Régime," *Choix culturels et mémoire*, Paris 2000 (*Histoire de la France*, eds. A. Burgière and J. Revel, 3), pp. 29-142

Chauvaud, F., *Les passions villageoises au XIXe siècle. Les émotions rurales dans les pays Beauce, du Hurepoix et du Mantois*, Paris 1995

Child, L. M., *Authentic Anecdotes of American Slavery*, Newburyport (RI) 1835

Child, L. M., *An Appeal in Favor of That Class of Americans Called Africans*, New York 1836

Christie, J. W., and D. L. Dumond, *George Bourne and The Book and Slavery Irreconcilable*, Baltimore 1969

Clapier-Valladon, S., "L'homme et le rire," *Histoire des moeurs* 2, Paris 1991, pp. 247-97

Clark, M. S., "A role for arousal in the link between feelings states, judgments, and behavior," *Affect and Cognition. The Seventeenth Annual Carnegie Symposium on Cognition*, eds. eadem and S. T. Fiske, Hillsdale (NJ) 1982, pp. 265-89

Clark, S., "The *Annales* historians," *The Annales School*, ed. idem, London 1999, 1 pp. 238-56 [orig., 1985]

Clore, G. C., "Cognitive phenomenology: feelings and the construction of judgment," *The Construction of Social Judgments*, eds. L. L. Martin and A. Tesser, Hillsdale (NJ) 1992, pp. 133-63

Clore, G. C., "Why emotions are felt," *The Nature of Emotions. Fundamental Questions*, eds. P. Ekman and R. J. Davidson, New York 1994, pp. 103-11

Cobet, J., "Herodotus and Thucydides on war," *Past Perspectives. Studies in Greek and Roman Historical Writing. Papers Presented at a Conference... 1983*, eds. I. S. Moxon et al., Cambridge (UK) 1986, pp. 1-18

Connor, W. R., "A post-modernist Thucydides?" *Classical Journal* 72 (1977) pp. 289-98

Connor, W. R., *Thucydides*, Princeton 1984

Connor, W. R., "Narrative discourse in Thucydides," *The Greek Historians. Literature and History*, Stanford 1985, pp. 1-17

Contat, N., *Anecdotes typographiques: ou l'on voit la description des coutumes, moeurs et usages singuliers des Compagnons imprimeurs*, ed. G. Barber, Oxford 1980

Corbier, M., "Maiestas domus Augustae," *Varia epigraphica. Atti del Colloquio internazionale di Epigrafia... 2000*, eds. G. Angelina Bertinelli and A. Donati, Faienza 2001, pp. 155-99

Cornelius, R. R., *The Science of Emotion. Research and Tradition in the Psychology of Emotions*, Upper Saddle River (NJ) 1996

Corrigan, J., *Business of the Heart. Religion and Emotion in the Nineteenth Century*, Berkeley 2002

Crespo, E., "A regional variation: emotions in Spain," *The Social Construction of Emotions*, ed. R. Harré, Oxford 1986, pp. 209-17

Cross, B., ed., *The Autobiography of Lyman Beecher*, 2 vols., Cambridge 1961

Cross, W. R., *The Burned-Over District. The Social and Intellectual History of Enthusiastic Religion in Western New York, 1800-1850*, Ithaca 1950

Damasio, A. R., *Descartes' Error. Emotion, Reason, and the Human Brain*, New York 1994

D'Andrade, R. G., "The cultural part of cognition," *Cognitive Science* 5 (1981) pp. 179-95

Darnton, R., *The Great Cat Massacre and Other Episodes in French Cultural History*, New York 1985

Davidson, J., "Dover, Foucault and Greek homosexuality: penetration and the truth of sex," *Past and Present* 170 (2001) pp. 2-51

Davis, D. B., "Some recent directions in cultural history," *American Historical Review* 73 (1968) pp. 696-707

Davis, H., *Leonard Bacon: New England Reformer and Antislavery Moderate*, Baton Rouge 1998

Dawes, R. M., "Behavioral decision making and judgment," *Handbook of Social Psychology*, ed. 4, eds. D. T. Gilbert et al., Boston 1998, 1 pp. 497-548

Debate at the Lane Seminary, Cincinnati: Speech of James A. Thome, of Kentucky...; Letter of the Rev. Dr. Samuel H. Cox..., Boston 1834

Delumeau, J., *Sin and Fear. The Emergence of a Western Guilt Culture, 13th-18th Centuries*, trans. E. Nicholson, New York 1990 [French original, *La péché...*, 1983]

De Martino, "I 'supplicia' dell'iscrizione di Pozzuoli," *Labeo* 21 (1975) pp. 211-14

Demos, J. P., *Entertaining Satan. Witchcraft and the Culture of New England*, New York 1982

Demos, J. [P.], *Past, Present, and Personal. The Family and Life Course in American History*, New York 1986

Descimon, R., and C. Jouhaud, "De Paris à Bordeaux: pour qui court le peuple pendant la Fronde?" *Mouvements populaires et conscience sociale XVIe-XIXe siècles. Actes du Colloque... 1984*, ed. J. Nicolas, Paris 1985, pp. 31-42

Dickens, M., *My Father As I Recall Him*, New York 1897

Dienstbier, R. A., "The role of emotion in moral socialization," *Emotion, Cognition, and Behavior*, eds. C. E. Izard et al., Cambridge (UK) 1984, pp. 483-514

Dillon, M. L., *Elijah P. Lovejoy, Abolitionist Editor*, Urbana (IL) 1961

Dillon, M. L., *Benjamin Lundy and the Struggle for Negro Freedom*, Urbana (IL) 1966

Dosse, F., *L'histoire en miettes. Des 'Annales' à la 'nouvelle histoire'*, ed. 2, Paris 1997

Duan, C., "Being empathic: the role of motivation to empathize and the nature of target emotions," *Motivation and Emotion* 24 (2000) pp. 29-49

Dumond, D. L., ed., *Letters of James Gillespie Birney, 1831-1857*, 2 vols., New York 1938

Dumond, D. L., *Antislavery Origins of the Civil War in the United States*, Ann Arbor 1939 [repr. 1959]

Dumond, D. L., *Antislavery: The Crusade for Freedom in America*, Ann Arbor 1961

Eckstein, A. M., *Moral Vision in The Histories of Polybius*, Berkeley 1995

Edmunds, L., *Chance and Intelligence in Thucydides*, Cambridge 1975

Elias, N., *The Civilizing Process. The History of Manners*, trans. E. Jephcott, New York 1978 [*Uber den Prozess der Zivilisation*, Basel 1939]

Ellgring, H., and B. Rimé, "Individual differences in emotional reactions," *Experiencing Emotion. A Cross-cultural Study*, eds. K. R. Scherer et al., Cambridge (UK) 1986, pp. 142-53

Ellsworth, P. C., "Sense, culture, and sensibility," *Emotion and Culture. Empirical Studies of Mutual Influence*, eds. S. Kitayama and H. R. Markus, Washington, D.C., 1994, pp. 23-50

Elster, J., *Alchemies of the Mind. Rationality and the Emotions*, Cambridge (UK) 1999

Engerman, S. L., and D. Eltis, "Economic aspects of the abolition debate," *Anti-Slavery, Religion, and Reform. Essays in Memory of Roger Anstey*, eds. C. Bolt and S. Drescher, Folkestone (UK) 1980, pp. 272-93

Epstein, D. F., *Personal Enmity in Roman Politics 218-43 BC*, London 1987

Erbe, M., "Historisch-anthropologische Fragestellungen der Annales-Schule," *Historische Anthropologie. Der Mensch in der Geschichte*, ed. H. Süssmuth, Göttingen 1984, pp. 19-31

Fajans, J., "The person in social context: the social character of Baining 'psychology'," *Person, Self, and Experience. Exploring Pacific Ethnopsychologies*, eds. G. M. White and J. Kirkpatrick, Berkeley 1985, pp. 367-97

Febvre, L., "History and psychology," *A New Kind of History: From the Writings of Febvre*, ed. P. Burke, New York 1973, pp. 1-12 [original in the *Encyclopédie française* 3 (1938)]

Ferrero, G., *Grandezza e decadenza di Roma*, 5 vols., Milano 1907

Ferry, A., *The "Inward" Language. Sonnets of Wyatt, Sidney, Shakespeare, Donne*, Chicago 1983

Finney, C. G., *Lectures on Revivals of Religion*, New York 1835 [repr. 1960, ed. W. G. McLoughlin]

Fischer, A. H., and A. S. R. Manstead, "The relation between gender and emotions in different cultures," *Gender and Emotion. Social Psychological Perspectives*, ed. A. H. Fischer, Cambridge (UK) 2000, pp. 71-94

Flandrin, J.-L., *Families in Former Times. Kinship, Household and Sexuality*, trans. R. Southern, Cambridge (UK) 1979 [French original, *Familles, parentés, maison, sexualité dans l'ancienne société*, Paris 1976]

Flaubert, G., *Oeuvres complètes. Correspondance*, ed. 2, 2nd series, Paris 1926; 3rd series, Paris 1927

Forgas, J. P., "Affect and social judgments: an introductory review," *Emotion and Social Judgments*, ed. idem, Oxford 1991, pp. 3-29

Forgas, J. P., "Introduction," *Feeling and Thinking. The Role of Affect in Social Cognition*, ed. idem, Cambridge (UK) 2000, pp. 1-28

Forgas, J. P., "Introduction: affect and social cognition," *Handbook of Affect and Social Cognition*, ed. idem, Mahwah (NJ) 2001, pp. 1-23

180   Feelings In History

Fornara, C. W., *The Nature of History in Ancient Greece and Rome*, Berkeley 1983

Forster, R., "Achievement of the Annales school," *The Annales School*, ed. S. Clark, London 1999, 2 pp. 178-95 [orig., 1978]

Fortenbaugh, W. F., et al., eds., *Theophrastus of Eresus. Sources for His Life, Writings Thought and Influence*, 2 vols., Leiden 1992

Fowler, D. P., "Epicurean anger," *The Passions in Roman Thought and Literature*, eds. S. M. Braund and C. Gill, Cambridge (UK) 1997, pp. 16-35

Fox, M., "Dionysius, Lucian, and the prejudice against rhetoric in history," *Journal of Roman Studies* 91 (2001) pp. 76-93

Fox, N., and R. A. Davidson, "Electroencephalogram asymmetry in response to the approach of a stranger and maternal separation in 10-month-old infants," *Developmental Psychology* 23 (1987) pp. 233-40

Fraser, J. W., *Pedagogue for God's Kingdom. Lyman Beecher and the Second Great Awakening*, Lanham (MD) 1985

Frigoglitti, J., *Bibliographie de Georges Lefebvre*, Paris 1972

Frijda, N. H., *The Emotions*, Cambridge (UK) 1986

Frijda, N. H., et al., "The influence of emotions on beliefs," *Emotions and Beliefs. How Feelings Influence Thoughts*, eds. iidem, Cambridge (UK) 2000, pp. 1-9

Fritz, K. von, "Poseidonios als Historiker," *Historiographia Antiqua. Commentationes Lovanienses in honorem W. Peremans*, Leuven 1977, pp. 163-93

Fromentin, V., *Denys d'Halicarnasse, Antiquités romaines*, I: *Texte et traduction*, Paris 1998

Gabba, E., "True history and false history in classical Antiquity," *Journal of Roman Studies* 71 (1981) pp. 50-62

Gabba, E., "The historians and Augustus," *Caesar Augustus. Seven Aspects*, eds. F. Millar and E. Segal, Oxford 1984, pp. 61-88

Galsterer, H., "A man, a book and a method: Sir Ronald Syme's Roman Revolution after 50 years," *Between Republic and Empire. Interpretations of Augustus and His Principate*, eds. K. Raaflaub and M. Toher, Berkeley 1990, pp. 1-20

Garrison, W. P. and F. J., *William Lloyd Garrison, 1805-1879: The Story of His Life Told by His Children*, 4 vols, New York 1885-1889 [repr. 1969]

Garrison, W. L., *Thoughts on African Colonization: or an Impartial Exhibition of the Doctrines, Principle and Purposes of the American Colonization Society...*, Boston 1832

Geertz, C., "Common sense as a cultural system," *Local Knowledge. Further Essays in Interpretive Anthropology*, New York 1983, pp. 73-93

Gerber, E. R., "Rage and obligation: Samoan emotion in conflict," *Person, Self, and Experience. Exploring Pacific Ethnopsychologies*, eds. G. M. White and J. Kirkpatrick, Berkeley 1985, pp. 121-67

Gillespie, J. B., "'The clear leadings of Providence:' pious memoirs and the problems of self-realization for women in the early nineteenth century," *Journal of the Early Republic* 5 (1985) pp. 197-221

Gillis, J. R., "From ritual to romance: toward an alternative history of love," *Emotion and Social Change. Toward a New Psychohistory*, eds. C. Z. and P. N. Stearns, New York 1988, pp. 87-121

Godechot, J., "En Languedoc et Gascogne au XVIIIe siècle: les paysans et les femmes contre les pouvoirs," *Mouvements populaires et conscience sociale XVIe-XIXe siècles. Actes du Colloque... 1984*, ed. J. Nicholas, Paris 1985, pp. 383-89

Goodheart, L. B., *Abolitionist, Actuary, Atheist: Elizur Wright and the Reform Impulse*, Kent (OH) 1990

Goodspeed, D. J., *The German Wars 1914-1945*, Boston 1977

Gowing, A. M., *The Triumviral Narratives of Appian and Cassius Dio*, Ann Arbor 1992

Grassotti, H., "La ira regia in Leon y Castilla," *Miscelanea de Estudios sobre instituciones Castellano-Leonensas*, ed. eadem, Bilbao 1978, pp. 3-132 [original in *Cuadernos de Historia de España* (Buenos Aires) 41-42 (1965) pp. 5-135]

Greven, P., *The Protestant Temperament. Patterns of Child-Rearing, Religious Experience, and the Self in Early America*, New York 1977

Grimké, Angelina, *Diary*, courtesy Manuscripts Division, William L. Clements Library, University of Michigan

Gueniffey, P., *La politique de la terreur. Essai sur la violence révolutionnaire 1789-1794*, Paris 2000

Guide to American Law. Everyone's Legal Encyclopedia, ed. 2, St. Paul 1983

Gundel, H. G., "Der Begriff Maiestas im Denken der augusteischen Zeit," *Politeia und res publica. Beiträge zum Verständnis von Politik, Recht und Staat in der Antiken*, ed. P. Steinmetz, Wiesbaden 1969, pp. 279-300

Hahn, I., "Appian und seine Quellen," *Romanitas-Christianitas. Untersuchungen zur Geschichte und Literatur der römischen Kaiserzeit Johannes Straub... gewidmet*, eds. G. Wirth et al., Berlin 1982, pp. 251-76

Hall, C. M., ed., *Nicolaus of Damascus' Life of Augustus. A Historical Commentary Embodying a Translation*, Northampton 1923

Hansen, C. H. and R. D., "Automatic emotion: attention and facial difference," *The Heart's Eye. Emotional Influences in Perception and Attention*, eds. S. Kitayama and P. M. Niedenthal, San Diego 1994, pp. 217-43

Harbsmeier, M., "Why do Indians cry?" *Culture and History* 1987, pp. 90-114

Hardman, C., "The psychology of conformity and self-expression among the Lohorung Rai of East Nepal," *Indigenous Psychologies. The Anthropology of Self*, eds. P. Heelas and A. Lock, London 1981, pp. 161-80

Harmand, J., *L'armée et le soldat à Rome de 107 à 50 avant notre ère*, Paris 1967

Harré, R., "An outline of the social constructionist viewpoint," *The Social Construction of Emotions*, ed. idem, Oxford 1986, pp. 2-14

Harris, W.V., "On war and greed in the second century B. C.," *American Historical Review* 76 (1971) pp. 1371-85

Harris, W.V., *Restraining Rage. The Ideology of Anger Control in Classical Antiquity*, Cambridge 2001

Hatch, N. O., *The Democratization of American Christianity*, New Haven 1989

Hawes, F., *Henry Brougham*, London 1957

Heelas, P., "Emotion talk across cultures," *Social Construction of Emotions*, ed. R. Harré, Oxford 1986, pp. 234-66

Hegel, G. F. H., *The Philosophy of History*, trans. J. Sibree, New York 1956

Hellegouarc'h, J., ed., *Velleius Paterculus, Histoire romaine*, text and Fr. trans., 2 vols., Paris 1982

Henry, S. C., *Unvanquished Puritan. A Portrait of Lyman Beecher*, Grand Rapids (MI) 1973

Hess, U., and G. Kirouac, "Emotion expression in groups," *Handbook of Emotions*, ed. 2, eds. M. Lewis and J. M. Haviland-Jones, New York 2000, pp. 368-81

Hexter, J. H., "Fernand Braudel and the *Monde Braudelien*...," *Journal of Modern History* 44 (1972) 480-539

Heyrick, E. C., *Immediate, Not Gradual Abolition; or, An Inquiry into the Shortest, Safest, and Most Effectual Means of Getting Rid of West Indian Slavery*, Boston 1838

Hinard, F., "La 'loi de Pouzzoles,'" *La mort au quotidien dans le monde romain... 1993*, Paris 1995, pp. 202-12

Hochschild, A. R., "The sociology of feeling and emotion: selected possibilities," *Another Voice. Feminist Perspectives on Social Life and Social Science*, eds. M. Millman and R. M. Kanter, Garden City (NY) 1975, pp. 280-307

Hölkeskamp, K.-J., *Die Entstehung der Nobilität. Studien zur sozialen und politischen Geschichte der römischen Republik im 4. Jhdt. v. Chr.*, Stuttgart 1987

Horsfall, N., *Cornelius Nepos. A Selection, including the Lives of Cato and Atticus*, Oxford 1989

Huizinga, J., *The Waning of the Middle Ages. A Study of the Forms of Life, Thought and Art in France and the Netherlands in the XIVth and XVth Centuries*, trans. F. Hopman, London 1924

Hume, D., *Essays Moral, Political, and Literary*, ed. 2, ed. E. F. Miller, Indianapolis 1987

Hunt, L., "French history in the last twenty years: the rise and fall of the *Annales* paradigm," *The Annales School*, ed. S. Clark, London 1999, 1 pp. 24-38 [orig., 1986]

Hyman, S. E., *The Tangled Bank. Darwin, Marx, Frazer, and Freud as Imaginative Writers*, New York 1962

Izard, C. E., "Emotion-cognition relationships and human development," *Emotions, Cognition, and Behavior*, eds. idem et al., Cambridge (UK) 1984, pp. 17-37

Izard, C. E., and B. P. Ackerman, "Motivational, organizational, and regulatory functions of discrete emotions," *Handbook of Emotions*, ed. 2, eds. M. Lewis and J. M. Haviland-Jones, New York 2000, pp. 253-64

Izard, C. E. et al., "Introduction," *Emotions, Cognition, and Behavior*, eds. iidem, Cambridge (UK) 1984, pp. 1-14

Jeffrey. J. R., *The Great Silent Army of Abolitionism. Ordinary Women in the Antislavery Movement*, Chapel Hill 1998

Jervis, A. E., "Talking heads. The iconography of mutilation in the Roman Republic," Diss. Stanford University 2001

Johnson, A. B., *A Treatise on Language*, ed. 2, ed. D. Rynin, New York 1947

Johnson, E., *Dickens, His Tragedy and Triumph*, 2 vols., New York 1952

Johnson, P. E., *A Shopkeeper's Millennium. Society and Revivals in Rochester, New York, 1815-1837*, New York 1978

Juster, S., "'In a different voice': male and female narratives of religious conversion in post-Revolutionary America," *American Quarterly* 41 (1989) pp. 34-62

Kahneman, D., et al., "Economic preferences or attitude expressions? An analysis of dollar responses to public issues," *Journal of Risk and Uncertainty* 19 (1999) pp. 203-37

Karcher, C. [L.], "Rape, murder, and revenge in 'Slavery's Pleasant Homes,' Lydia Maria Child's antislavery fiction and the limits of genre," *Women's Studies International Forum* 9 (1986) pp. 323-32

Karcher, C. L., *The First Woman in the Republic. A Cultural Biography of Lydia Maria Child*, Durham 1994

Keller, C., *The Second Great Awakening in Connecticut*, New Haven 1942

Keltner, D., et al., "Beyond simple pessimism: effects of sadness and anger on social perception," *Journal of Personality and Social Psychology* 64 (1993) pp. 740-52

Kidd, I. G., *Poseidonius, II. The Commentary*, 2 vols., Cambridge (UK) 1988

Kidd, I. G., *Poseidonius, III. The Translation of the Fragments*, Cambridge (UK) 1999

Kienast, D., *Augustus, Prinzeps und Monarch*, ed. 3, Darmstadt 1999

Kierdorf, W., "Freundschaft und Freundschaftskündigung," *Saeculum Augustum* 1: *Herrschaft und Gesellschaft*, ed. G. Binder, Darmstadt 1987, pp. 223-45

Kitayama, S., et al., "Culture, emotion, and well-being: good feelings in Japan and the United States," *Cognition and Emotion* 14 (2000) pp. 93-124

Kitayama, S., and H. R. Markus, "Introduction," *Emotion and Culture. Empirical Studies of Mutual Influence*, eds. iidem, Washington (D.C.) 1994, pp. 1-19

Kitayama, S., and P. M. Niedenthal, "Introduction," *The Heart's Eye. Emotional Influences in Perception and Attention*, eds. iidem, San Diego 1994, pp. 1-14

Kneppe, A., *Metus Temporum. Zur Bedeutung von Angst in Politik und Gesellschaft der römischen Kaiserzeit des 1. und 2. Jhdts. n. Chr.*, Stuttgart 1994

Kober, M., *Die politischen Anfänge Octavians in der Darstellung des Velleius und dessen Verhältnis zur historiographischen Tradition. Ein philologischer Quellenvergleich: Nikolaos von Damaskus, Appianos von Alexandria, Velleius Paterculus*, Würzburg 2000

Kögler, H. H., and K. R. Steuber, "Introduction: empathy, simulation, and interpretation in the philosophy of social science," *Empathy and Agency. The Problem of Understanding in the Human Sciences*, eds. iidem, Boulder (CO) 2000, pp. 1-61

Konner, M. J., "Do we need enemies? The origin and consequences of rage," *Rage, Power, and Aggression*, eds. R. A. Glick and S. P. Roose, New Haven 1993, pp. 173-93

Krentz, P., "Fighting by the rules: the invention of the hoplite agôn," *Hesperia* 71 (2002) pp. 23-39

Lange, C. G., and W. James, *The Emotions*, Baltimore 1922

Lanson, G., *Nivelle de la Chaussée et la comédie larmoyante*, Paris 1887

Lazarus, R. S., "On the primacy of cognition," *American Psychologist* 39 (1984) pp. 124-29

Lazarus, R. [S.], "Universal antecedents of the emotions," *The Nature of Emotion. Fundamental Questions*, eds. P. Ekman and R. J. Davidson, New York 1994, pp. 163-71

Le Breton, D., *Les passions ordinaires. Anthropologie des émotions*, Paris 1998

Ledoux, J. E., "Cognitive-emotional interactions in the brain," *The Nature of Emotion. Fundamental Questions*, eds. P. Ekman and R. J. Davidson, New York 1994, pp. 216-23

Leeper, R. W., "The motivational and perceptual properties of emotions as indicating their fundamental character and role," *Feelings and Emotions. The Loyola Symposium*, ed. M. B. Arnold, New York 1970, pp. 151-68

Lefebvre, G., *Etudes sur la Révolution française*, ed. 2, Paris 1963

Lefebvre, G., *The Great Fear of 1789. Rural Panic in Revolutionary France*, trans. J. White, New York 1973

Leighton, S. R., "Aristotle and the emotions," *Essays on Aristotle's Rhetoric*, ed. A. O. Rorty, Berkeley 1996, pp. 206-37

Lendon, J. E., "Athens and Sparta and the coming of the Peloponnesian War," *Cambridge Companion to the Age of Pericles*, ed. J. Samons (New York 2004) — pre-publication manuscript kindness of the author

Lepore, J., "Historians who love too much: reflections on microhistory and biography," *Journal of American History* 88 (2001) pp. 129-44

Lerat, B., *Le terrorisme révolutionnaire 1789-1799*, Paris 1989

Levenson, R. W., "The intrapersonal function of emotion," *Cognition and Emotion* 13 (1999) pp. 481-504

Leventhal, H., "The integration of emotion and cognition: a view from the perceptual-motor theory of emotion," *Affect and Cognition. The Seventeenth Annual Carnegie Symposium of Cognition*, eds. M. S. Clark and S. T. Fiske, Hillsdale (NJ) 1982, pp. 121-56

Levy, R. I., "Emotion, knowing, and culture," *Culture Theory. Essays on Mind, Self, and Emotion*, eds. R. A. Shweder and R. A. LeVine, Cambridge (UK) 1984, pp. 214-37

Little, S. L., *The Branded Hand; A Dramatic Sketch. Commemorative of the Tragedies at the South in the Winter of 1844-5*, Pawtucket (RI) 1845

Lloyd, G. E. R., *Demystifying Mentalities*, Cambridge (UK) 1990

Loasby, B. J., "The imagined, deemed possible," *Behavioral Norms, Technological Progress, and Economic Dynamics. Studies in Schumpeterian Economics*, eds. E. Helmstädter and M. Perlman, Ann Arbor 1996, pp. 17-31

Loewenstein, G., and J. S. Lerner, "The role of affect in decision making," *The Handbook of Affective Science*, eds. R. J. Davidson et al., Oxford 2002, pp. 619-42

Loewenstein, G. F., et al., "Risk as feelings," *Psychological Bulletin* 127 (2001) pp. 267-86

Loreto, L., *Guerra e libertà nella repubblicana romana. John R. Seeley e le radici della Roman Revolution di Ronald Syme*, Roma 1999

Loriga, S., "La biographie comme problème," *Jeux d'échelles. La micro-analyse à l'expérience*, ed. J. Revel, Paris 1996, pp. 209-31

Lowenstein, R., "Exuberance is rational," *New York Times*, Feb. 11, 2001, Section 6 p. 68

Luhmann, N., *Love as Passion. The Codification of Intimacy*, trans. J. Gaines and D. L. Jones, Cambridge (UK) 1986

Lundberg, M. J., *The Incomplete Adult: Social Class Constraints on Personal Development*, Westport (CT) 1974

[Lundy, B.], *The Life, Travels and Opinions of Benjamin Lundy, Including His Journeys to Texas and Mexico...*, Philadelphia 1847 [ed. anon.]

Lutz, C. [A.], "Ethnopsychology compared to what? Explaining behavior and consciousness among the Ifaluk," *Person, Self, and Experience. Exploring Pacific Ethnopsychologies*, eds. G. M. White and J. Kirkpatrick, Berkeley 1985, pp. 35-79

Lutz, C. A., *Unnatural Emotions. Everyday Sentiments on a Micronesian Atoll & Their Challenge to Western Theory*, Chicago 1988

Lyon, B., "Marc Bloch: did he repudiate *Annales* history?" *The Annales School*, ed. S. Clark, London 1999, 4 pp. 200-12 [orig. 1985]

MacMullen, R., "Romans in tears," *Classical Philology* 75 (1980) pp. 254-55

MacMullen, R., *Changes in the Roman Empire. Essays in the Ordinary*, Princeton 1990

MacMullen, R., "Hellenizing the Romans (2nd century B. C.)," *Historia* 40 (1991) pp. 419-38

MacMullen, R., *Sisters of the Brush. Their Family, Art, Life, and Letters 1797-1833*, New Haven 1997

MacMullen, R., *Sarah's Choice 1828-1832*, New Haven 2001

Magnino, D., *Appiani Bellorum civilium liber tertius. Testo critico, introduzione, traduzione e commento*, Firenze 1984

Magnino, D., "Le 'Guerre Civili' di Appiano," *Aufstieg und Niedergang der römischen Welt*, ed. H. Temporini, II 34, 1, Berlin 1993, pp. 523-54

Malcovati, H., *Oratorum Romanorum fragmenta*, 3 vols., Torino 1930

Malitz, J., *Die Historien des Poseidonius*, München 1983

Mandrou, R., *Introduction to Modern France 1500-1640. An Essay in Historical Psychology*, trans. R. E. Hallmark, New York 1976 [French original, 1961]

Mandrou, R., *La France aux XVIIᵉ et XVIIIᵉ siècles*, 6th ed. augmented by M. Cottret, Paris 1997

Manuwald, B., *Cassius Dio und Augustus. Philologische Untersuchungen zu den Büchern 45-56 des dionischen Geschichtswerkes*, Wiesbaden 1979

Marks, M., ed., *Memoirs of the Life of David Marks, Minister of the Gospel*, Dover (NH) 1846

Marsden, G. M., *The Evangelical Mind and the New School Presbyterian Experience. A Case Study of Thought and Theology in Nineteenth Century America*, New Haven 1970

Mastrogregori, M., *Il manoscritto interrotto di Marc Bloch*, Pisa 1996

Mathews, D. G., "Orange Scott: the Methodist Evangelist as revolutionary," *The Antislavery Vanguard: New Essays on the Abolitionists*, ed. M. Duberman, Princeton 1965, pp. 71-101

Matlack, L. C., *The Life of Rev. Orange Scott in Two Parts*, New York 1848 [repr. 1970]

McGushin, P. C., *Sallustius Crispus: Bellum Catilinae. A Commentary*, Leiden 1977

McKivigan, J. R., *The War Against Proslavery Religion. Abolitionism and the Northern Churches, 1830-1865*, Ithaca 1984

Meier, C., *Caesar*, ed. 2, Berlin 1982

Mellers, B., et al., "Emotion-based choice," *Journal of Experimental Psychology: General* 128 (1999) pp. 332-45

Meltzer, M., et al., eds., *Lydia Maria Child. Selected Letters, 1817-1880*, Amherst 1982

Middleton, R. R., "Emotional style: the cultural ordering of emotions," *Ethos* 17 (1989) pp. 189-201

Moore, R. L., "Religion, secularization, and the shaping of the culture industry in antebellum America," *American Quarterly* 41 (1989) pp. 216-42

Morsbach, H., and J. W. Tyler, "A Japanese emotion: amae," *Social Construction of Emotions*, ed. R. Harré, Oxford 1986, pp. 289-307

Namier, L., "Human nature in politics," *The Listener* 50 (1953) pp. 1077-79 [repr. idem, *Personalities and Powers*, London 1955]

Narrative of the Revival of Religion in the County of Oneida... in the Year 1826, Utica 1826

Needles, E., *An Historical Memoir of the Pennsylvania Society for the Abolition of Slavery...*, Philadelphia 1848

Nevins, A., ed., *The Diary of Philip Hone 1828-1851*, 2 vols., New York 1927 [repr. 1969]

Nussbaum, M. C., *Upheavals of Thought. The Intelligence of Emotions*, Cambridge (UK) 2001

Oakley, J., *Morality and the Emotions*, London 1992

Oatley, K., *Best Laid Schemes. The Psychology of Emotions*, Cambridge (UK) 1982

Oexle, O. G., "Das Andere, die Unterschiede, das Ganze: Jacques Le Goffs Bild des europäischen Mittlealters," *The Annales School*, ed. S. Clark, London 1999, 4 pp. 318-41 [orig., 1990]

Oniga, R., *Il confine conteso. Lettura antropologica di un capitolo sallustio* (Bellum Iurgurthinum 79), Bari 1990

Oost, S. I., "Thucydides and the irrational. Sundry passages," *Classical Philology* 70 (1975) pp. 186-96

Ortony, A., et al., *The Cognitive Structure of Emotions*, Cambridge (UK) 1988

Orwin, C., *The Humanity of Thucydides*, Princeton 1994

Palmer, B. W., ed., *Selected Letters of Lucretia Coffin Mott*, Urbana 2002

Panksepp, J., *Affective Neuroscience. The Foundations of Human and Animal Emotions*, New York 1998

Panksepp, J., "Emotions as natural kinds within the mammalian brain," *Handbook of Emotions*, ed. 2, eds. M. Lewis and J. M. Haviland-Jones, New York 2000, pp. 137-56

Panksepp, J., "Affective consciousness and the instinctual motor system. The neural sources of sadness and joy," *The Caldron of Consciousness. Motivation, Affect and Self-Organization – an Anthology*, eds. R. D. Ellis and N. Newton, Amsterdam 2000-a, pp. 27-54

Paret, P., "Commentary on 'Psychoanalysis in History,'" *Psychology and Historical Interpretation*, ed. W. McK., Runyan, New York 1988, pp. 121-25

Partington, W., ed., *The Private Letter-Books of Sir Walter Scott. Selections from the Abbotsford Manuscripts*, New York 1930

Pasoli, E., *Le Historiae e le opere minore di Sallustio*, ed. 2, Bologna 1967

Paul, G. M., *A Historical Commentary on Sallust's Bellum Jugurthinum*, Liverpool 1984

Pease, J. H., "The Freshness of Fanaticism: Abby Kelley Foster: An Essay in Reform," Diss. University of Rochester 1969

Pease, W. H. and J. H., *Bound With Them in Chains: A Biographical History of the Anti-Slavery Movement,* Westport (CT) 1972

Pédech, P., *La méthode historique de Polybe,* Paris 1964

Peter, H., *Historicorum Romanorum reliquiae,* ed. 2, 2 vols., Stuttgart 1967

Peters, E., and P. Slovic, "The springs of action: affective and analytical information processing in choice," *Personality and Social Psychology Bulletin* 26 (2000) pp. 1465-75

Peterson, N. P., "Iz zapisok byvshego uchitelia," ("Recollections of a former teacher"), *Mezhdunarodnyi tolstovskii al'manakh (International Tolstoy Almanac),* Moscow 1909, pp. 257-262 [reprinted in L. N. Tolstoi, *V vospominaniiakh sovremennikov v dvukh tomakh,* Moscow 1978, pp. 122-26]

Phillips, W., *Speeches, Lectures, and Letters,* Boston 1863

Pitocco, F., "Introduzione. Ritorno alle radici. Febvre, Bloch e la storia della mentalità," *Storia delle mentalità,* ed. idem, 1: *Interpretazioni,* Roma 1996, pp. 9-100

Plutchik, R., "Measuring emotions and their derivatives," *The Measurement of Emotions,* eds. idem and H. Kellerman, San Diego 1989, pp. 1-35

Premerstein, A. von, *Vom Werden und Wesen des Prinzipats,* München 1937

Raaflaub, K., *Dignitatis contentio. Studien zur Motivation und politischen Taktik im Bürgerkrieg zwischen Caesar und Pompeius,* München 1974

Rankin, J., *Letters on American Slavery, Addressed to Mr. Thomas Rankin, Merchant at Middlebrook, Augusta Co., Virginia,* Boston 1833

Rauzduel, R., *Sociologie historique des Annales,* Paris 1999

Reddy, W. M., *The Navigation of Feeling. A Framework for the History of Emotions,* Cambridge (UK) 2001

Reeve, J., *Understanding Motivation and Emotion,* ed. 2, Fort Worth 1997

Revel, J., "Introduction," *Histories. French Constructions of the Past,* eds. idem and L. Hunt, trans. A. Goldhammer et al., New York 1995, pp. 1-63

Revel, J., "Micro-analyse et construction du social," *Jeux d'échelles: la micro-analyse à l'expérience,* ed. idem, Paris 1996, pp. 15-36

Rice, C. D., "Literary sources and the revolution in British attitudes to slavery," *Anti-Slavery, Religion, and Reform. Essays in Memory of Roger Anstey,* eds. C. Bolt and S. Drescher, Folkestone (UK) 1980, pp. 319-34

Ricoeur, P., "L'écriture de l'histoire et la représentation du passé," *Annales* 55 (2000) pp. 731-47

Robinson, P., "Why do we believe Thucydides? A comment on W. R. Connor's 'Narrative discourse in Thucydides'," *The Greek Historians. Literature and History,* Stanford 1985, pp. 19-23

Röcke, W., "Die Faszination der Traurigkeit. Inszenierung und Reglementierung von Trauer und Melancholie in der Literatur des Spätmittelalters," *Emotionalität. Zur Geschichte der Gefühle*, eds. C. Benthien et al., Köln 2000, pp. 100-118

Rogivue, E., *L'amitié d'affaires. Essai de sociologie économique*, Lausanne 1938

Romilly, J. de, *Histoire et raison chez Thucydide*, Paris 1956

Rood, T., *Thucydides: Narrative and Explanation*, Oxford 1998

Rosaldo, M. Z., *Knowledge and Passion. Ilongot Notions of Self and Social Life*, Cambridge (UK) 1980

Rosaldo, M. Z., "Toward an anthropology of self and feeling," *Culture Theory. Essays on Mind, Self, and Emotion*, eds. R. A. Shweder and R. A. LeVine, Cambridge (UK) 1984, pp. 137-57

Rose, W. L., "'Iconoclasm has had its day': abolitionists and freedmen in South Carolina," *The Antislavery Vanguard: New Essays on the Abolitionists*, ed. M. Duberman, Princeton 1965, pp. 178-205

Rosenwein, B. H., "Controlling paradigms," *Anger's Past. The Social Uses of an Emotion in the Middle Ages*, ed. eadem, Ithaca 1998, pp. 233-47

Rosenwein, B. H., "Worrying about emotions in history," *American Historical Review* 107 (2002) pp. 821-45

Rudd, J. D., "A perception of hierarchy in eighteenth-century France: an epistolary etiquette manual for the Controller General of Finances," *French Historical Studies* 17 (1992) pp. 791-801

Russell, J. A., "A circumplex model of affect," *Journal of Personality and Social Psychology* 39 (1980) pp. 1161-78

Russell, J. A., "Measures or emotion," *The Measurement of Emotions*, eds. R. Plutchik and H. Kellerman, San Diego 1989, pp. 83-111

Sacks, K. S., "Historiography in the rhetorical works of Dionysius of Halicarnassus," *Athenaeum* 61 (1983) pp. 65-87

Sacks, K. S., *Diodorus Siculus and the First Century*, Princeton 1990

Saint-Simon, L. de R., *Mémoires*, 8 vols., Paris 1983-88

Salmon, P., *Histoire et critique*, ed. 3, Paris 1990

Sandall, R., *The Culture Cult: Designer Tribalism and Other Essays*, Boulder (CO) 2001

Sauder, G., "Der empfindsame Leser," *Das weinende Saeculum. Colloquium der Arbeitsstelle 18. Jahrhundert, Gesamthochschule Wuppertal, Universität Münster... 1981*, Heidelberg 1983, pp. 9-23

Scanlon, T. F., *The Influence of Thucydides upon Sallust*, Heidelberg 1980

Scherer, K. R., "Emotion serves to decouple stimulus and response," *The Nature of Emotion. Fundamental Questions*, eds. P. Ekman and R. J. Davidson, New York 1994, pp. 127-36

Scherer, K. R., et al., "Emotional experience in cultural context: a comparison between Europe, Japan, and the USA," *Facets of Emotion. Recent Research*, ed. idem, Hillsdale (NJ) 1988, pp. 5-30

Schieffelin, E. L., "Anger, grief, and shame: toward a Kaluli ethnopsychology," *Person, Self, and Experience. Exploring Pacific Ethnopsychologies*, eds. G. M. White and J. Kirkpatrick, Berkeley 1985, pp. 168-82

Schrijvers, P. H., "Invention, imagination et théorie des émotions chez Cicéron et Quintilien," *ACTUS. Studies in Honour of H. L. W. Nelson*, ed. J. den Boeft and A. H. M. Kessels, Utrecht 1982, pp. 395-408

Schumpeter, J. A., *The Theory of Economic Development*, Cambridge 1934

Schwarz, N., "Happy and mindless, but sad and smart? The impact of affective states on analytic reasoning," *Emotion and Social Judgments*, ed. J. P. Forgas, Oxford 1991, pp. 55-71

Schwarz, N., "Emotion, cognition, and decision making," *Cognition and Emotion* 14 (2000) pp. 433-40

Scott, J. W., "The Sears case," *Gender and the Politics of History*, ed. 2, New York 1999, pp. 167-77

Seabury, S., *Autobiographical Sketch* [ca. 1831], ed. R. B. Mullin, as *Moneygripe's Apprentice. The Personal Narrative of Samuel Seabury III*, New Haven 1989

Ségur, A. de, *Vie du comte Rostopchine, gouverneur de Moscou en 1812*, ed. 3, Paris 1883

Shiller, R. J., *Market Volatility*, Cambridge 1989

Shorter, E., *The Making of the Modern Family*, New York 1975

Showers, C. J., "Self-organization in emotional contexts," *Feeling and Thinking. The Role of Affect in Social Cognition*, ed. J. P. Forgas, Cambridge (UK) 2000, pp. 283-307

Shweder, R. A., "Preview," *Culture Theory. Essays on Mind, Self, and Emotion*, eds. idem and R. A. LeVine, Cambridge (UK) 1984, pp. 1-24

Shweder, R. A., "'You're not sick, you're just in love.' Emotions as an interpretive system," *The Nature of Emotions*, eds. P. Ekman and R. Davidson, Oxford 1994, pp. 32-44

Simon, P., *Freedom's Champion : Elijah Lovejoy*, Carbondale (IL) 1994

Smith, C. A., and L. D. Kirby, "Affect and cognitive appraisal processes," *Handbook of Affect and Social Cognition*, ed. J. P. Forgas, Mahwah (NJ) 2001, pp. 75-92

Solomon, R. C., "Getting angry. The Jamesian theory of emotion in anthropology," *Culture Theory. Essays on Mind, Self, and Emotion*, eds. R. A. Shweder and R. A. LeVine, Cambridge (UK) 1984, pp. 238-54

Solomon, R. C., *A Passion for Justice. Emotions and the Origins of the Social Contract*, Reading (MA) 1990

Sommers, S., "Understanding emotions: some interdisciplinary considerations," *Emotion and Social Change. Toward a New Psychohistory*, eds. C. Z. and P. N. Stearns, New York 1988, pp. 23-38

Sorokin, P. A., *Social and Cultural Dynamics*, 4 vols., New York 1937-41

Sorokin, P. A., *The Crisis of Our Age. The Social and Cultural Outlook,* New York 1942

Souriac, R., "Mouvements paysans en Comminges au XVIᵉ siècle," *Mouvements populaires et conscience sociale XVIᵉ-XIXᵉ siècles. Actes du Colloque... 1984,* ed. J. Nicolas, Paris 1985, pp. 273-85

Sousa, R. de, *The Rationality of Emotion,* Cambridge 1987

The South Vindicated from the Treason and Fanaticism of the Northern Abolitionists, Philadelphia 1836

Speicher, A. M., *The Religious World of Antislavery Women. Spirituality in the Lives of Five Abolitionist Lecturers,* Syracuse 2000

Spiro, M. E., "Some reflections on cultural determinism and relativism with special reference to emotion and reason," *Culture Theory: Essays on Mind, Self, and Emotion,* eds. R. A. Shweder and R. A. LeVine, Cambridge (UK) 1984, pp. 323-46

Spiro, M. E., "Anthropology and human nature," *Ethos* 27 (1999) pp. 7-14

Sprague, W. B., *Lectures on Revivals of Religion,* New York 1832

Stahl, H.-P., "Speeches and course of events in Books Six and Seven of Thucydides," *The Speeches in Thucydides. A Collection of Original Studies with a Bibliography,* ed. P. A. Stadter, Chapel Hill 1973, pp. 60-77

Stanton, H. B., *Random Recollections,* ed. 2, New York 1886

Stearns, C. Z., "'Lord help me walk humbly': anger and sadness in America, 1570-1750," *Emotion and Social Change. Toward a New Psychohistory,* eds. eadem and P. N. Stearns, New York 1988, pp. 39-68

Stearns, C. Z., and Stearns, P. N., *Anger. The Struggle for Emotional Control in America's History,* Chicago 1986

Stearns, P. N., and C. Z. Stearns, "Emotionology: clarifying the history of emotions and emotional standards," *American Historical Review* 90 (1985) pp. 813-36

Stewart, J. B., *William Lloyd Garrison and the Challenge of Emancipation,* Arlington Heights (VA) 1992

Stewart, J. B., "Joshua Giddings, antislavery violence and Congressional politics of honor," *Antislavery Violence. Sectional, Racial, and Cultural Conflict in Antebellum America,* eds. J. R. McKivigan and S. Harrold, Knoxville (KY) 1999, pp. 167-92

Stone, L., *The Family, Sex and Marriage in England 1500-1800,* New York 1977

Stowe, H. B., *A Key to Uncle Tom's Cabin; Presenting the Original Facts and Documents Upon Which the Story is Founded ...,* Boston 1853

Strasburger, H., "Umblick im Trümmerfeld der griechischen Geschichtsschreibung," *Historiographia Antiqua. Commentationes Lovanienses in honorem W. Peremans,* Leuven (1977) pp. 3-52

Swerdlow, A., "Abolition's conservative sisters. The Ladies' New York City Anti-Slavery Societies, 1834-1840," *The Abolitionist Sisterhood. Women's Political Culture in Antebellum America,* eds. J. F. Yellin and J. C. Van Horne, Ithaca 1994, pp. 31-44

Syme, R. *The Roman Revolution*, Oxford 1939

Syme, R., *Tacitus*, 2 vols., Oxford 1958

Syme, R., "Thucydides," *Proceedings of the British Academy* 1962, pp. 39-56

Syme, R., *Sallust*, Berkeley 1964

Taine, H., *Les origines de la France contemporaine*, 1: *l'Ancient Régime*, ed. 6, Paris 1887

Taine, H., *Hippolyte Taine, sa vie et sa correspondence*, 4 vols., Paris 1902-07

Taine, H., *Histoire de la littérature anglaise*, 12th ed., Paris 1905

Tappan, L., *The Life of Arthur Tappan*, New York 1870 [repr. 1970]

Thoits, P. A., "The sociology of emotions," *Annual Review of Sociology* 15 (1989) pp. 317-42

Thompson, L., "The printing and publishing activities of the American Tract Society from 1825 to 1850," *The Papers of the Bibliographical Society of America* 35 (1941) pp. 81-114

Thompson, W. E., "Fragments of the preserved historians – especially Polybius," *The Greek Historians. Literature and History*, Stanford 1985, pp. 119-39

Tolstoy, L., *War and Peace*, trans. R. Edmonds, London 1957

Tomkins, S. S., "The psychology of commitment: the constructive role of violence and suffering for the individual and for his society," *The Antislavery Vanguard. New Essays on the Abolitionists*, ed. M. Duberman, Princeton 1965, pp. 270-98

Toqueville, A. de, *Democracy in America*, trans. H. Reeve, 4 vols., London 1836-40

Toulmin, S., *Cosmopolis. The Hidden Agenda of Modernity*, New York 1990

Tudesq, A. J., "Les survivances de l'Ancien Régime: la noblesse dans la société française de la première moitiè du XIXe siècle," *Ordres et classes. Colloque d'histoire sociale... 1967*, ed. C. E. Labrousse, Paris 1973, pp. 199-214

Turner, J. H., *On the Origins of Human Emotion. A Sociological Inquiry into the Evolution of Human Affect*, Stanford 2000

Turner, L. D., *Anti-Slavery Sentiment in American Literature Prior to 1865*, Port Washington (NY) 1929 [repr. 1966]

Uchitelle, L., "Following the money, but also the mind," *New York Times*, Feb. 11, 2001, Section 3 p. 1

Van Bezooijen, R., et al., "Recognition of vocal expressions of emotion. A three-nation study to identify universal characteristics," *Journal of Cross-Cultural Psychology* 14 (1983) pp. 387-406

Van Brockhoven, D. B., "'Let your names be enrolled.' Method and ideology in women's antislavery petitioning," *The Abolitionist Sisterhood. Women's Political Culture in Antebellum America*, eds. J. F. Yellin and J. C. Van Horne, Ithaca 1994, pp. 179-99

Veyne, P., *Comment on écrit l'histoire. Essai d'épistémologie*, Paris 1971

Veyne, P., *Le pain et le cirque: sociologie historique d'un pluralisme politique*, Paris 1976

Veyne, P., *Bread and Circuses. Historical Sociology and Political Pluralism,* abridged trans. by B. Pearce, London 1992

Vielmetter, G., "The theory of holistic simulation: beyond interpretivism and postempericism," *Empathy and Agency. The Problem of Understanding in the Human Sciences,* eds. H. H. Kögler and K. R. Steuber, Boulder (CO) 2000, pp. 83-102

Vincent-Buffault, A., *The History of Tears. Sensibility and Sentimentality in France,* Houndsmills (UK) 1991 [*Histoire des larmes XVIIIe-XIXe siècles,* Paris 1986]

Vital, D., *A People Apart. A Political History of the Jews in Europe 1789-1939,* Oxford 1999

Vovelle, M., "Les larmes et la mort au siècle des Lumières," *Das weinende Saeculum. Colloquium der Arbeitsstelle 18. Jahrhundert, Gesamthochschule Wuppertal, Universität Münster... 1981,* Heidelberg 1983, pp. 181-91

Vovelle, G., *La mentalité révolutionnaire. Société et mentalités sous le Révolution française,* Paris 1985

Walbank, F. W., "ΦΙΛΛΙΠΠΟΣ ΤΡΑΓΩΙΔΟΥΜΕΝΟΣ. A Polybian experiment," *Journal of Hellenic Studies* 58 (1938) pp. 55-68

Walbott, H. H., and K. R. Scherer, "Assessing emotion by questionnaire," *The Measurement of Emotions,* eds. R. Plutchik and H. Kellerman, San Diego 1989, pp. 55-82

Walsh, P. G., *Livy. His Historical Aims and Methods,* Cambridge (UK) 1961

Walters, R. G., *American Reformers 1815-1860,* New York 1978

Wandruska, M., "Unterwegs zu einer anthropologischen Linguistik," *Der ganze Mensch. Aspekte einer pragmatischen Anthropologie,* ed. H. Rössner, München 1986, pp. 127-45

Weil, R., "Histoire et intelligence chez Thucydide," *l'Information littéraire* 19 (1967) pp. 201-09

Weiner, B., "The emotional consequences of causal attributions," *Affect and Cognition. The Seventeenth Annual Carnegie Symposium of Cognition,* eds. M. S. Clark and S. T. Fiske, Hillsdale (NJ) 1982, pp. 185-209

Weld, T. D., *American Slavery As It Is: Testimony of a Thousand Witnesses,* New York 1839 [repr. 1968]

Wenzel, S., *The Sin of Sloth: Acedia in Medieval Thought and Literature,* Chapel Hill 1960

Wheeldon, M. J., "'True stories': the reception of historiography in antiquity," *History as Text. The Writing of Ancient History,* ed. A. Cameron, London 1989, pp. 36-63

Whissell, C. M., "The Dictionary of Affect in Language," *The Measurement of Emotion,* eds. R. Plutchik and H. Kellerman, San Diego 1989, pp. 113-131

White, G. M., "Representing emotional meaning: category, metaphor, schema, discourse," *Handbook of Emotion,* ed. 2, eds. M. Lewis and J. M. Haviland-Jones, New York 2000, pp. 30-44

White, G. M., and C. Lutz, "The anthropology of emotions," *Annual Review of Anthropology* 15 (1986) pp. 403–36

White, S. D., "The politics of anger," *Anger's Past. The Social Uses of an Emotion in the Middle Ages*, ed. B. H. Rosenwein, Ithaca 1998, pp. 127–52

Wiebe, R. H., *The Opening of American Society. From the Adoption of the Constitution to the Eve of Disunion*, New York 1984

Wierzbicka, A., "Emotion, language, and cultural scripts," *Emotion and Culture. Empirical Studies of Mutual Influence*, eds. S. Kitayama and H. R. Markus, Washington, D. C., 1994, pp. 133–96

Wigham, E., *The Anti-Slavery Cause in America and Its Martyrs*, London 1863 [repr. 1970]

Williams, S. J., *Emotion and Social Theory. Corporeal Reflections on the (Ir)rational*, London 2000

Wiseman, T. P., "Practice and theory in Roman historiography," *History* 66 (1981) pp. 375–93

Wiseman, T. P., "The origins of Roman historiography," *Historiography and Imagination. Eight Essays on Roman Culture*, Exeter (UK) 1994, pp. 1–22

Wistrand, E., *Caesar and Contemporary Society*, Göteborg 1978

Wolf, H. C., *On Freedom's Altar. The Martyr Complex in the Abolition Movement*, Madison (WI) 1952

Woodman, A. J., *Velleius Paterculus. The Caesarian and Augustan Narrative (2.41-93)*, Cambridge (UK) 1983

Woodman, A. J., *Rhetoric in Classical Historiography. Four Studies*, London 1988

Wright, A., "The death of Cicero. Forming a tradition: the contamination of history," *Historia* 50 (2001) pp. 436–52

Wyatt-Brown, B., "Conscience and career: young abolitionists and missionaries," *Anti-Slavery, Religion, and Reform. Essays in Memory of Roger Anstey*, eds. C. Bolt and S. Drescher, Folkestone (UK) 1980, pp. 183–203

Wyman, L. B., "Reminiscences of two abolitionists," *New England Magazine* 27 (1902-1903) pp. 536–50

Yavetz, Z., "The Res Gestae and Augustus' public image," *Caesar Augustus. Seven Aspects*, eds. F. Millar and E. Segal, Oxford 1984, pp. 1–36

Yellin, J. F., *The Intricate Knot: Black Figures in American Literature, 1776-1863*, New York 1972

Zajonc, R. B., "Feeling and thinking. Preferences need no inferences," *American Psychologist* 35 (1980) pp. 151–75

Zajonc, R., "On the primacy of affect," *American Psychologist* 39 (1984) pp. 117–23

Zajonc, R. B. , "Emotions," *Handbook of Social Psychology*, ed. 4, eds. D. Gilbert et al., New York 1998, 1 pp. 591–632

Zinn, H., "Abolitionists, freedom-riders, and the tactics of agitation,"
  The Antislavery Vanguard: New Essays on the Abolitionists, ed. M.
  Duberman, Princeton 1965, pp. 417-51

INDEX

Made in the USA
San Bernardino, CA
26 January 2016